# Supervision Strategies for the First Practicum

## Second Edition

### Susan Allstetter Neufeldt, PhD
University of California, Santa Barbara

AMERICAN
COUNSELING
ASSOCIATION

**SUPERVISION STRATEGIES FOR THE FIRST PRACTICUM, Second Edition**

10 9 8 7 6 5 4 3 2 1

**American Counseling Association**
5999 Stevenson Avenue
Alexandria, VA 22304

Director of Publications
Carolyn Baker

Publishing Consultant
Michael Comlish

Cover art by Max Neufeldt

Cover design by BonoTom Studio

**Library of Congress Cataloging-in-Publication Data**

Neufeldt, Susan Allstetter.
   Supervision strategies for the first practicum / by Susan
Allstetter Neufeldt. — 2nd. ed.
     p.   cm.
   Includes bibliographical references.
   ISBN 1-55620-218-0 (alk. paper)
   1. Psychotherapists—Supervision of.  2. Counselors—Supervision
of.  3. Psychotherapy—Outlines, syllabi, etc.  4. Counselling—
Outlines, syllabi, etc.  I. Title.
RC459.N48    1999
616.89'14'07155—dc21                        98-49915
                                              CIP

*To my family in Santa Barbara: Max, Carla, Bill, and Jane*

# TABLE OF CONTENTS

# FOREWORD TO THE FIRST EDITION

In 1992 I wrote in concluding a review on the empirical literature on supervision, "Will there ever be a manual with step-by-step procedures for the practice of supervision? I think not" (Holloway, 1992b, p. 206)

Now 2 years later I find myself faced with and intrigued by a manual of supervision. The authors have worked at creating a guide to understanding how to do supervision within a training context. They have anchored their thinking in the cognitive development literature and Schön's conceptualization of the reflective practitioner. From this conceptual foundation, they have identified tasks and strategies to illustrate how one might teach a novice counselor in supervision. It is a complicated task they have set out for themselves.

How can a manual lay out *a priori* what might occur and how one might respond to the myriad situations that we face in the act of teaching another how to be a psychotherapist? Because both the delivery of therapy and supervision are constructed in human interaction, the delivery of the service, or instruction itself, will change the understanding of the situation on a moment-to-moment basis. The trainee must be trained to adapt to the unfolding needs of the client. The supervisor's task includes articulating layers of thinking, understanding, and conceptualizing the client and the counseling relationship. The manual, through illustration of interactions around specific tasks, seeks to educate the supervisor. The authors might ease the would-be supervisor's anxiety by describing a week-by-week process of teaching if trainees and clients acted in a predictable manner. However, the contextual factors of supervision—including the institutional setting, the characteristics and problems of the client, and the trainee's and supervisor's self-presentation, theoretical orientation, cultural identification, and learning style—play a role in the supervisor's understanding of a particular problem presented by a particular trainee in supervision.

The authors have drawn from empirical and practical knowledge to predict the most probable supervisory needs and appropriate strategies for the novice counselor. These anchors of knowledge are the scaffolding on which the manual's illustrations take shape. The supervisor can use this scaffolding to build a unique and effective teaching strategy relevant to the issues presented by the trainee and the trainee's counseling work.

This manual serves, then, as an illustration of what might be an event and a way to approach such an event in supervision. It is an important effort to create a meaningful illustration of how one might practice supervision to enhance the development of the reflective practitioner. Although the artistry of supervision remains elusive, it is identifying what we do in supervision that ultimately leads us to asking the relevant questions about what we do.

To finish the opening quotation: " . . . the best of supervision will appear in the creative moments of an accomplished supervisor with an engaged student" (p. 206).

Elizabeth L. Holloway
University of Wisconsin–Madison

# FOREWORD TO THE
# SECOND EDITION

This is not a "little" book on clinical supervision. For starters, Neufeldt, Iversen, and Juntunen were the first authors to offer us any form of manualized supervision, something that had been called for (e.g., Holloway, 1992b) but not expected in the foreseeable future. Second, they attempted to pair something as concrete as a manual with something as imprecise as reflective practice. Third, they resisted the urge to land in one supervisory theoretical camp; that is, though offering one cohesive approach to counseling to their trainees, they managed to offer a manual that could be used with a variety of approaches. Finally, with this edition, Neufeldt has addressed both the heart of supervision (evaluation) and the ethical context for supervision.

The outline for this supervision manual derives from Stenack and Dye's (1982) research on the discrimination model (Bernard, 1979). Specifically, the Stenack and Dye list of interventions make up the strategies for introductory supervision. Neufeldt follows these with advanced strategies and detailed outlines for two semesters of clinical instruction for supervisees. The beauty of the manual is in its modeling. There are innumerable books on counseling process that model therapeutic questioning, reflecting, and summarizing. Examples of supervisor interventions, however, are scant and scattered. Borders (1992) addressed the issue of learning to "think like a supervisor"; Neufeldt has helped new supervisors speak like supervisors. It should be noted that slickly delivered interventions are not offered as the stuff of supervision; rather, the authors help the new supervisor to pair language with the goal of developing a functional and healthy supervisory relationship. The relationship is assisted by the manual, not replaced by it.

In my opinion, the most ambitious facet of this text is the author's attempt to introduce reflective practice to the counselor-in-training. It is both reasonable and tempting to assume that reflectivity is the purview of the mature therapist and, therefore, beyond the responsibility of the instructor of a first practicum. Neufeldt has not allowed us the luxury of a reductionist view of training. Rather, affirming Skovholt, Rønnestad, and Jennings's (1997) suggestion that it takes 15 years for a counselor or psychotherapist to become expert in an extremely complex field, the author asserts that the deliberate practice of reflection must begin at the beginning. Furthermore, she holds herself to a high standard in this regard: "To qualify as a reflective event, reflectivity must have consequences; the trainee must change" (p.7, this volume). Neufeldt delves into the tenets of developmental supervision with this assertion. In effect, she outlines educators' responsibility to usher their trainees out of stagnation, through confusion, and toward integration (Loganbill, Hardy, & Delworth, 1982). Neufeldt makes a case that what is taught early in one's training is relevant to what is to come. Although the author has chosen Teyber's (1997) interpersonal process approach as the conceptual base for trainees, she asserts (rightly, I believe) that this text can be used supervising trainees of other theoretical persuasions. This is so because Teyber's model emphasizes the therapeutic relationship and the process of therapy, factors all counselors must address. Their choice of a single approach to counseling is also part of Neufeldt's assertion that the field has oversimplified the issue of structure or the lack of it within supervision. Whereas most authors have addressed structure in terms of supervisory interventions, the author has encouraged the reader to think of the novice trainee's need for structure as conceptual. In other words, she has chosen a particular model of counseling precisely to have more freedom to use a variety of interventions in supervision. This is a refreshing and thought-provoking look at the whole topic of learning environment.

The first edition of *Supervision Strategies for the First Practicum* provided its readers with a hands-on tool for conducting supervision. The second edition is of even more assistance because of its inclusion of a discussion of both evaluation and ethical guidelines. Because neither evaluation nor ethical practice can be isolated from the practice of supervision, these topics not only add content to the book but context as well. Neufeldt has offered the mental health professions a well-organized and inviting introduction to the supervision process. It is a unique and highly worthwhile contribution to the supervision literature.

Janine M. Bernard
Fairfield University

# PREFACE

When I joined the faculty of the graduate program in counseling clinical/school psychology at the University of California, Santa Barbara after years as a practitioner, there was no basic text on supervision. Since that time, several excellent books on supervision theory have appeared, but none describes just how to go about conducting supervision on a day-to-day basis. With the able assistance of two graduate student supervisors, Cindy Lee Juntunen and Janet Noble Iversen, I set out in 1992 to develop a manual that would provide step-by-step assistance to beginning supervisors as they work with novice counselors and therapists.

We developed and described supervision strategies and demonstrated their use with trainees enrolled in a basic counseling skills course and practicum. In 1995 the first edition of this book appeared under all of our names after we had used the strategies and modified the text over a 3-year period. Since that time, Cindy Juntunen and Janet Iversen have gone on to distinguished careers as a professor at the University of North Dakota and a psychologist in private practice in Santa Barbara. I continue to use the manual as I work with novice supervisors and counselors.

Numerous professionals have used that first manual at sites around the country. Some have used it, as I do, in teaching courses on supervision and counseling. Others have used it as a guide to providing supervision for practicing professionals. Although gratified at its wide use, I became increasingly aware of the manual's deficiencies. Finally I proposed the development of a new edition, to incorporate recent research, particularly in the area of reflectivity as well as supervisor and counselor training, and a chapter on ethics and evaluation. Strategies have been modified, and some lessons are completely different. On the whole, I feel that this edition fits the way we can now best help supervisors work effectively with their supervisees.

This book is divided into three major parts. The first contains an introduction in which we discuss our commitment to supervisor and counselor development. We do not believe that students come to graduate training as receptacles waiting to be filled with all the knowledge they need. We ask students to collaborate with us in learning how to work with therapists and clients. In chapter 2 we provide ethical guidelines for supervisors as they work with counselors-in-training. Research indicates that future professional supervisors, whether in academic settings or in practice, learn their ethical practices when they are in training. Ethical guidelines for useful evaluation are included. In both the practical and ethical dimensions, we encourage supervisors and counselors to reflect on their practice continuously from the perspectives of professional experience, personal and professional values, and research literature.

The second part explores supervision strategies and the case conceptualization model. In chapter 3 we describe basic supervision strategies and illustrate each with a vignette. In chapter 4 we describe a model of case conceptualization and advanced supervision strategies that combine teaching, counseling, and consulting functions.

The third part provides the setting for supervision: a practicum course for first-year counseling students. The first term, outlined in chapter 4, focuses on building a relationship with clients, and we delineate plans for each week. We suggest what each class should include and describe weekly supervision sessions in detail. Vignettes illustrate supervision in action. The second term, outlined in chapter 5, focuses on conceptualization of cases and the process of counseling.

I am grateful to the graduate students in the UCSB program for their participation as supervisors and beginning counselors. Without their willingness to use the manual, to work with one another, and to give me feedback on the usefulness of both the supervision strategies and the practicum course, we could not have prepared the present manuscript. The comments of Mary Lee Nelson, Tom Skovholt, Helge Rønnestad, Janine Bernard, Elizabeth Holloway, Dennis Kivlighan, and other colleagues have shaped what follows. I appreciate the willingness of Carla Neufeldt to read and edit the entire manuscript. Jules Zimmer and James Wells have supported my development as a therapist, teacher, and supervisor for more than 25 years, and Billy Allstetter has supported my development as a writer. I am grateful to my Santa Barbara family, to whom this edition is dedicated, for their patience and support as I sat at the computer with my back to them. Carolyn Baker at the American Counseling Association has provided encouragement and support for both editions of the book.

# ABOUT THE AUTHOR

Susan Allstetter Neufeldt received her B.A. and M.A. from Stanford University and her Ph.D. from the University of California, Santa Barbara. She was in private practice for 15 years before returning to the university to head the Ray E. Hosford Clinic, a training facility for graduate students and a service provider for the community. In addition to being author of numerous articles and chapters on supervision over the past 8 years, she also lectures and consults with professionals nationally and internationally.

# PART I

# INTRODUCTION AND ETHICAL FRAMEWORK

# CHAPTER 1

# INTRODUCTION TO SUPERVISION AND COUNSELOR DEVELOPMENT

Although numerous authors (Bernard & Goodyear, 1998; Holloway, 1992b; Holloway & Neufeldt, 1995; Rønnestad & Skovholt, 1998; Watkins, 1997a; Wiley & Ray, 1986) have recognized that supervision is critical in the preparation of counselors and psychotherapists,* there is to date no other manual developed for the process (Bernard & Goodyear, 1998). This supervision manual, which is organized around a coherent theory of training, can aid practitioners as they learn to supervise counselors and therapists. It also can help experienced supervisors refine their skills.

The manual is designed primarily for supervisors of beginners. Holloway (1995) stated that the goal of supervision is to enhance supervisees' effective professional functioning. In other words, supervisors endeavor to assist students with a good grasp of declarative (academic) knowledge and to develop procedural knowledge, the ability to put that academic knowledge into practice with actual clients (Binder & Strupp, 1997). Supervision strategies intended to facilitate this process are defined and explained in part 2 (chapters 3 and 4). Our strategies can be used by those who work with beginners, advanced trainees, interns, or practicing clinicians. Examples, however, illustrate supervision as it is carried out with first-year practicum students.

Because supervision takes place in a professional environment and involves the welfare of both supervisees and clients, we have added a chapter (part 1, chapter 2) that outlines the ethical responsibilities of supervisors. Included in that chapter are recommendations for careful evaluation of supervisees in a manner that supports their development as therapists while serving the gatekeeping function (Bernard & Goodyear, 1998) necessary to protect the public from incompetent practitioners.

We ground our approach in theories of counselor development and in theories of education. This has required us to consider all aspects of the training experience, because supervision does not occur in a vacuum. To

---

*Throughout this manual the terms *counselor, psychotherapist*, and *therapist* will be used interchangeably, as will the terms *counseling, psychotherapy*, and *therapy*.

provide a context for the strategies, ethics, and evaluation of trainees, we outline a beginning practicum course and associated practicum supervision in part III (chapters 5 and 6). Specific supervision strategies are suggested and examples of supervision are provided for each week. It is not necessary to follow our practicum outline to use the manual to train supervisors; examples from the supervision segments will be useful in many situations.

We anticipate that a number of players operate in the training environment. In this manual, we refer to the supervisors-in-training as *supervisors*, the counselor trainees as *trainees*, and the instructor of the practicum course as *instructor*. A *master supervisor* works with the supervisors-in-training on a weekly basis. In some settings, the master supervisor is the same person as the course instructor.

Three ideas have informed our model: (a) development of counselors and supervisors into reflective practitioners (Neufeldt, 1994b, 1997, 1999; Neufeldt, Karno, & Nelson, 1996); (b) employment of practices known to promote the progression of novices into experts (Ericsson, Krampe, & Tesch-Romer, 1993; Rosenberg, 1998); and (c) use of the supervisory relationship as the catalyst for change (Holloway, 1995; Rønnestad & Skovholt, 1998). The assumptions about counselor and therapist learning used to construct the manual are described in the following sections.

## RESEARCH AND THEORY

Historically, it has been difficult to determine which supervision activities are effective and when (Bernard & Goodyear, 1998; Holloway & Hosford, 1983). As Binder (1993) suggested, however, despite the lack of empirical data, "such problems are sufficiently critical to the therapy training endeavor to warrant even speculative discussion" (p. 305). In the last 25 years, research on counselor development and supervisor activity in general has provided insight into the development and training of therapists.

### The Process of Counselor Development

Much discussion of counselor supervision has focused on counselor development (Bernard & Goodyear, 1998; Borders, 1989; Fong, Borders, Ethington, & Pitts, 1997; Stoltenberg, McNeill, & Crethar, 1994). Models of counselor development have proliferated (Blocher, 1983; Hogan, 1964; Loganbill, Hardy, & Delworth, 1982; Stoltenberg & Delworth, 1987; Stoltenberg, McNeill, & Delworth, 1998), and researchers have offered some support for changes in counselors during training that are consistent with these models (Borders, 1989; Fong et al., 1997; Heppner & Roehlke, 1984; Hill, Charles, & Reed, 1981; Worthington, 1987). They have not, however, effectively described how therapists move from one developmental stage to the next (Holloway, 1987).

Not until Skovholt and Rønnestad's (1992) extensive qualitative study of 100 therapists, who ranged from untrained paraprofessionals to therapists with 40 years' experience, did a picture emerge of therapist development throughout the professional life-span. Skovholt and Rønnestad (1992) found therapists who had stagnated and in many cases left the profession along with therapists who developed through a series of stages along the novice-expert continuum from "Conventional Thinking, [in other words] using what one naturally knows," (p. 14) to "Integrity, [in which] experience-based generalizations and accumulated wisdom are primary" (p. 16). At each stage, they postulated, a therapist faces a challenge. How the therapist handles it determines whether he or she proceeds into the developmental track, a period of moratorium, or the stagnation track.

The challenge occurs when the therapist is "stuck" (Skovholt, personal communication, May 18, 1994) and is uncertain about what underlies events in session or what to do next. Along with Stoltenberg and Delworth (1987), Skovholt and Rønnestad (1992) believed that development can occur when the Piagetian assimilation-accommodation balance (Ginsburg & Opper, 1969) is disrupted. When trainees encounter a problem in therapy that fits their prior cognitive system or organizing structure, they sense no tension between their internal organization and their external experience. They readily incorporate the new experience into the old structures, a process Piaget called *assimilation* (Flavell, 1985). When trainees learn basic skills, such as restatement and open-ended questioning, they assimilate them into their preexisting structure of conversational responses. Their skills increase, but the trainees do not progress to a new stage of development.

However, when trainees encounter a problem in therapy that does not fit their preexisting cognitive structures, tension ensues between their internal organization and their external experience. Piaget called this tension *disequilibrium* (Rosen, 1985). For instance, when trainees encounter the first clients to demand excessive attention, they discover that what they might do to help a friend, such as talk at any hour of day or night, lend money, or provide shelter, are inappropriate in the counseling relationship. This requires trainees to change their internal model of helping, or to accommodate their internal structures, to set limits in psychotherapy and build working alliances with clients. Trainees are initially uncomfortable with the tension of disequilibration, but resolving it provides the impetus for progression to new levels of professional development.

Accommodation and development can occur successfully, according to Skovholt and Rønnestad (1995), when therapists use the process of "continuous profesional reflection"* (p. 125) in an atmosphere of support and challenge.

## Development of the Reflective Practitioner

Skovholt & Rønnestad (1995) described continuous professional reflection as "a central developmental process. It consists of three essential aspects: ongoing professional and personal experiences, a searching process with others within an open and supportive environment, and active reflection about one's experiences" (p. 141).

Likewise, Donald Schön (1983, 1987) described reflective practice. The task of the reflective practitioner, he said, is to conduct practice as a continuous form of scientific inquiry that allows the practitioner to frame problems and modify them appropriately to devise solutions unique to particular situations. It encourages experimentation and the use of unexpected results as valid information (Neufeldt & Forsyth, 1993). It is more than mere cogitation about what has happened; reflectivity includes both thought and the actions that result from it (Copeland, Birmingham, de la Cruz, & Lewin, 1993). Schön (personal communication, February 16, 1994) suggested that a trainee who exhibits a high level of reflective inquiry in supervision is willing to be confused and vulnerable, to entertain a new idea, and to test it in session with a client. The supervisor must support the trainee's confusion and experimentation.

Because Schön, Skovholt, Rønnestad, and Copeland all spoke to the concept of reflectivity, Neufeldt, Karno, and Nelson (1996) sought to determine whether they were referring to the same concept, and if so, what qualities defined it. They interviewed these four theorists along with Elizabeth Holloway, a recognized expert on counselor and therapist supervision. From their initial interviews, they extracted a preliminary model of reflectivity, which they submitted to the experts for comments in a subsequent interview. There was substantial agreement among the experts on the components of reflectivity as they would occur in supervision, which is described next.

Trainees can only reflect when they are cognitively complex, able to tolerate ambiguity, and open to ideas, and when they work in a safe supervisory relationship, within an environment in which questioning is valued. Reflectivity begins with a problem or dilemma, a place in which a trainee feels stuck and unsure of how to proceed. The process involves attention to the therapist's own actions, emotions, and thoughts in the counseling session, and to the interaction between the client and the

---

*Throughout this chapter, the term *reflection* refers only to a process of thinking; it does not refer to a response a counselor makes to mirror a client's statement or feelings.

therapist. Reflective trainees search for understanding, with openness to a variety of alternatives. To understand their clinical experiences, they use formal theory along with their own past personal and professional experiences. In addition, they attend to their own experience during the session in question as a source of understanding. A reflection of some depth has meaning and clarity. To qualify as a reflective event, the thought process must have consequences; the trainee must change. After reflecting in supervision, trainees should change their behavior in their next counseling sessions. In addition, they may also understand their clients, the counseling process, or themselves differently as a result of reflecting.

With that in mind, the supervisor should create an interpersonal environment that supports the searching process and active reflection on ongoing counseling practice (Neufeldt & Forsyth, 1993; Rønnestad & Skovholt, 1993). This is consistent with theories of counseling and psychotherapy (Kiesler, 1982; Strong, 1968; Strong & Claiborn, 1982; Teyber, 1997). Also, it is similar to Argyris and Schön's (1974) Model II for developing effectiveness with people in a variety of professions. Model II includes challenging ongoing professional practice within a milieu where valid information is sought, free and informed choice of actions is advocated, and an internal commitment to carrying out those choices is encouraged. The atmosphere of mutuality is enhanced because discussion proceeds collaboratively on the basis of "directly observable categories" (Argyris & Schön, 1974, p. 90) rather than evaluative statements.

Mutuality moves us away from "teacher-centered" or "student-centered" approaches to training; we join our students and gather around the "great things" (Palmer, 1998a, p. 107). Together we draw on our objective research-based knowledge, and our subjective emotional experiences as we seek to understand. Our questions include: How does human development occur? How do we understand people's problems in living (Szasz,1974)? What different ways do we know, from research, personal experience, and professional experience, to help particular people change and grow?

## Facilitation of Practitioners' Progression Toward Expertise

Skovholt, Rønnestad, and Jennings (1997) described counselor's developmental path toward professional expertise, the elegant procedural knowledge of the highly skilled practitioner. Although Dawes (1994) demonstrated that experience alone does not differentiate successful from unsuccessful practitioners, Skovholt et al. (1997) argued that much of the research that compares inexperienced to experienced practitioners is based on comparisons of master's students or master's degree holders with doctoral students or graduates with only a few additional years of experience. Ericsson and Lehmann (1996) argued that 10 years is a minimum time for expertise to develop in any area, but Skovholt et al. (1997) suggested that it takes 15 years for a counselor or psychotherapist to become an expert in this complex field. Expert psychotherapists are marked by their voracious desire to learn, reflectivity and self-awareness, comfort with complexity and ambiguity, openness and nondefensiveness, emotional maturity, exceptional interpersonal skill, and the practice of self-care with awareness of how their emotional health impacts their work (Jennings & Skovholt, in press). Experience alone does not necessarily provide the means to evaluate one's practice and develop further.

Critical to the development of expertise is deliberate practice, rather than simple experience. To make practice more deliberate means that practitioners must examine their behavior in light of its results. Dawes (1994) suggested that to improve, learners must understand what constitutes an incorrect response or error in judgment and receive consistent, clear feedback when errors are made. This is consistent with Henry, Schacht, Strupp, Butler, and Binder's (1993) finding that the most effective supervisor on a particular project explored specific therapy interactions with supervisees and encouraged them to state their intentions and examine the results of their interventions. We have incorporated this approach into our supervision strategies.

We believe that such examination of particular clinical events facilitates the reflective process and ultimately promotes the development of expertise. We join Rønnestad and Skovholt (1993) and Schön (1987) in the belief that examining one's clinical work on a regular basis is as important as practicing specific skills for therapist development. Use of the reflective process allows counselors and therapists to develop after formal training has been completed (Skovholt & Rønnestad, 1995), and provides a means for them to practice in a deliberate fashion over the 10–15 years it takes to become an expert. Supervision, therefore, must encourage both. This manual shows the supervisor how to nurture counselors' nascent abilities to reflect and act.

## CONSTRUCTION OF THE BASIC PRACTICUM

In the outline we provide for a practicum course, we attend to the developmental process described by Skovholt and Rønnestad (1992, 1995) and incorporate strategies to encourage an interactional environment that is conducive to both skills acquisition and practice in reflective process. We match the course to the needs of students in their first practicum experience as described in the literature.

After several years of experimentation, we now believe that it is important for graduate students to learn one theoretical approach well to learn to function within a theoretical paradigm and to critique its limitations. Wampold and his colleagues (Wampold et al., 1997) have shown, in a comprehensive meta-analysis, that no therapeutic method produces outcomes superior to any other. Nonetheless, we believe that beginning therapists must have some theoretical basis for beginning to think about clients and their interactions with their therapists. Research indicates that beginning therapists want structure in their early practicum and supervisory experiences (Heppner & Roehlke, 1984; Stoltenberg et al., 1994; Worthington, 1987). Although some (e.g., Lambert & Arnold, 1987) have suggested that structure is most effectively provided as training in specific skills, we conceptualize structure in a different fashion. First, we propose that structure be offered in terms of theory, that is, in terms of a way to look at the phenomena of counseling interactions. This idea of theory as a lens through which to view behavior of both clients and counselors is consistent with the reflective process we advocate throughout the manual. At the same time, the trainee can evaluate the theory in terms of its ability to explain or predict client behavior or apply effective interventions. We encourage the trainee to question the theory's predictive validity and usefulness throughout the course.

Second, we offer deliberate practice in both listening and responding, consistent with research on the novice-expert path. Our intention, however, is not to produce therapists who emit skills but rather to provide a basis from which they can examine their work with clients. Can a given counselor listen carefully enough to restate content, which only requires listening to words, or can he or she reflect feeling, which requires attention to nonverbal and paraverbal behavior? And how does that therapist know when he or she is accurate? This engages the counselor in looking at the effects of the intervention on the client. Does the client frown, look away, nod, or respond by saying either, "No, that's not it," or "Yes, exactly!" In this way the therapist begins to develop the ability to receive feedback in session directly from the client, which in the long run is the only way to assess errors in therapist behavior or judgment, which is so necessary for the development of expertise. Naturally, the ability to assess client response to interventions becomes more complex as case conceptualization and interventions become more complex.

We use an interpersonal process approach (Teyber, 1997), supplemented with Hill and O'Brien's (1999) delineation of helping skills, for beginners in our program because it provides a basis for understanding the relationship and process aspects of counseling and psychotherapy. In addition, it is consistent with our view of supervision as an interactive process that can be a model for the counseling relationship. Regardless of theoretical approaches trainees may later learn, we believe that they must understand the nature of the therapeutic relationship and the process of therapy. As Wampold et al. (1997) acknowledged, common factors account for differences in therapeutic results, and chief among the common factors is the quality of the therapeutic relationship. This does not mean, however, that this manual is useful only for interpersonal process counseling. We have made every effort to provide supervision strategies that can be used with a variety of orientations; we simply suggest that a specific approach be used with beginners.

## Goals

We selected a primary goal for each term of the beginning practicum, based on skills necessary for therapists, and we organized the curriculum around that goal. The first term's curriculum is focused on relationship skills, because research indicates that a good relationship between therapist and client is positively associated with outcome (Beutler, Machado, & Neufeldt, 1994; Sexton & Whiston, 1994). The course instructor introduces the idea of the therapeutic relationship and provides experiences that illustrate its importance. To teach skills in relationship building, the instructor helps students develop ways to listen empathically to the client and respond concretely so that the client feels understood. Supervisors help trainees understand the working alliance, the transference relationship, and the real relationship (i.e., the realistic as opposed to the fantasized aspects of the relationship) as described by Gelso and Carter (1985, 1994). Throughout the course, the instructor offers an environment that is facilitative and collaborative so that experimentation is valued and risks can be taken, in spite of the intense anxiety beginning trainees feel (Skovholt & Rønnestad, 1992, 1995; Rønnestad & Skovholt, 1993).

The second term's curriculum is concentrated on case conceptualization. The ability to conceptualize cases is a complex skill (Fong et al., 1997; Holloway & Wampold, 1986). Although trainees can quickly learn basic therapeutic skills in a variety of counseling approaches, they find it considerably more difficult to formulate cases with particular clients (Greenberg & Goldman, 1988; Shaw, 1984). This manual provides a model for case conceptualization, which incorporates the presenting problem, the observable characteristics of clients, results of any standardized assessments, clients' history and ability to form relationships, environmental factors, counseling goals, and change strategies. We show case conceptualization in a variety of settings in which counselors may be expected to work, from counseling centers to schools to mental health agencies. As trainees begin to see their own clients and view videotapes and records of their colleagues' clients, they are questioned by supervisors on each aspect of case conceptualization until trainess consistently develop satisfactory case formulations.

Again, after experimentation with a multitheoretical approach, we have concluded that it is easier for trainees to learn the process of case conceptualization within one theoretical orientation in a manner that later can be applied to others. Our model can be applied within most theoretical frameworks.

## Matching the Curriculum to Trainee Developmental Characteristics

We provide experiences matched to the cognitive patterns of beginning therapists, as described by researchers. Borders (1989), in her study of trainee thinking, reported some similarities in the thoughts of all beginners. "Their few planning statements," she said, "indicated a lack of goals and direction over sessions. Similarly, the focus on events in the present session precluded recognition of themes and patterns" (p. 167). In other words, they were overwhelmed by events in their sessions and confused about what to do next. This suggests a need for some structure during early training, which is consistent with findings about beginners' preferences (Heppner & Roehlke, 1984; Reising & Daniels, 1983; Worthington, 1987; Worthington & Roehlke, 1979).

We plan the first quarter's experiences so that each week new skills are developed in class and deliberately practiced in role-play sessions with other trainees. Skills include those needed to set up appointments, begin and end sessions, respond empathically to client concerns, set appropriate boundaries, and respond effectively to common emergency situations. Toward the end of the first term, trainees meet with volunteer clients from an undergraduate class and practice their new skills in a limited number of sessions. During the second term they conduct intake interviews and meet with their first community clients. In this way they move from structured, predictable experiences with their colleagues to the increasingly unpredictable experiences provided by real clients.

Along with Rønnestad and Skovholt (1993), we believe that too much structure in the initial practicum invites passive learning. Some of students' desire to be told how to counsel is analogous to clients' desire to be told how to live. To develop as reflective practitioners, students must grapple with their own ideas, questions, and thoughts from the outset. As they learn to work with clients, they must struggle to understand what is going on and to respond, based on the integration of their experiences with self, life, exposure to counselor education and psychotherapy research, and interaction with particular clients. If too much structure is provided, trainees are likely to develop an external orientation (Rønnestad & Skovholt, 1993), that is pay more attention to what others tell them about their work than to their own sense of it. This can discourage further development (Skovholt

& Rønnestad, 1992). Like therapists who must help clients discover their own answers, instructors and supervisors must tolerate trainees' anxiety as they search for ways to work with particular clients.

We assume that supervisors develop through the same process as counselors. They will encounter both expected and unexpected situations as they work with trainees. If they reflect on their own training as counselors along with the results of specific supervisory interventions, they will grow in competence.

## Multicultural Emphasis

Because society is diverse, we are committed to training therapists to be responsive to cross-cultural influences. As shown by scholars (Atkinson, Morten, & Sue, 1998; Sue & Sue, 1990; Tanaka-Matsumi & Draguns, 1997), clients from different cultures often have different expectations of psychotheraphy. To respond respectfully to those differences and to use culturally appropriate interventions, therapists must be culturally sensitive. We use *cultural differences* to include those of ethnicity, race, gender, sexual orientation, and religion. Though here we discuss the infusion of a multicultural approach into the supervision of therapists, we join LaFromboise and Foster (1992) and Stone (1997) in recommending that the entire training program within which the supervision occurs be culturally sensitive. All training in cultural sensitivity cannot occur in supervision or practica.

Fischer, Jome, and Atkinson (1998) have provided a compelling model of multicultural counseling. Specifically, they have conceptualized multicultural counseling as use of the validated common factors (Wampold et al., 1997) when counseling in a cultural context. Four factors are elaborated with cultural emphases. First, the therapeutic relationship is enhanced when the counselor demonstrates knowledge of and respect for the client's culture and situates the client's problem in a cultural context (Atkinson & Lowe, 1995). Furthermore, understanding of the frequent experiences of oppression and common power differentials in the broad culture between racial and ethic majority and minority groups, men and women, and straight and gay individuals can promote trust-building within the counseling relationship. Second, a cultural understanding of the client's problem allows the therapist to communicate a shared worldview. Third, when the counselor explains the client's problem in the context of the client's worldview, the client is more likely to feel hopeful and believe that counseling can help. Fourth, the client is more likely to accept and use counseling interventions when they are consistent with and explained in terms of cultural rituals or culturally accepted healing processes. We ask supervisors to use this model in helping counselors to work with clients of cultures both different from and similar to their own. Throughout the first-year practicum, supervisors ask trainees to consider the influence of the client's cultural background and the therapist's cultural background on case conceptualization and psychotherapy.

Likewise, supervisors are encouraged to consider the impact of cultural similarities and differences within the supervisory dyad and select culturally sensitive strategies to enhance the relationship. There is considerably less research available on multicultural supervision than on multicultural counseling (Bernard & Goodyear, 1998; Leong & Wagner, 1994). We would argue, however, that some of the principles elaborated by Fischer et al. (1998) about multicultural counseling can be applied in the context of multicultural supervision. In establishing the supervisory relationship, for instance, supervisors can demonstrate respect for a trainee's cultural background, whether or not it resembles the supervisor's own. The issues of power differential are particularly salient because supervision is obviously a relationship between individuals of unequal power. Fong and Lease (1997) described some problems that may occur between the White supervisor, for instance, and the minority trainee, as unintentional racism, power dynamics, trust and the supervisory alliance, and communication issues. Such concerns are illuminated by research showing differences in supervisor responses to male and female supervisees (Nelson & Holloway, 1990) or the reluctance of minority supervisees to raise the issue of race with European American supervisors until the supervisor does so (Kleintjes & Swartz, 1996). It is not clear from current supervision research that differences of sexual orientation affect the power differential in the supervisory relationship as they sometimes do in the world outside the training setting, but we recommend that if a trainee self-identifies as gay, lesbian, or bisexual, the heterosexual supervisor should check in with the trainee regarding his or her feelings about supervision by a straight supervisor. We have encountered supervision situations in which the sexual preference of the trainee challenged the religious beliefs of the supervisor.

In our program, as in an increasing number of other training programs, often the supervisor is a member of a racial or ethnic minority or is female, and the trainee is a male or a member of the same or a different racial or ethnic group. In this instance, the supervisor is advised to raise the issue of racial, ethnic, and gender differences (Priest, 1994) as well.

Additionally, numerous authors (Bernard & Goodyear, 1998; Cook, 1994; Fong & Lease, 1997) have pointed out that supervisors may be at a lower level of racial identity development than supervisees. This is an issue to be addressed in training programs by the master supervisor. If the supervisor of the student supervisors believes that the level of racial or ethnic identity development of the supervisor-in-training is below that of the counseling trainee, the master supervisor must intervene. Initially, this may involve discussion with the supervisor-in-training to address the issues and conduct additional assessment of the problem. If the supervisor's level of development is significantly below that of the trainee and this is interfering with the satisfactory practice of supervision, the master supervisor must arrange for a transfer of the trainee to another supervisor. Careful supervision of both supervisors and trainees is central to our approach.

## HOW TO USE THIS MANUAL

Our belief in reflective process seems to conflict with the idea of a manual. We use our manual, however, like a course in a foreign language and as a stimulus for further development. If beginning supervisors can learn the vocabulary (i.e., the supervision strategies), they can then facilitate reflective inquiry on the part of trainees. Supervisors are encouraged to use selected strategies in supervision and reflect on their impact on trainees and themselves, both during and after their meetings. Like Fogel (1990), we believe that supervisors should encourage doubting and creative innovation; therefore, we encourage our supervisors-in-training to question and modify strategies, once they have tried them, and to determine when they should be implemented for maximum effect. In other words, we recommend that supervisors have an opportunity to experience their own searching process in the supportive environments of individual and group supervision.

One way we have encouraged supervisor reflection is with the use of written journals. Student supervisors are asked to write weekly about their experiences both of providing supervision to trainees and of being supervised by the master supervisor. The master supervisor then responds with written comments to the ideas of the supervisors-in-training. Neufeldt, Doucette-Gates, and Carvalho (1998) examined a selection of the journals written by supervisors-in-training over two quarters. In a qualitative analysis, they found that supervisors were three times as likely to record reflective comments as they were to make any other statements. We do not know, of course, whether that would have occurred with different supervisors-in-training, but it suggests that reflectivity can be promoted by the use of journal writing.

To place supervision in context, we have included a chapter on ethics and evaluation (chapter 2) that particularly applies to the supervision of beginning counselors. Ethical principles of supervision are explained, with particular application to use with trainees in a graduate program. Following that is a method of trainee evaluation developed in a fashion consistent with the ethical responsibilities of supervisors. It can readily be modified for use by supervisors in nonacademic settings.

With our goals and the trainees' needs in mind, we have developed a variety of strategies for supervisors to use. Bernard (1979) described three roles taken by supervisors, as teacher, counselor, and consultant. Stenack and Dye (1982), in a factor analytic study, catalogued supervisor functions into each category. We have used Stenack and Dye's list to organize our beginning supervision strategies, and we have added advanced strategies later in the manual that combine teaching, counseling, and consulting roles. We describe precise supervisor behaviors to delineate each strategy in accordance with our guiding principles.

Although the descriptions of the supervision strategies may not match those in the minds of Bernard (1979) or Stenack and Dye (1982), they provide a basis for the education and evaluation of supervisors. In particular, we provide vignettes that illustrate how to draw the trainees into a reflective, collaborative process of learning from the client, the supervisor, and their peers. This allows supervisors to help trainees recognize when they are stuck, reflect on what happens in sessions, make hypotheses, and experiment.

Following each vignette, we present examples to illustrate them and commentary on those examples. The strategy descriptions and vignettes enable supervisors to develop specific supervision skills, which can be evaluated by themselves and their master supervisor.

Part II of this manual, in chapters 3 and 4, describes supervision strategies and the case conceptualization model and evaluation. Basic supervision strategies (with vignettes to illustrate) are delineated in chapter 3, advanced strategies in chapter 4. Practicing supervisors may use the first section to expand their supervisory skills without using the second section, which is directed at a first practicum experience.

Part III of the manual is directed toward a first practicum experience and outlines a two-term practicum course. In chapter 5 we specify the first-term course outline as well as the supervisory behaviors for each week's supervision session that parallel classroom activities and respond to trainee counseling experiences with peers and voluntary clients. Again, we provide vignettes to illustrate their use. In chapter 6 we present a specific course outline for the second term, but we assume that supervisors are more skillful at making supervisory choices by then, and we instruct supervisors to use the strategies most appropriate to the material presented by the trainee. In all supervision sessions we assume the client is part of the supervisory relationship (Holloway, 1992a, 1992b, 1995). Because clients are not predictable, supervision sessions are sure to vary in terms of their adherence to the manual.

Each term's curriculum includes 15 lessons and supervision sessions with appropriate supervisory strategies. Ten of these, we feel, are essential in each quarter of a two-quarter course. The additional lessons are provided for use in a two-semester course, and some of these additional lessons can be substituted for some of the initial 10, according to the instructor's preference. Students in our program, who tend to be academically strong but clinically inexperienced, take their initial counseling and practicum course in the second quarter of their first year of graduate study. Prior to taking the practicum course, they have studied basic counseling theories, and concurrent with the practicum, they take courses in multicultural issues and ethics. At other sites, some adjustments to the course might be made to accommodate specific student populations and their prior academic or clinical experiences.

In specifying strategies and developing vignettes, we have made the assumption that practicum counseling occurs in a facility equipped with video cameras. We recognize, however, that not all sites are so equipped, and all references to the use of videotapes can be applied to the use of audiotapes. In cases where supervisors and trainees do not have access to tapes of sessions, supervisors can obtain considerable information from the trainees' verbal descriptions of counseling interactions and written process notes. Argyris and Schön (1974, p. 47) have provided a model for process notes to encourage reflective inquiry.

Henry, Strupp, Butler, Schacht, and Binder (1993) reported that use of therapy manuals increases accurate demonstration of skills, and we encourage supervisors to adhere closely to the supervision manual. Because these researchers also reported that increased hostility and diminished warmth sometimes accompany therapists' efforts to adhere to manualized strategies, we encourage diligent attention to the quality of the supervisory relationship. In turn, the master supervisor needs to attend to the relationship he or she has with the supervisors-in-training and address the potential for these problems directly with them.

One way to diminish frustration with the use of precise strategies is to help supervisors-in-training personalize the strategies by attending to language. At the same time that we describe strategies in precise terms, we encourage trainees to find their own words to implement them. Most experienced therapists can remember attending a workshop on a new therapeutic method and coming home to implement the new method—only to see it fall flat. Until therapists or supervisors make methods their own, with language that fits their own personal styles, no strategy is likely to be effective. Rambo and Shilts (1997) recommended that therapists-in-training "play with" language, and we recommend that supervisors do the same.

We propose that master supervisors meet with supervisors-in-training on a regular basis. They should attend to the complex relationships among clients, counselor trainees, and supervisors. They can nourish the supervisors' reflective processes and invite supervisors to experience their own confusion, make hypotheses, and test them. By thinking aloud about their own ideas and interventions in supervision, master supervisors demonstrate reflective processes for the supervisors-in-training. In these ways they model good supervision.

# CHAPTER 2

# ETHICAL SUPERVISION AND EVALUATION OF BEGINNING COUNSELORS

In this chapter, we provide an ethical framework for the instruction and supervision of beginning counselors and explain how they can be evaluated in an ethical fashion. In subsequent chapters, we carefully describe strategies designed to promote the development of trainee competence in clinical thinking and practice. Without attention to ethics and values, however, education of all kinds becomes merely a technical exercise, a process that "dissects life and distances us from the world" (Palmer, 1998b, p. 25). This chapter delineates the ethics and evaluation procedures that guide all of the strategies and examples presented later in the book.

Counseling and psychotherapy are intimate activities, based in a caring and respectful relationship. Likewise, the supervision relationship must be handled with attention to care (Gilligan, 1982) and justice (Kohlberg, 1984). Kitchener (1984) advanced ethical principles of respect for autonomy, nonmalificence, beneficence, justice, and fidelity, to which Meara, Schmidt, and Day (1996) added the principle of veracity. Meara et al. also proposed that psychologists demonstrate virtue, that is, they should desire to do what is good, show vision and discernment, acknowledge the role of affect or emotion in evaluating conduct, demonstrate self-understanding and awareness, and make moral decisions in the context of the community in which an action takes place.

The Association for Counselor Education and Supervision (1995) has developed a set of ethical guidelines specifically to govern the practice of supervision, and all associations of professional counselors provide rules for the practice of supervision within their ethical codes. Ladany, Lehrman-Waterman, Molinaro, and Wolgast (in press) examined not only the ACES ethical code for supervisors but also the guidelines elaborated by the American Association for Marriage and Family Therapy (AAMFT, 1991), the American Counseling Association (ACA, 1995), the American Psychiatric Association (1995), the American Psychological Association (APA, 1992), the American School Counselor Association (1992), and the National Association of Social Workers (NASW, 1996). From these they extrapolated 18 arenas of ethical practice, 16 of which apply to counselors-in-training. These delineate the two responsibilities, described by Vasquez (1992), of supervisors to ensure trainee ethical understanding and behavior within counseling and to conduct themselves ethically within the supervisory relationship.

In their careful study of supervisee complaints about supervisor ethical violations, Ladany et al. (in press) found that a third of the complaints focused on inadequate evaluation and feedback procedures. This complaint appeared almost twice as often as the next most frequently mentioned one. Because of this concern, we believe that particular attention needs to be paid to the area of evaluation and feedback.

In the following pages we provide practical suggestions for supervision of beginning counselors and therapists that flesh out the areas of ethical practice described by Ladany et al. (in press), organized by the general categories defined by Vasquez (1992). We include specific proposals for feedback and evaluation of supervisees. From time to time, exercises or examples illustrate the suggestions. In addition, we describe responsibilities of the supervisee within the supervisory relationship, as elaborated by Worthington and Gugliotti (1997).

## PROCEDURES TO ENSURE TRAINEE ETHICAL UNDERSTANDING AND PRACTICE

To teach ethical principles to beginning therapists and enable them to use these principles in practice is among the most important tasks of counselor educators and supervisors. In most training programs, one course focuses on ethical guidelines within the profession. It is the task of supervisors, however, to enable trainees to turn that declarative knowledge into procedural knowledge they can demonstrate in counseling practice. Supervisors are ultimately responsible for the ethical behavior of the trainees under their supervision (Bernard & Goodyear, 1998; Corey, Corey, & Callanan, 1998). How supervisors can encourage trainee ethical performance is described below. Attention is focused on professional roles and site standards, disclosure to clients, ethical behavior and responses to ethical concerns, sexual and other dual-role issues, multicultural sensitivity toward clients (APA, 1993), crisis management, and termination issues.

### Explicit Site Procedures

Trainees usually understand ethical principles, but they may be unclear as to how they can most efficiently carry them out. When a program has its own practice site or training clinic on campus, it is possible to establish procedures that enable trainees to proceed ethically. On the other hand, when trainees practice in an agency outside the campus, it is the task of faculty supervisors to make sure there are procedures in place at the off-campus site to promote ethical practice. We elaborate specific procedures below.

*Disclosure of training status and client consent.* When clients come for counseling, they must be told that they will be working with counselors-in-training and consent to that before the process begins. At a site-based training clinic, this is initially explained over the telephone and often in written materials sent to clients or provided when clients come in for intake interviews. Following up, counselors explain their training status to clients at the first meeting and describe the procedures for supervision, such as audiotaping or videotaping, and the name and licensing status of their supervisor. They relate exactly who will know what happens in sessions (e.g., the supervisor and other members of the confidential group) and the ways in which confidentiality will be protected. In addition, they explain the state-mandated legal limits to confidentiality (e.g., when the client presents a danger to self or others or when the client describes child abuse). In addition, if research is routinely conducted at the site, procedures to ensure client anonymity and confidentiality should be explained. How the client can contact the therapist or other professionals in an emergency should also be described.

Before proceeding, counselors ask clients to consent formally to these procedures by signing a consent form that outlines them in writing. If the client is unwilling to do so, the therapist graciously accepts the refusal and makes a referral to other agencies who might serve the client's needs.

Such a detailed explanation and consent form enable both clients and counselors to understand exactly what can be expected. In addition, supervisors and other program officials should make clear to trainees the consequences of violations of these procedures for supervision, crisis management, and confidentiality.

*Record keeping.* All site supervisors must provide guidance in record keeping. Clear outlines of intake reports, progress notes, billing records, and termination forms, along with examples of each, can help beginners to manage paperwork appropriately. Supervisors must monitor all records to train counselors under their supervision and to ensure that records meet ethical standards for record keeping.

*Emergency and reporting procedures.* Counselors need to understand exactly how to recognize a potential emergency and what to do to address it. Although every effort is made to select clients for beginning therapists who will not be at risk for suicide, active on-site drug use, or other acting-out behavior, it is not always possible to predict with certainty that these issues will not arise in a training facility (Neufeldt, 1994a). As a consequence, procedures should be clear and a supervisor should be available on-site to assist counselors or even intervene directly when potential emergencies arise.

Similarly, supervisors should elaborate procedures for situations in which counselors are legally required to make official reports. In most states, counselors must report the occurrence of child abuse or the reasonable suspicion that clients may harm themselves or others (Corey et al., 1998). The legal procedures should be clear to trainees, and a supervisor should be available on-site to assist them in making these legally mandated reports.

Advance training is an important component of supervision for emergencies. It is helpful to model likely emergency situations and ask counselors to role-play with their colleagues or supervisors before they face actual emergency situations. We incorporate this modeling and practice into the practicum course described in Part III of this manual.

*Termination.* Termination procedures should likewise be spelled out. Trainees should know how and when to broach the topic of termination with clients, and what is likely to ensue. As well, they should understand that "mini-terminations" occur each time they go on vacation, and they must be prepared to discuss their clients' feelings with regard to these pauses in counseling.

Although ideally counselors and clients arrive at termination decisions strictly on the basis of clinical factors, other factors sometimes make termination a more one-sided affair. Clients sometimes decide unilaterally that they do not want to come to sessions anymore. Furthermore, the individuals who use low-cost counseling services often have unstable job and living situations that make them more likely to move away before therapy is completed to everyone's satisfaction. On the other hand, counselors in training programs frequently make unilateral changes too as they move on to other sites or end their training (Teyber, 1997); in these instances, cases often need to be transferred to other therapists. In all of these cases, counselors need to be trained to discuss with their clients the feelings clients have regarding termination. Likewise, counselors need to talk out their own feelings about termination with their supervisors so that they will not act them out with their clients.

Trainees should know exactly what is required in terms of paperwork for both case transfers and termination. Often a form to evaluate the counseling relationship or the success of counseling to that point is included. To ensure that clients fill these forms out without bias, they can be told that the counselors will not see what they have written. Counselors are asked to make certain that such confidentiality is maintained. In addition, some sites require follow-up procedures, and counselors need to know what they must do to follow up on clients and explain that to the clients at the time of termination.

## Response to Ethical Issues as They Arise in the Counseling Process

Specific procedures can be spelled out for many situations, such as the beginning of counseling or termination, but many ethical issues arise in an ongoing fashion. The supervisor is enjoined to address these as they arise. Two of these, however, seem to be particularly problematic for trainees (Ladany et al., in press; Ladany et al., 1997), and ways to address them are elaborated below.

*Sexual feelings.* Trainees usually understand that they are not to have sexual or romantic relationships with their clients. This knowledge, however, sometimes makes it difficult for trainees to discuss sexual or romantic feelings they may have toward their clients. In a qualitative study by Ladany et al. (1997), trainees stated that they are sometimes more invested, caring, and attentive than usual to the clients toward whom they have sexual feelings and are sometimes more distant, distracted, and lacking in objectivity. Nonetheless, they said in this and another study (Ladany, Hill, Corbett, & Nutt, 1996) that they do not report these feelings to their supervisors. Although Worthington and Gugliotti (1997) argued that it is the trainee's responsibility to report his or her feelings in supervision, trainees indicated that they did not do so because of poor supervisory alliances or fears that supervisors would be unable to help or would view the trainee more negatively after the disclosure. Consequently, it is the supervisor's task to recognize a trainee's uncharacteristic concern for or distance from one client and inquire about such feelings. Such inquiries should be handled sensitively through the careful use of strategy 7, "Explore trainee feelings during the counseling session" (discussed in chapter 3). This is a significant concern to trainees, who mentioned in two studies (Ladany et al., in press; Ladany et al., 1997) that sexual attraction was not adequately addressed by supervisors or in training programs.

*Multicultural sensitivity toward clients.* Specific strategies for developing empathy toward clients from cultures other than the trainees' own and ways of addressing multicultural issues are elaborated in the practicum course outlined in Part III. Some of the ethical components are addressed here. The American Psychological Association (1993) outlined guidelines for the provision of services to ethnic, linguistic, and culturally diverse populations, and all ethical codes for counselors and psychologists prohibit discrimination on the basis of all or most of the following: race, ethnicity, gender, age, differential abilities, religion, economic status, and sexual orientation. Nevertheless, counselors may be unaware of assumptions they may hold toward clients who differ from themselves along these dimensions (Ivey, Ivey, & Simek-Morgan, 1993). In addition, trainees reported

(Ladany et al., in press) that supervisors sometimes made multiculturally insensitive remarks about clients.

It is the supervisor's task to inquire about trainee feelings toward clients who differ from themselves. In addition, supervisors should model sensitivity to cultural issues. In particular, supervisors must familiarize themselves with the social and cultural experiences of the clients their supervisees treat to provide supervision to trainees in a culturally appropriate fashion. Perhaps more important, they must examine their own feelings and attitudes toward any clients seen by their trainees who differ from themselves. Pedersen (1991) argued that all individual differences can be conceptualized and addressed as cultural differences, and this definition broadens the area in which supervisors should address their own and their trainees' feelings. This issue is not addressed by the ACES (1995) ethical code for supervision, but Ladany et al. (in press) described it as a necessary component of supervisor ethical behavior.

## ETHICAL BEHAVIOR WITHIN THE SUPERVISORY RELATIONSHIP

Supervisors, who must adhere to ethical principles as therapists and teach them to their trainees, must also conduct themselves in a caring and just way within the supervisory relationship. The bulk of discussion of supervisor ethics in the literature (see, for example, ACES, 1995; Bernard & Goodycar, 1998; Corey et al., 1998) focuses on the supervisor's respectful and fair treatment of supervisees. Suggestions are made below to address the ethical issues outlined by Ladany et al. (in press).

### Supervisor Training in Supervision

The ACES (1995) ethical standards for supervision stated that training in supervision is a necessary prerequisite for supervisors' assumption of that role. On behalf of ACES, Borders et al. (1991) outlined a desirable curriculum for supervisor training. Supervised practice of supervision is also recommended. To ensure adequate training of supervisors, the National Board for Certified Counselors currently offers a credential for supervisors of national certified counselors.

Unfortunately, few supervisors of counselors or other mental health workers have actually received explicit training in supervision (Corey et al., 1998). Although professional organizations and state licensing boards sometimes specify a necessary amount of post-licensure practice experience for supervisors, they seldom require training focused on the task of guiding less-experienced professional therapists. Consequently, it is up to supervisors themselves to obtain the training they never received in graduate school. One way is to read books and attend courses on counseling supervision. This manual offers numerous practical suggestions for supervision, and more complete books on theory and research, such as Bernard and Goodyear's (1998) *Fundamentals of Clinical Supervision* or Watkins's (1997b) *Handbook of Psychotherapy Supervision*, offer a broader picture of the field as a whole.

Novice supervisors need to be supervised on their own supervision of counseling trainees. Professionals who are beginning to supervise can often call universities in local or nearby communities to obtain names of experienced supervisors. Those who wish to become national certified counselors can call the National Board for Certified Counselors to obtain the names of certified supervisors near them. However they obtain it, novice supervisors can enhance their own skills by securing such guidance of their work with professional counselors less experienced than themselves.

## Establishment of Expectations

Supervisors lay the groundwork for ethical practice within supervisory relationships when they specify requirements and procedures at the outset. Trainees are characteristically very anxious when they begin their first practicum experience (Skovholt & Rønnestad, 1995). Understanding what is expected of them can allay some of that anxiety.

*Orientation to professional roles and consent for supervision.* Surprising as it may seem to longtime practitioners, many trainees do not know what to expect in supervision. They do not know how they should behave and what they can anticipate from their supervisors. In situations in which beginning counselors are supervised by supervisors-in-training, under the direction of a master supervisor who also teaches the basic counseling course, beginning counselors can be particularly confused about professional roles.

At the beginning of such a course, the master supervisor can explain exactly how the course will be conducted and what the roles of each participant are. Along with a syllabus, the instructor explains how often the class will meet and how often students will meet with their student supervisors. The responsibilities of each person, the instructor and master supervisor, the student supervisor, and the trainee, are outlined. In particular, the instructor states that all counseling and supervision sessions must be audiotaped or videotaped for supervisory purposes. Such an explicit policy can prevent most conscious ethical violations by either supervisors or trainees.

*Limits to confidentiality.* Trainees need to know from the beginning exactly what is and is not confidential and from whom. Nothing, for instance, that is told to the student supervisor can be kept in confidence from the master supervisor, who is ultimately responsible for trainee competence and behavior. Because all sessions are videotaped, trainees can expect that whatever they do in supervision may be shown in the supervisor's own supervision group. Knowing that they will be videotaped enables trainees to decide what to share with their student supervisors.

Concurrently, the members of the supervisor group need to establish a policy of confidentiality among themselves. Trainees need to know that whatever they discuss in supervision will not be mentioned by the supervisors outside of supervision class. This is particularly important to stress because trainees are usually all members of the same training program and so function as peers in settings outside of supervision. Who the "stars" of the practicum group are and which trainees are struggling are not appropriate subjects for program-wide gossip. To further limit the possibility of disrespectful gossip, we ask supervisors-in-training not to discuss the trainees assigned to their colleagues, even among themselves, outside of the supervision class.

As a rule, what is discussed in supervision will not be shared with other faculty or staff. Exceptions to this occur, however. Evaluations of trainee performance will naturally become part of the public record, and when the master supervisor deems it necessary, he or she must share concerns about trainee impairment or needs with appropriate faculty members. It is a good policy for master supervisors to promise their supervisees (i.e., all supervisors-in-training and counselors-in-training) that they will notify them in advance when they plan to speak with other faculty about them. In this way, distrust is limited and the supervisory relationship is enhanced. Naturally, the supervisee whose questionable performance is under discussion with other faculty may not feel particularly pleased about it, but other supervisees can know that they will not be denigrated behind their backs.

All course policies, such as the requirement to videotape or audiotape sessions, along with limits to confidentiality, should also be spelled out in writing. Trainees and the course instructor and supervisors should sign the written statement of policies, and each should keep a copy for future reference. This limits possibilities for misunderstanding.

*Session boundaries and respectful treatment.* Knowing when and where supervision will occur makes it possible for trainees to prepare. In the event that the supervisor needs to cancel a session or cut it short, he or she should give adequate notice and offer to reschedule. Once in a session, trainees have the right to expect their supervisor's full attention and to be free from interruptions. In short, supervisors need to treat the times scheduled with trainees as carefully as therapists treat time with clients.

*Crisis coverage and intervention.* As indicated earlier, supervisors are responsible for the management of emergencies. They need to be in a place where they can be easily reached, in person or by telephone, during all trainee sessions. With beginners, it is particularly important to have a student supervisor or faculty supervisor at the site when counseling sessions take place. Supervisors should encourage trainees to come out of the session for advice whenever a situation arises that may require emergency procedures or legally mandated reporting. Written policies for supervisors at any site should delineate emergency procedures in detail, so that both supervisors and trainees know exactly what to do and when. It is not possible for even the most experienced supervisor to prevent some negative outcomes with clients, but a competent supervisor can assist the trainee to carry out the best possible procedures. If these fail to prevent a client suicide, for instance, the supervisor is there to help the trainee with the feelings that naturally occur at such times.

*Written procedures for summative evaluation.* At the very first meeting, the supervisor needs to explain the criteria and procedures for evaluation to be done at the end of the academic term. A written list of tasks to be completed successfully, such as "Trainee will see three volunteer clients for a total of three sessions each," or "Trainee will demonstrate the ability to elicit the client's feelings toward the counselor during the session," clarify expectations. Likewise, a copy of a final evaluation form should be presented.

The form should include all areas on which trainees will be evaluated. We have found that a good evaluation form covers the areas of clinical and relationship skills, professional presentation and behavior, knowledge demonstration, and agency behavior, and provides a 5-point scale, with an explanation for each rating. Each number does not represent a grade, but rather the amount of supervision the trainee still needs in that area. It is important to reiterate this point with the high-achieving students who make up our graduate programs. Explaining that "No one is expected to score over a 2 or 3 in the performance areas during the first year because you are only at the beginning of your training, and if you could function without supervision at this point, why would you need further practicum experiences?" is helpful in alleviating trainee anxiety. Furthermore, written comments that include particular examples of trainee performance illuminate the ratings in each area. A number by itself is seldom helpful; behavioral observations provide a direction for the trainee's future development of skill. It is inappropriate to evaluate the person's personality or character. If the trainee exhibits impaired performance, a statement about the performance should suffice. Instead of writing, for instance, "The trainee is inhibited and passive in dealing with clients," the supervisor can write, "The trainee needs to speak more frequently in session and provide the client with reflections of feeling, restatements of content, and occasional interpretations, so that the client can see that the counselor understands his or her experiences."

No evaluation form should simply be handed to the trainee. Instead, the course instructor and student supervisor should meet with the trainee at a time scheduled in advance. Trainees should be asked to prepare for evaluation by thinking about their strengths in counseling as well as areas they need to develop further. Discussion of these should occur before the written evaluation is presented. Trainees and supervisors develop goals toward which the trainee can work during the next practicum course, whether or not that supervisor will be involved.

It is also helpful to elicit trainees' comments about their experiences in the course. Although some students may hesitate to speak up in this setting and respond more easily to the anonymous course evaluations provided in class, soliciting their opinions during the meeting conveys the belief that evaluation goes both ways and that supervisor performance is also open for discussion.

Discussion is followed by an opportunity for each person to read the written evaluation. Questions about any comment are solicited. The supervisor and course instructor sign the evaluation, and the trainee is likewise asked to sign to show simply that he or she has read the evaluation. Supervisors then tell the trainee to come back if any questions later surface about any comment or rating. Trainees are also told what to do if they disagree with any rating (e.g., that they may file a written statement of their position along with the evaluation).

We use a similar form with student supervisors, adapted to include skills and tasks appropriate to that arena. Likewise, we suggest that the master supervisor meet individually with each student supervisor at the end of the academic term to discuss his or her performance and future goals.

## Ongoing Ethical Behavior

Explicit expectations go a long way to make practicum policies and expectations clear, but every ethical dilemma cannot be anticipated and written into a plan at the beginning of the course. In fact, we often put in policies to handle the dilemmas that arose the year before—and then the same situations do not arise! The supervisor must be prepared to deal ethically with the ongoing issues of both supervision and counseling.

*Formative evaluation and consistent monitoring of supervisee activities.* Many trainee complaints listed by Ladany et al. (in press) revolved around inadequate ongoing feedback. Among these were objections to surprising comments in the summative course evaluations, for example, "I was very surprised to find that she was unsatisfied with my work. I had never been evaluated or critiqued." No trainee should be surprised by negative comments at the final evaluation. Instead, feedback on inadequate performance should be given clearly and frequently during the term.

Henry, Schacht and associates (1993) reported that supervisors who provided explicit feedback about specific aspects of therapist performance promoted improvement in those areas. Trainees want that feedback, and their complaints (e.g., "supervisor gives little feedback," and "supervisor never listened to my audiotapes"; Ladany et al., in press) demonstrate their dissatisfaction when they do not get it. Trainees have a right to know what their supervisors are thinking and how they can improve. Failure to provide it is a serious ethical violation because in that instance, the supervisor fails to provide the most essential task of supervision.

Some authors (e.g., Bernard & Goodyear, 1998; Knapp & VandeCreek, 1997) have recommended that supervisors document their supervision sessions in writing, just as therapists keep progress notes on clients. Possible formats for documentation appear in Bernard & Goodyear's (1998) book. When they write out their concerns about trainee performance, supervisors can consider ways to address them in future sessions. This can encourage more consistent feedback from one supervision session to the next.

*Expertise and competency issues.* Supervisors are expected to have expertise with the client problems that appear in the cases they supervise (Bernard & Goodyear, 1998; Corey et al., 1998; Knapp & VandeCreek, 1997). When they do not, they are advised to refer the case to another trainee or refer the trainee to another supervisor. When this is not possible (e.g., when an unanticipated problem, such as an unusual eating disorder, is disclosed well into the therapy process and there is no other supervisor available for this trainee), the supervisor can consult with another therapist on a regular basis about the case (Bernard & Goodyear, 1998).

Likewise, supervisors should ensure in each instance that a client is assigned to a trainee with adequate skill to take on the challenge the client presents. This is a judgment call; the supervisor balances the trainee's need to learn new skills with the client's needs for adequate treatment. Consequently, the supervisor really needs to ensure that the trainee possesses sufficient resources to build a relationship with the client and develop the needed specific skills with careful supervision.

*Dual roles.* Sexual relationships between current trainees and supervisors are clearly prohibited by all ethical codes (Corey et al., 1998). Nevertheless, evidence that graduate students (Pope, Levenson, & Schover, 1979; Miller & Larrabee, 1995) have had sexual relationships with faculty members abounds. Sexual feelings between supervisors and their supervisees (Bernard & Goodyear, 1998; Ladany et al., 1996; Larrabee & Miller, 1993) naturally arise and need to be discussed, though trainees are hesitant to do so (Ladany et al., 1996; Ladany et al., 1997). Supervisors are reminded that feelings talked out are less likely to be acted out. Bernard and Goodyear (1998) suggested that trainees and supervisors may pursue a sexual relationship subsequent to their supervisory relationship. We recommend, however, that supervisors, like therapists, not end their supervisory roles simply to pursue such a relationship. Many academic institutions now have rules that prohibit any student-professor sexual contact, and we encourage faculty supervisors not to pursue relationships with supervisees until the trainees have graduated.

Nonsexual dual roles within the university setting are ubiquitous and unavoidable (Goodyear & Sinnett, 1984). It is important to make certain that the supervisor does not abuse, exploit, or harm the trainee in any way (Bernard & Goodyear, 1998). Student supervisors are in a unique position with regard to trainees because they are usually all students in a single graduate program. They have numerous other contacts. Before assigning trainees to supervisors, it is wise to ask student supervisors to let the master supervisor know if they have a close personal or romantic relationship with any trainee, currently work closely on a research project with a trainee, or if they have had negative interactions or feelings toward a particular trainee. In those cases, it is best to assign the trainee to another supervisor. Beyond that, supervisors regularly have classes and informal social interactions with trainees, and it would be unreasonable to expect that they not attend certain classes or social events for fear of encountering their trainees. Instead, they are encouraged to discuss the issues with trainees at their first meeting and explain that their current roles prohibit close friendships. They can together develop informal rules for managing their relationship outside supervision. When in doubt in a particular situation, student supervisors are expected to seek supervision.

It is important to remember that cultural values affect trainees' perceptions of the relationship they have with supervisors. One European American trainee in our experience was surprised to discover that a Latina trainee believed her supervisor did not like her because she "did not speak to me when we passed in the hallways," and this affected the supervisory relationship. Only when another supervisor, also a Latina, informed the European American that in Latin cultures one always acknowledges one's acquaintances at any encounter did the supervisor understand the way the extrasession behavior had been perceived.

*Differentiating supervision from psychotherapy and counseling.* Supervisors are enjoined to avoid therapeutic relationships with their trainees (Kitchener, 1988; Neufeldt & Nelson, in press; Whiston & Emerson, 1989) and prohibited from taking on trainees as counseling clients by ethical codes (Bernard & Goodyear, 1998; Corey et al., 1998). Rosenblatt and Mayer (1975) identified a therapeutic approach to supervisees as one of the supervisory styles most objectionable to trainees, but Ladany et al. (in press) stated that only 5% of the trainees they surveyed reported that inappropriate counseling occurred in their supervisory relationships. This is a complex topic because at times counseling behaviors (Bernard, 1979) are desirable responses from supervisors (Neufeldt & Nelson, in press).

Exploration of trainee feelings and emotions may become necessary in carrying out a critical task of supervision, as Vasquez (1992) pointed out:

> One of the most important responsibilities of a supervisor is to assess the supervisee's limitations, blind spots, and impairments in order to protect the welfare of the supervisee's clients. . . . A goal for supervisors is thus to promote the supervisee's self-awareness and ability to recognize personal issues that could negatively affect the therapeutic process. (p. 199)

To assess trainee limitations, encourage self-awareness, and protect clients, supervisors need to use the counseling behaviors of supervision identified in this manual (strategies 7–12). In particular, trainees need to understand when their own feelings and reactions interfere with their responses to clients (Neufeldt & Nelson, in press; Whiston & Emerson, 1989) or, in contrast, when these feelings may illuminate their understanding of a client (Neufeldt & Nelson, in press).

Supervisors teach reflective self-questioning when they encourage trainees to notice their feelings. Useful supervisor observations facilitate this process. Stating, for instance, "At that point you seemed to draw back and look away from the client. What was happening for you then?" helps trainees notice their own shifts in behavior as cues to question themselves. They are then in a position to identify feelings that prevent them from responding as they might wish to do. When the issues that interfere with therapy have been identified, however, supervisors encourage trainees to address those feelings themselves (Whiston & Emerson, 1989). Often the clarification of feelings is enough; having attended to their internal processes, trainees can set them aside to attend to the client. If not, they can explore their own dynamics with other professionals away from the supervision environment.

In other instances, their own feelings inform a therapist about the client. If, for instance, a trainee's initial response to the supervisor's question about withdrawing is, "I don't know why I feel that way with this client; it is different from my usual response," this provides another teaching opportunity. Trainees can learn that their feelings are like those of others in the client's life, for example, and so understand the client's experience more effectively. Likewise, identifying their own reactions allows therapists to avoid reenacting their clients' usual experiences in session (Teyber, 1997).

Beyond these situations, discussion of trainee feeling is necessary on those few occasions when the trainee's transitory personal issues intrude upon supervision (Neufeldt & Nelson, in press). For instance, a trainee who has just been rejected from a desired internship placement may be so distraught that supervision cannot proceed until those feelings are addressed. Acknowledgment of feelings needs to be brief and focused, and if the trainee is still too overwhelmed to focus on supervisory tasks, then supervision should be postponed.

Although supervisors may ethically explore feelings in all of the previously described situations, they need to limit the exploration to issues that currently affect their trainees' professional functioning. Investigation of personal history or deep probing of trainee dynamics is inappropriate, because trainees may not know how to draw the line between counseling, which is a nonjudgmental activity, and supervision, in which evaluation is required.

*Respect for trainee ideas and alternative perspectives.* Although not among the primary ethical concerns noted by supervisors, respect for alternative perspectives ranked with confidentiality as the second most-often listed complaint of trainees about supervisors (Ladany et al., in press). Like other training models, ours recommends the use of a single theoretical orientation. Trainees, however, seemed to object not to the actual use of a particular approach but to a lack of respect for the trainee's theoretical perspective, with statements like, "My supervisor has strong preference for her orientation, thus comments made about other orientations, including mine, are at times disrespectful," and "the supervisor is all knowing and it is his way or else" (Ladany et al., in press).

It is unreasonable to ask supervisors to know and use all orientations to a level of competence. With beginners it is furthermore inadvisable. It is, however, important for supervisors to maintain an air of respect toward trainees. It is not only respectful but practical to show acceptance of their ideas and feelings if we are interested in hearing trainees. If we ridicule any of their ideas, even if they espouse astrology as a means of therapy, we create an atmosphere in which creative ideas cannot be tried. (This does not mean that we may not question the predictive validity of astrology as a therapeutic approach.)

As a value, we strongly believe in mutuality, and we believe it comes into play here. We ask trainees to treat us and our ideas with respect, and we must treat them and their ideas with respect. In the same vein, we talk directly to trainees about mutuality of expectations in other areas. We offer, for instance, to participate in any experiences that they may find difficult, such as acting as clients with real issues in role-plays and showing our own work with clients (with client permission) to the group.

In the same way, we address mutuality early in supervision when we talk about evaluation. We state that we will speak directly to trainees about any criticisms we have of their work, and we ask trainees to speak directly with us about their objections about ours. We state that we will try not to give any surprises in their final evaluations, that everything written there will have been told to them earlier, and we ask that they not surprise us in the anonymous written evaluations they hand in. We recognize that this is sometimes an impossible standard for trainees, because of their very real fears of retaliation for their critical remarks, but we believe it can work to some degree. We have found that when trainees do offer criticism, if we respond by listening to and considering what they have to say in a respectful manner, they will continue to talk openly with us. This creates a climate of trust. Likewise, if we talk about them disrespectfully to other students or to faculty, the word usually gets back in some way, and the sense of mutual respect and trust is lost.

By our response to trainees and their ideas, we provide the kind of ethical climate that can lead to a good supervisory working alliance, as Ladany et al. (in press) have shown. When we make our expectations for performance and our evaluation procedures clear from the very first meeting, when we demonstrate ethical and respectful treatment of clients, when we respond positively to trainee ideas and thinking, when we are honest and consistent in our feedback, when we make the boundaries between supervision and other activities clear, and when we recognize the power of our position and conduct ourselves judiciously and never exploit trainee or client vulnerability, we demonstrate our commitment to professional ethics. How we treat our trainees will shape how they treat not only clients but their own trainees in the future.

# PART II

# SUPERVISION STRATEGIES AND CASE CONCEPTUALIZATION

All strategies in part II's two chapters have been designed to provide a supervisory environment of support and challenge that nourishes counselor development. Strategies 1 through 17 are in chapter 3; strategies 18 through 28 are in chapter 4. Holloway (1995) emphasized that involvement in the supervisory relationship enables the supervisee to grow and develop into an effective professional therapist. Vignettes included in these chapters illustrate the collaborative nature of the relationship and show how supervisors assist trainees to take the necessary steps to turn their academic, declarative knowledge into the procedural knowledge necessary for practice. In each vignette, supervisors encourage trainees to talk about the client, the counseling relationship, counseling theories and strategies, ethical implications, and the interpersonal process of supervision.

Each strategy is designed to encourage reflective inquiry on the part of the trainee. We believe that trainees enter a graduate program with experience in life and human relationships along with their undergraduate academic preparation, and that supervisors are wise to acknowledge and build on that. Instead of immediately telling trainees what to do with a given client, supervisors in our examples first question trainees about their experiences in session and their thoughts and feelings about them. In this way, we incorporate the practice of reflective process that is essential for professional development both during training and beyond. Our long-term goal is the development of the reflective practitioner who can self-evaluate and gradually develop the expertise available 10 to 15 years after training is completed (Skovholt, Rønnestad, & Jennings, 1997).

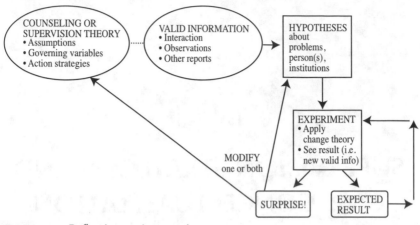

**FIGURE 1.** *Reflection on Interventions*

A reflective counselor examines what happens in practice in a particular way. Figure 1 illustrates reflective examination of counseling and is based on Argyris and Schön's (1974) Model II.

The counselor begins with a theory of counseling. In training, this is likely to be one of the major orientations, such as family systems, cognitive-behavioral, psychoanalytic, Gestalt, or interpersonal process. Each theory is based on assumptions, governing variables, and action strategies. The counselor uses the theory to look at information based on interactions with the client in sessions, observations in other situations (such as school), and reports such as formal assessments or medical records. From this perspective, the counselor makes hypotheses about the presenting problem or problems in session and the nature of the client or client system (e.g., the family or school). At this point the counselor plans an action, consistent with the theory, to test the hypothesis and experiments in session. If the counselor obtains the expected result, he or she can proceed with the next action experiment. If the result is a surprise, however, the counselor needs to modify the hypothesis. When results do not match theory on a consistent basis, the counselor may modify the theory.

To regard unexpected results as information rather than as failure is a challenge for novice counselors. Typically they want to get the expected results, to allay their anxiety about their own performance. In this situation, it is difficult for supervisors to resist telling them what to do. This is even more true for novice supervisors, who tend to be "highly supportive and/or didactic, concrete, structured, and task-oriented" (Borders & Fong, 1994, p. 281). This manual assists novice supervisors to handle novice-counselor anxiety and encourage reflective practice.

All supervision strategies have been designed for use by supervisors-in-training. As a consequence, the strategies are very specific. They emphasize encouraging trainee exploration and building on what trainees already know—even what they don't realize they know. Questioning is focused on what the therapist has experienced in session or what the client has done, that is, highlighting what to attend to rather than what to do next. The strategies are designed to break the common habit of constant focus on the client and what to do with the client. Even Carl Rogers, who told Rod Goodyear (1982), "my major goal is to help the therapist to grow in self-confidence and to grow in understanding of the therapeutic process," said in the same interview, "Often when I see a tape of an interview or even hear a tape of an interview, somehow my feeling very strongly is 'Move out of that chair; let me take over' because I really have a love of doing therapy."

Practicing the strategies with colleagues or other beginning supervisors helps fix the approach in place. We believe it is important that supervisors integrate the principles behind the strategies with their own personal styles, their natural use of language, their personal life experiences and professional experiences as therapists and supervisors, and their ongoing work with particular supervisees. It is critical for the master supervisor to use reflective inquiry when training supervisors. Unless supervisors experience opportunities to reflect on their own work, they will be unable to provide similar opportunities for the counselors they train.

# CHAPTER 3

# EFFECTIVE STRATEGIES FOR INTRODUCTORY SUPERVISION

Determining the basic strategies each supervisor should learn proved surprisingly easy. We examined the research and determined that more research supported the social role model described by Bernard (1979) than any other. Bernard differentiated among supervisor roles in her discrimination model. Furthermore, Stenack and Dye (1982) delineated specific functions for each role. In one of several studies validating Bernard's model, Stenack and Dye (1982) administered a list of supervisor behaviors to 36 supervisors and trainees and asked participants to indicate which were teacher, counselor, or consultant functions. The teaching and counseling roles were clearly differentiated, and the consultant role was less so. On the basis of the comprehensive list of supervisor functions that made up each role in Stenack and Dye's (1982) study, we developed our initial strategies.

We took the functions listed by Stenack and Dye (1982), described them in behavioral terms, and defined each as a strategy. In addition, we have added a strategy to their list of functions by dividing one behavior to make two strategies (7 and 8). The strategy names are quoted from Stenack and Dye; the explanations are ours and reflect our principles for working within the supervisory relationship to encourage reflective practice. Each strategy is listed under the teacher, counselor, or consultant role designated in Stenack and Dye's (1982) study and provides a basis for developing supervisory skill.

Although research on supervisor development is at an early stage (Borders & Fong, 1994; Watkins, 1995), we presume that development proceeds along a novice-expert continuum. In his studies of teachers, Berliner (1988) reported that novice instructors benefit from the use of "standard lesson forms and scripts" (p. 22) as they practice their craft. Rosenberg (1998) developed a supervisor training program that incorporated the deliberate practice, self-reflection, and ongoing corrective feedback that seem to be necessary for the development of expertise in any area (Ericsson & Lehmann, 1996). We suggest that the supervisor learns from practice with specific strategies as well. The 17 beginning strategies (listed in Table 1) should be rehearsed individually in role-play with colleagues before they ɪbserved counseling session interactions.

2. ᴀ‌_____ ɪelor to provide a hypothesis about the client.

3. Identify appropriate interventions.

4. Teach, demonstrate, or model intervention techniques.

5. Explain the rationale behind specific strategies and interventions.

6. Interpret significant events in the counseling session.

7. Explore trainee feelings during the counseling session.

8. Explore trainee feelings during the supervision session.

9. Explore trainee feelings concerning specific techniques or interventions.

10. Encourage trainee self-exploration of confidence and worries in the counseling session.

11. Help the trainee define personal competencies and areas for growth.

12. Provide opportunities for the trainee to process their own affect and defenses.

13. Provide alternative interventions or conceptualizations for trainee use.

14. Encourage trainee brainstorming of strategies and interventions.

15. Encourage trainee discussion of client problems and motivations.

16. Solicit and attempt to satisfy trainee needs during the supervision session.

17. Allow the trainee to structure the supervision session.

---

are used with trainees. As supervisors practice them, they should reflect on their experiences with colleagues and trainees and receive feedback on their performance. In this way, they can evaluate when and how to use the strategies and modify them in ways that are consistent with their own styles. They can make them their own and use them effectively in a variety of situations.

## TEACHER FUNCTIONS

When the supervisor functions as a teacher, he or she instructs the trainee. Instruction, however, does not mean "the banking concept of education" (Freire, 1993, p. 53), in which the students are "receptacles" and the teacher "deposits" knowledge. Freire described an effective teacher as one who is a "teacher-student" among "student-teachers" (p. 61). In the teaching strategies described below, the supervisor proposes problems to the student therapists, and together they work to understand and solve them.

The supervisor draws on professional research and past clinical and teaching experiences (Neufeldt, Doucette-Gates, & Carvalho, 1998), and the trainee draws on objective knowledge or any prior subjective experiences in social interactions, work settings, or psychotherapy (as client, counselor, or paraprofessional helper).

## 1. Evaluate Observed Counseling Session Interactions

In this mode, the supervisor is directly observing or listening to tapes of counseling sessions. While observing, the supervisor considers whether the trainee's behaviors serve the intention of the trainee at this time in session, are appropriate for this client at this time and in the context of the client's cultural history, and illustrate good use of counseling skill. Following the observation, the supervisor elicits the trainee's feelings about performing as a counselor. The supervisor acknowledges the trainee's observations, explores them and validates the trainee's thought process, presents the trainee with additional observations about his or her performance, and checks with the trainee to see what he or she has made of the supervisor's comments.

Critical to the feedback delivered is an understanding of the trainee's reasoning in making the original intervention in session. Like Piaget (J. M. Zimmer, personal communication, October 13, 1998), we need to be curious about our students' apparent errors. My colleague, Yukari Okamoto (personal communication, February 6, 1998) described questioning a child about mathematics. She was initially surprised by a child's "wrong" answer. She had told the preschool child, "Here is half a pizza. Here are the two glasses of water a child would need to drink with a half pizza. Now," she asked, "here is a whole pizza. How many glasses would a child need with it?" "One," answered the child. Puzzled, Okamoto asked how he had reached his conclusion. "Oh," he said, "if you ate a whole pizza and drank four glasses of water, you'd be sick!" Only after she inquired about his reasoning and understood it could Okamoto proceed with teaching.

In the same way, if we fail to understand our trainees' process of deciding when and how to intervene, we may miss good reasoning and lose an opportunity to teach. Should the trainee, for instance, suggest to a client that she make a barbecue dinner on the back porch for her husband, we may think that the counselor is giving advice inappropriately. The trainee, however may simply wish to test whether the client cares enough about her husband to make this effort on his behalf. Once we understand that reasoning, we are in a position to help the trainee design a new strategy to ascertain the client's feelings without giving inappropriate advice.

Although we do not specify it in every strategy, we recommend that supervisors frequently ascertain how trainees make sense of what the supervisor has offered. Anyone who has ever taught students and then tested them recognizes that students construct what teachers say in very different ways. Questioning students about this is consistent with both interaction and reflective process theories and was reported by Schön (D.A. Schön, personal communication, February 16, 1994) as a strategy he used with supervisor-therapist dyads in Europe.

*To illustrate:*

*Supervisor:* As you observed yourself reflecting feelings to John [a friend who played the role of the client] how did you feel about it?

*Trainee:* I always dislike listening to myself—it sounds so odd. But as I listened, I thought I got his mood right, that he was depressed, and I said so.

*Supervisor:* Yes. How did you get the sense that he was depressed?

*Trainee:* Well, he said a lot of things that indicate depression like "I feel like crying," and "I think about her all the time," and he looked sad.

*Supervisor:* Your thinking makes sense. I think you made a good hypothesis, that John might be depressed. However, that's a diagnostic word and sounds kind of analytical. Clients sometimes hear diagnostic words as pronouncements about them. What you just said to me, that he looked sad, might have fit better as a reflection to use with the client. What do you think about that?

*Trainee:* Yeah, I see what you mean. Sad is a feeling that everyone understands, and the client might feel that I am trying to understand his experience rather than categorizing him.

*Supervisor:* Exactly!

In this way the supervisor validates the trainee's perception and develops the trainee's skill further by encouraging the trainee to use different language with a client. When the supervisor asks the trainee what he or she thinks, the supervisor is checking to see how the trainee integrated what the supervisor said.

## 2. Ask Counselor to Provide a Hypothesis About the Client

Developing hypotheses about clients and testing them out is the basis of a reflective approach to therapy. In this strategy, the supervisor encourages the trainee to take the first step. He or she asks the trainee to describe the client's behavior in the session, and then invites the trainee to suggest several ideas about the client. These ideas may be hypotheses about the client's internal experience, the origins of the client's behavior, the cultural context of the client's behavior, or the degree to which the client's behavior might be old or new. The supervisor encourages the trainee to develop several hypotheses, to invite flexibility and creativity. The supervisor then asks the trainee to select a hypothesis to explore further in session.

*To illustrate:*

*Supervisor:* Tell me what you see the client doing in this part of the session.

*Trainee:* Hmmm. He is shifting around in his chair a lot.

*Supervisor:* Yeah . . . and what else?

*Trainee:* Gee, as I look at it again, I see that he wasn't looking at me much, even though earlier he was looking me right in the eye . . . and his mouth looks funny. . . .

*Supervisor:* Now that you see that, what do you imagine is happening inside of him?

*Trainee:* Boy . . . I didn't notice it then, but I think he was about to cry and he was trying not to.

*Supervisor:* What do you think that was all about? What happened right before that?

*[They rewind the tape and look at the segment again.]*

*Trainee:* Hmm . . . he was talking about his sister's marriage . . . maybe he is worried about her or misses her or something . . . I don't know . . . but something about her.

*Supervisor:* Yeah, that might be right. What other hypotheses do you have?

*Trainee:* Hmm—maybe he got upset before that, when we were talking about work.

*Supervisor:* How do you want to start checking these ideas out?

*Trainee:* Well, I could just ask him if he is worried about his sister.

*Supervisor:* Yeah, that might be a place to start.

For this strategy and in this vignette, the supervisor takes a rather Socratic approach and encourages the trainee to observe the client more carefully and then develop hypotheses based on the observations. Trainees in beginning practica often fall silent when faced with questions (Holloway & Wampold, 1983), presumably because they really do not know what to say or are fearful of giving the "wrong answer." With this in mind, the supervisor in this vignette focused the initial questions on what was clearly observable on the videotape. Once the trainee was engaged in thinking about the client's behavior, the supervisor solicited hypotheses about the client's internal experience. Some trainees' anxiety, however, may be so intense that even the initial question is too tough. In that case, the supervisor can state what he or she sees on the videotape, and then make a remark designed to encourage the trainee, such as "You know this client better than I; what do you think that facial expression and body movement might mean?" Once the trainee provides a hypothesis, then the supervisor uses it to solicit further ideas.

## 3. Identify Appropriate Interventions

We have interpreted this to mean helping the trainee to identify interventions and choose among those suggested. After asking the trainee to select a hypothesis to explore (strategy 2), the supervisor encourages the trainee to consider interventions that would allow the trainee to validate or reject the hypothesis.

The supervisor invites the trainee to suggest appropriate interventions for this purpose. If the trainee seems stuck and unable to think of any, the supervisor names one or two interventions and then asks for more from the trainee. Following the trainee's suggestions, the supervisor may generate additional interventions. The supervisor prompts the trainee to choose one of the interventions to explore the hypothesis; he or she makes certain that the chosen option suits the trainee's personal style. It may be a new intervention or one the trainee has used before, and it moves the trainee to the next step in reflecting process: action.

*To illustrate:*

*[In this situation, the trainee has hypothesized that a client is afraid to show how angry he is at the way he believes he is being treated in graduate school.]*

*Supervisor:* That's quite a hypothesis. Can you conceive of some ways to explore it further?

*Trainee:* Well, let's think . . . I could simply paraphrase what I hear, by saying, "You are saying that you have a lot to do and you don't really think you have been told how to do it," which might get at it.

*Supervisor:* Yes . . . what else can you think of?

*Trainee:* I could just give the old minimal verbal response, "Mmm-hmm," or "Tell me more about that."

*Supervisor:* Those are both possibilities. Let me add a few and then you can decide what best fits this client and your own style. You could confront the client, by describing the discrepancy you see between his words and his facial expression.

*Trainee:* Yeah, I see that.

*Supervisor:* Or you could simply reflect what you think he is feeling, by saying something like, "I'm getting the feeling that you are pretty angry right now. Am I correct?"

*Trainee:* Well, that's direct!

*Supervisor:* Yes. it's funny how we can have hypotheses in our heads about clients and fail to say them out loud. Sometimes that's the easiest way. Is there anything else you might want to try?

*Trainee:* I can't think of anything more right now.

*Supervisor:* Okay. Now the question is, which one is most likely to get the information you want and which would be most comfortable for you?

*Trainee:* Well, although he might get around to exploring this hypothesis if I just paraphrased or gave a minimal response, I can see that he might not. . . . So I think the confrontation or the reflection is most likely to elicit some confirmation or disconfirmation of my hypothesis.

*Supervisor:* I think you're right. . . . Now which is comfortable for you and which are you willing to try?

*Trainee:* I'm not sure I'm that comfortable with either one . . . but I could probably do them. I guess I'd rather try the confrontation, because it is just a matter of describing what I see.

*Supervisor:* Okay. And remember—it is as useful to discover that your hypothesis is invalid as to find it confirmed. Either way gives you a direction for your next move.

In this vignette, the supervisor solicited possibilities from the trainee before providing any strategies and then showed the trainee how to select among them by asking appropriate questions. Again, if the trainee had become silent when asked for some interventions, the supervisor could have suggested one or two. It is always tricky to figure out how to proceed here, because giving a suggestion too soon sometimes stops students from making any of their own, but waiting too long can just aggravate their anxiety to the point where they cannot think creatively. It is the supervisor's primary task to develop a relationship with the trainee that enables the supervisor to assess the situation and act within it on the basis of what the trainee needs (and not on the desire of the supervisor to come up with ideas, despite the ideas' cleverness).

## 4. Teach, Demonstrate, or Model Intervention Techniques

In this mode, the supervisor first describes an intervention verbally. He or she may provide written instructions as well. Then the supervisor either plays a videotape in which he or she models the intervention or acts out the intervention in a role-play with the trainee. Following demonstration of the technique, the supervisor asks the trainee to role-play the technique with several goals and situations in mind. Then the supervisor asks the trainee about his or her experience during the encounter. This allows the trainee to reflect on the interaction between the two participants. Role-playing may include simple verbalizations of responses or more complex interactions with the supervisor or another trainee as client.

*To illustrate:*

*Supervisor:* You are wanting to make the client feel that you understand her feelings, I think.

*Trainee:* Yes.

*Supervisor:* I want to show you one way to do that. In class last week, did you feel understood by your partner in your mock session?

*Trainee:* Yeah. Some of the things she said to me let me know that she really understood my feelings.

*Supervisor:* How did she do that?

*Trainee:* Well, I don't know . . . let's see . . . she seemed really interested in what I was saying. And at one point she said something about my being hurt, and I realized that I really was hurt.

*Supervisor:* So she reflected your feelings accurately, and you felt understood?

*Trainee:* Yeah.

*Supervisor:* Okay . . . today let's practice accurate reflection of feelings.

*Trainee:* All right . . . but I'm really not sure how to go about it.

*Supervisor:* Sure. Let's do a brief role-play of reflections. We can videotape it and then look at the videotape. First, I'll be the counselor. Would you be willing to be the client for a bit and share some of your feelings?

*Trainee:* Sure.

*Supervisor:* Okay. So go ahead and start. Just talk about something that matters to you and you feel comfortable sharing with me, but not something that you would want a lot of counseling on.

*Trainee:* Okay. . . . Well, I've been pretty stressed lately.

*Supervisor:* You feel stressed.

*Trainee:* Yes. I find that I am behind in everything, and I wake up at night worrying about all the things I have to do.

*Supervisor:* So you are anxious about that—enough to wake you up.

*Trainee:* Yes. In the past I've always been able to get everything done that I needed to and have even had time left over. I always got good grades before.

*Supervisor:* It sounds as if you are a bit disappointed that you can't do that anymore.

*Trainee:* Yeah, I am.

*Supervisor:* Okay . . . let's stop here, even though there is a lot we could say about that. Here is the videotape. *[They look at the videotape segment.]* Did you feel that my reflections were accurate?

*Trainee:* Yeah. I suppose that's why I just kept going.

*Supervisor:* Yes, and you kept talking about feelings. Did you notice that I didn't ask you anything about your thoughts and so you just responded with feelings?

*Trainee:* Yes.

*Supervisor:* Okay . . . let's reverse it. I'll be the client. Here goes: I've been working really hard lately, and I'm worried that I'm awfully irritable at home. My daughter is getting kind of crabby with me.

*Trainee:* Oh—you're a little worried.

*Supervisor:* Yes. Actually I'm quite worried! I keep trying to be nicer.

*Trainee:* You feel that you haven't done enough nice things lately.

*Supervisor:* Yes. I haven't taken her anywhere lately, and I get annoyed with very small things.

*Trainee:* You get annoyed with small things?

*Supervisor:* Yes, like dishes left on the counter and shoes left in the living room, and things I don't usually fuss over. Okay . . . let's stop here and play the tape. *[They watch the videotape.]* Did you think that you were able to keep the exchange focused on feelings?

*Trainee:* Well, partly. But you know, somehow it got off, because all of a sudden we were talking about details of what you were doing, and that didn't allow for more feelings.

*Supervisor:* Yes, right. Do you have a sense of where it "got off"?

*Trainee:* Well, it started when I said, "You feel that you haven't done enough nice things lately."

*Supervisor:* Exactly. Do you see why?

*Trainee:* Not really. . . .

*Supervisor:* Well, let me help here. You used the word *"feel"* but you weren't talking about a feeling. You were talking about a thought, the thought about not doing nice things.

*Trainee:* I don't get it.

*Supervisor:* Well, let's see if I can make it clearer. When you add the word *that* to *feel*, you can probably substitute the word *think* for *feel*. Whenever you could substitute the word *think* for *feel* and not change the meaning, you are probably not talking about a feeling. We often say, "I feel that" when we mean "I think that," such as, "I feel that statistics should be taught after research design." A real feeling statement along that line might be "I feel overwhelmed by statistics." Do you see now?

*Trainee:* Yeah, I get it.

*Supervisor:* What else could you have said?

*Trainee:* Well, a reflection for your sentence about not being nice enough might be something like, "You feel inadequate."

*Supervisor:* Sure . . . perfect! Now . . . let's think about where you might use this with a client.

*Trainee:* Well, if I really wanted to learn about the person's feelings, it sounds as if I could begin to reflect the feelings I hear . . . but what if I'm wrong?

*Supervisor:* The client will usually tell you! For instance, if you had said, "You feel inadequate," I might have responded, "No, I just feel sad about it." Because your use of the word *inadequate* focused on a feeling, even one I did not think described me, I would have given you a more accurate feeling back. Your use of a feeling word would have gotten you a feeling, even if it was different from the one you originally hypothesized.

*Trainee:* I see.

*Supervisor:* What other situations might be appropriate for reflections?

*Trainee:* Well, maybe if the person was one of those people who gives a zillion details about what is happening—and I still don't know what it feels like to them?

*Supervisor:* Yeah, that's a good example. Anything else?

*Trainee:* Well, if I just wanted the client to know I understood.

*Supervisor:* Sure.

In this example, after querying the trainee, the supervisor has modeled the intervention, provided the trainee with a chance to practice, and helped the trainee discover where things went awry. Then the supervisor encouraged the trainee to generate ideas for use in actual counseling situations. Although this was an illustration of modeling a very basic skill, the same strategy could be used with a more complex counseling skill.

## 5. Explain the Rationale Behind Specific Strategies and Interventions

After a specific intervention has been suggested for use with a particular client, the supervisor asks the trainee what might be expected to happen in a session if this intervention were used. The supervisor explores the possible meaning of the intervention with reference to the client's gender, ethnicity, and cultural background. The supervisor builds on the trainee's responses and further explains the rationale and intention for the use of this intervention.

*To illustrate:*

*[In this case, the student therapist has agreed to use more silence with a client.]*

*Trainee:* Okay, I think I can be silent more of the time. It's a challenge for me, though, and I'm worried that the client will just get anxious if I sit there and stare at him.

*Supervisor:* Yeah, that's always a concern. If he gets anxious, how will you know?

*Trainee:* You know, probably I'm the one who's going to get anxious. The client probably doesn't feel as responsible for the session as I do.

*Supervisor:* Yes, that's just the point, isn't it?

*Trainee:* What do you mean? . . . Oh, I see. You mean I'm feeling as if I'm responsible for the session, but the client needs to feel responsible to bring up what matters to him.

*Supervisor:* Exactly. And so if you stop talking all the time, what's likely to happen with this highly responsible European American man?

*Trainee:* He'll probably take charge.

*Supervisor:* Sure. And that's important, especially because you are female. In my experience, many men think women know all about feelings (C.D. Hollister, personal communication, May 12, 1991) and it's important for you to leave this client room to think about his own feelings and talk about them, however slowly they may emerge.

Now, your client is a European American man, and even in this feeling area, he's likely to think he should do something if you don't. So he'll probably talk if you are quiet. And his being able to talk about what matters to him would build your alliance.

But, as you know, different cultural groups, depending on their level of assimilation, might need different things in the early counseling sessions to form an alliance with you.

*Trainee:* Yeah, I thought about that with my African American client. I actually tried to be silent with her, and it didn't go over well. She seemed a bit impatient with that silence, like, "When are we going to get on with it?"

*Supervisor:* So silence seemed to work against building a good working alliance with her. Why do you think that was?

*Trainee:* Well, I learned in my cross-cultural counseling class that African Americans often expect more advice and suggestions from counselors.

*Supervisor:* So silence can seem like incompetence—or worse, that this is some kind of trick.

*Trainee:* Exactly.

*Supervisor:* So what did you do with her then?

*Trainee:* Well, I decided to ask her some specific questions about her problem, and I told her I wanted to know these things so we could make a plan. And of course, that's much more comfortable for me; I know how to do that from being an academic tutor.

*Supervisor:* And how did that seem to work?

*Trainee:* It went much better. I can show you that videotape next.

*Supervisor:* Good, I'd like to see it. And remember, once you've got a good alliance going, there might be times later on when silence is appropriate, when you want to give her time to experience her feelings, for instance. We can use a variety of interventions with our clients of various cultural backgrounds, but how we time them is often more important for alliance building than which ones we actually use.

*Trainee:* Yeah, I can see that.

The point here is not that any observations about ethnic or gender groups are necessarily accurate. Rather, the supervisor encourages the therapist to use interventions that will promote a good alliance with the client, and that means taking gender and culture into account. To do that, the supervisor and the counselor discuss some possible interventions to use at particular times with particular types of clients. It is one way to explore the rationale behind an intervention.

In this example, the trainee had some familiarity with multicultural counseling. If that had not been the case, the supervisor could have provided some of the research-based information on cultural preferences that was elicited from the trainee here.

## 6. Interpret Significant Events in the Counseling Session

As in strategy 2, the supervisor asks the trainee to generate ideas about the client. In particular, the supervisor asks for ideas that connect the client's external behavior with cultural background and previous life events, and with potential internal processes. Building on those, the supervisor proceeds to flesh out the outline presented by the trainee and then, if it is appropriate, offers alternative interpretations as well. Then the supervisor asks the trainee how he or she will know if the interpretation is correct.

After the trainee presents one or more possibilities, the supervisor may suggest additional ones. The supervisor asks the trainee what it would mean for further counseling if the interpretation were correct. This strategy is most useful after a therapist has seen a client for a while and already has a few ideas about the client. Even then, it is often difficult for a beginner to trust his or her ideas about a client, and so the supervisor encourages the flow of ideas.

*To illustrate:*

*Supervisor:* You've been seeing this client for a while. We just looked at a segment in which he was talking about how angry he was that his wife was getting fat while he was willing to exercise to stay fit. I know from what you've said previously that you've developed some ideas about this client. What do you think that anger was about?

*Trainee:* Well . . . you mean, after I stop being annoyed at him for being a male chauvinist and wanting a thin woman?

*Supervisor:* Yeah. Those feelings are important, and we'll come back to them. They may tell you quite a bit about how he affects his wife! They can also tell you something about what he might be trying to stir up in you. But let's let that part go for a bit, and just assume that he wasn't trying to get a reaction from you, and that he was just expressing a feeling he has. How do you understand this particular feeling . . .

*Trainee:* I'm not sure what you mean.

*Supervisor:* Well, you know something about his background and his life. That might help you.

*Trainee:* Do you mean, about how he has achieved a lot?

*Supervisor:* I'm not sure; I don't know him as well as you do. But it sounds as if you have some ideas here. Tell me about that and how you think it fits in.

*Trainee:* Well, he grew up in a lower-class family, and he worked really hard to make it—and he has. He is very bright and he is a successful accountant. That's meant that he has had to be pretty disciplined. So I guess he resents that his wife isn't as disciplined and is "just letting herself go."

*Supervisor:* So why do you think that would make him as mad as he is in the segment we just watched?

*Trainee:* Well, this might be stretching it.

*Supervisor:* Good. That's what I want you to do—just play with ideas here.

*Trainee:* Okay. Well, he says that his family sort of ran to extremes. I mean, he really counted on his mother when he was small. Then his mother started having a few drinks "with the girls" after work. After a while, when his mother drank, she just didn't have one drink; when she started drinking, she got drunk, and I think she even went into the drunk tank in the jail a few times. That was pretty awful for him. And he really admired his older sister, and then after his sister left home and got married, she came back to visit, and she had turned into an obese person. So maybe he thinks his wife's getting fat is just the beginning of her going downhill, and she's going to let him down, too.

*Supervisor:* Okay. So you think he might experience any sign of letting oneself go as an indication that everything is going to collapse. And then he's going to be left with a different person than he thought he married?

*Trainee:* Yeah, that's it.

*Supervisor:* Okay, that's a nice interpretation and one you might want to test out. Tell me how you might put your interpretation to him.

*Trainee:* I could say something like, "Sometimes when you talk about how your wife is getting fat, you get really upset, more upset than, say, when you actually argue with her about something. And I'm wondering if you are afraid she is just going to turn into a fat person like your sister and you are going to be left with someone totally different from the person you married?"

*Supervisor:* Hey, that sounds great! And how will you know whether this interpretation is correct?

*Trainee: [laughs]* If he says, "Oh yes, right, how did you think of such a clever interpretation?" then I'll know. But seriously, if he seems to think about it and then says, "Yes, you might be right," and gives me, say, another example that is like that, then I'll know.

*Supervisor:* But what if he doesn't? What if he just says, "Well, maybe, but my sister's getting fat didn't upset me that much."

*Trainee:* Well, I guess I'd think I was wrong.

*Supervisor:* You could be. And I'd always take what the client says as the most important data about whether my hypothesis is correct. You might store it away, however, just in case your interpretation turns out to be correct and it comes up again in another way when the client might be more ready to hear the interpretation. A good interpretation needs to be accurate, but it also can be accurate and fail to clarify things for the client because the timing isn't right.

In this situation, the supervisor encouraged the trainee to pursue ideas, no matter how far-fetched they might seem. Then the supervisor followed the trainee's hunch and restated the interpretation in a slightly simpler fashion. When the trainee put it into words, the supervisor asked the trainee how it might be validated. At the end, the supervisor added some information about a good interpretation's needing both accuracy and timing to be effective in counseling.

## COUNSELOR FUNCTIONS

When supervisors assume the counseling role, they encourage trainees' internal exploration in the context of interactions with the supervisor and with the client. This is consistent with Skovholt and Rønnestad's (1995) model of development and is another aspect of reflective inquiry.

It is here that ethical considerations most often come into play. As described in chapter 4, the supervisor needs to encourage self-reflection and yet must not cross the line and become a therapist to the trainee—even if the trainee seems to want that. Thus the supervisor walks the fine line of asking about feelings, as experienced in both counseling sessions and during supervision, and yet limiting the exploration of those feelings. Sometimes the discussion touches on broader issues in the trainee's personal life, but the supervisor always moves it back to the interaction with the particular client. This maintains the focus of supervision and avoids the development of a dual role with the trainee.

Strategies for counselor functions are described in this section.

### 7. Explore Trainee Feelings During the Counseling Session

Trainees must learn to accept and use their feelings to understand their clients and themselves. The supervisor aids this process by encouraging the trainee to notice feelings during counseling and consider their meaning. This is quite difficult for beginners because they often believe they should not have these feelings—that they should always like their clients and feel empathy toward them—when in fact, they might experience them as quite annoying or unattractive at times. If counselors do not acknowledge these feelings, however, they might act them out (Teyber, 1997). Discussion of the feelings with the supervisor, on the other hand, enables them to avoid acting them out in counseling sessions.

To carry out this strategy, the supervisor explains that it is important for the trainee to use feelings as data about the client while refraining from acting on them in session. In supervision, the trainee can be asked such general questions as, "Do you like this client?" "Do you feel comfortable with her?" "Do you feel inadequate when dealing with her?" As the trainee responds, the supervisor can explore further to help the trainee assess whether his or her feelings are similar to those the client evokes in others;

this might help the trainee to understand the client's difficulties in relationships. In this case, the information about the client's relationship behavior can allow the trainee to formulate additional hypotheses and strategies for use in counseling. It is also an opportunity to encourage the trainee to make a response that is unlike the response of others in the client's life, a noncomplementary response. It is important to help the trainee choose a response here, as it will determine where the session goes next.

On the other hand, the client may remind the trainee of someone in the trainee's past or belong to a group of people, including a gender, ethnic, or sexual-orientation group, who regularly evoke such feelings in the trainee. In this event, the supervisor invites the trainee to explore the feelings further. The supervisor allows him or her to express feelings in supervision but does not interpret the counselor's feelings or turn the meeting into a counseling session. Again, the supervisor points out that these are important feelings for the trainee and might be considered further, either when the trainee is alone or with a friend or professional, but that the trainee must guard against behavior that reveals the feelings to the client.

Whenever the trainee becomes emotional during the discussion, the supervisor stays with the trainee and allows the trainee to experience his or her feelings. Then the discussion is returned to the counseling session with a question that explores the circumstances that differentiate the counseling session from other experiences.

*To illustrate:*

*[In this situation, the supervisor is exploring the trainee's feelings during a counseling session that was just shown on a videotape.]*

*Supervisor:* When she began to cry, you moved back slightly. What were you feeling then?

*Trainee:* Gee, I don't know. I guess I just didn't want her to cry.

*Supervisor:* Tell me about that.

*Trainee:* Well, I don't like it when people get really upset. It just makes me uncomfortable . . . I never have liked it much.

*Supervisor:* Do you know what that's about?

*Trainee:* I'm not sure . . . you know, now that you mention it, I used to come home from school hoping that my mother wouldn't be upset and crying . . . she was depressed a lot when I was a kid. She would lie around on her bed or on the couch. I could cope with it if she was just sleeping or watching TV, though I didn't like it much—I didn't bring any friends home after school. She didn't pay much attention to me when she was like that, and I could go out and play and stuff. But sometimes I would come home and she would be crying, and then she would want to talk to me about things . . . and I never knew what to do! I felt scared and kind of helpless; I kept wishing my dad would come home and get me out of this.

*Supervisor:* So when you felt alone with her and responsible, you just wanted to be out of there.

*Trainee:* Yeah . . . And I guess part of wanting to be a counselor was wanting to be able to help people like that.

*Supervisor:* But when they start acting like your mother and crying, you get uneasy in the way you did when you were little?

*Trainee:* Yeah, I do.

*Supervisor:* I can imagine! How do you think this situation with your client is like the situation with your mother?

*Trainee:* Well, there's a person who's unhappy who wants help from me.

*Supervisor:* Sure. And yet you are different now from the child who was listening to his mother.

*Trainee:* I suppose so, but it doesn't feel like it.

*Supervisor:* Now you are an adult.

*Trainee:* Well, I suppose I'm grown up *[laughs]*.

*Supervisor:* Yes, you're not dependent on the client for your own well-being.

*Trainee:* You're right. If she doesn't get better, I'll probably be able to get dinner and get my work done and get to school and stuff.

*Supervisor:* Sure. And you know more now about helping people.

*Trainee:* Well, by now I know something about counseling, I guess. I may not know a lot yet, but I know more than I did as a kid. . . .

*Supervisor:* And you're not alone here the way you were as a child. You have people here at the clinic to ask for advice about it, if it gets out of hand.

*Trainee:* Yeah, I guess I do have more resources now.

*Supervisor:* Do you think that you could remind yourself of that when a client gets upset?

*Trainee:* Yes.

*Supervisor:* And then maybe you could stand to listen to your client longer, without withdrawing.

*Trainee:* Yes, that might help. I'll try that.

In a real supervision session, such an exchange would take much longer to develop. Still, the vignette illustrates the focus first on the feelings of the trainee and then on a strategy to handle them in the counseling session.

## 8. Explore Trainee Feelings During the Supervision Session

This strategy employs the behaviors of strategy 7 in the context of the relationship between the trainee and the supervisor. Again, it is tricky to maintain the line between supervision and counseling—or supervision and friendship. Yet if feelings are not discussed, they may interfere with the trainee's ability to experiment and learn. Because trainees seldom bring up their feelings toward their supervisors (Ladany et al., 1996), it is up to the supervisor to attend closely to each trainee and initiate discussions when feelings might be interfering with the supervisory process. When exploring the trainee's feelings in the supervisory session, the supervisor begins with a self-disclosure, which includes a hypothesis about the trainee. It might include a behavioral reference along with a hypothesis. The trainee can respond, and the supervisor explores the feelings further.

*To illustrate:*

*[In this situation, exploration of the trainee's feelings in the supervision session provides an opportunity to explore the supervisory relationship.]*

*Supervisor:* When you were watching that segment of tape, you frowned, and I imagined that you were embarrassed about showing that segment of tape to me. Am I correct?

*Trainee:* No, well . . . yeah, I guess I was.

*Supervisor:* Tell me a little about that feeling.

*Trainee:* Well, this probably seems silly. But I've been working with you for a few months now, and you've been pretty positive about my skills.

*Supervisor:* Yeah. And?

*Trainee:* And, well, I don't feel as good about my counseling sometimes as you seem to.

*Supervisor:* Oh?

*Trainee:* So I need help with this, but I hate to let you down.

*Supervisor:* And you think I might be disappointed somehow. What do you imagine that I might think about you now that I've seen this session?

*Trainee:* Oh, that I'm not really as good as you thought, or I should have handled that situation better.

*Supervisor:* So you have been thinking that I have pretty high expectations for you.

*Trainee:* Well, sort of. But really—this is hard to say—I like you a lot, and I guess I think that you like me, and I've been thinking that you liked me for being a good counselor.

*Supervisor:* Okay. I'm wondering if I have given you that impression by something I've done. If I liked you because you never made any mistakes, there would be nothing I could teach you.

*Trainee:* No, I don't think it's something I've gotten from you. And I guess it doesn't make sense *[laughs]*. What would you have to do if I already knew everything?

*Supervisor: [Laughs in return]* And why would you be here if you did?

In this vignette, the supervisor and trainee have faced a difficult situation for the trainee and explored it at a medium level of depth appropriate to the training relationship. In an effort to look into the interaction, the supervisor asked whether the supervisor might have contributed to the trainee's perception. By exploring these issues, they have reaffirmed what the function of each is for the other in the relationship. Yet the supervisor did not stray into talking about all the things that were attractive and pleasing about the trainee or how much the supervisor did like the trainee, which could have intensified the personal aspect of the relationship. Instead, the supervisor maintained the focus on the supervisory interaction and its purpose.

## 9. Explore Trainee Feelings Concerning Specific Techniques or Interventions

This strategy is designed to help the trainee think about how well a strategy fits his or her personal style. At the same time, the trainee is encouraged to try the strategy and experiment with it, to add to his or her counseling repertoire. For any therapist, learning to use a new technique is difficult. It takes time to shape a new technique into a tool that a therapist can use successfully. Part of that shaping is understanding the feelings one has when trying something new.

As techniques are introduced, supervisors ask how trainees feel when using them. The supervisor observes and describes the trainee's facial expression during discussions or role-plays of new interventions. When the trainee acknowledges the accuracy of the observation, the supervisor proceeds to explore the trainee's feelings. Such exploration is brief, limited to probes that help the trainee explore the relationships between in-session and in-life behaviors. It is sometimes helpful to remind the trainee that part of becoming a therapist is learning to initiate questions, make observations, and confront issues with a client that would be impolite to initiate with a friend.

*To illustrate:*

*Supervisor: [After watching a videotape segment]* Your forehead wrinkled and your shoulders tightened when you delivered that confrontation. Did you notice that?

*Trainee:* Yes, I guess so.

*Supervisor:* What do you think that was about?

*Trainee:* I don't know; I got pretty uncomfortable.

*Supervisor:* Well, when you are with your friends, are you usually comfortable confronting them with inconsistencies?

*Trainee: [Laughs]* No I guess you know by now that I don't like to offend people, and I'll go out of my way to avoid it!

*Supervisor:* Yeah, that's what I thought. Do you think that might be part of your cultural heritage too?

*Trainee:* Oh, yeah, of course. And confronting someone who is older than I am feels particularly inappropriate.

*Supervisor:* So if you were counseling an older person from your own cultural background, a confrontation might really interfere with the development of a good working alliance.

*Trainee:* Absolutely. But this client is European American.

*Supervisor:* Yes. And a confrontation is appropriate at this point in the session—and might even help the alliance. But I can see that for you to practice confrontation in counseling means going against what you feel and have been taught is polite behavior in social situations.

*Trainee:* You bet! No wonder I'm having a hard time.

*Supervisor:* Sure. And the respect for others you learned to show is an asset in counseling. You don't seem to need to rush in and say something; you can wait and let the person's story unfold. On the other hand, there are times when counselors have to be more confrontive than they would be in social situations. It's really tricky to learn to do things you wouldn't do in polite conversation. Yet you have to find out different things from clients. If clients just needed social conversation, they could go to their friends. They come to us for something different.

*Trainee:* I guess you're right. So I'm going to have to practice quite a lot of confrontations until I get more comfortable.

*Supervisor:* You're exactly right. Good for you! It will take time to learn to go against 25 years of conditioning!

In this situation the supervisor has explored what was on the videotape and appropriately raised cultural issues without going into an extensive discussion of the meaning and feelings associated with confrontation. In addition, the supervisor has differentiated between counseling and ordinary conversation in an effective manner.

## 10. Encourage Trainee Self-Exploration of Confidence and Worries in the Counseling Session

Trainees will vary in confidence as they begin counseling. All trainees, however, will experience some anxiety as they begin to use new counseling behaviors (Skovholt & Rønnestad, 1992, 1995). The supervisor can assist by talking with the trainee about performance fears before the trainee experiences the first session. If the trainee acknowledges some anxiety or lack of confidence, the supervisor encourages exploring those feelings.

After feelings have been explored, the supervisor can suggest that the trainee think about a prior experience of doing something new. He or she can add that it is especially useful to recall experiences in which the trainee anticipated failure and then completed the task successfully. With such experiences in mind, the trainee can go into the new experience of counseling reminded of the process of doing something new and difficult.

*To illustrate:*

*Supervisor:* We've been working on role-playing situations for a while now. And yet it is usually hard to begin with a real client you've never met.

*Trainee:* Yeah, I'm a little nervous about it.

*Supervisor:* That's not unusual in a situation like this. It means you're paying attention and doing something new! What are some of the thoughts going around in your head now?

*Trainee:* Oh, that I'll never remember everything that I've learned or that I'll just panic—or that the person will know that I don't know what I'm doing and won't want to work with me. And what if the client has nothing to say and just looks at me?

*Supervisor:* Those are some pretty common thoughts. Can you remember any situation you were ever in before that was like this?

*Trainee:* Let's see . . . actually, I can. When I was becoming a teacher, I went out for student teaching. I remember the first lecture I ever gave. It was on the European Economic Community and I was sweating the whole time.

*Supervisor:* And what happened?

*Trainee:* It turned out that they didn't know anything about it and they got sort of interested. Once the kids began asking me questions, I got more relaxed and started just talking with them about it.

*Supervisor:* That does sound a lot like this situation. It sounds if you didn't know everything about teaching when you began, but you knew enough to start, and that once you could see what the others' needs were, you could relax.

*Trainee:* Yeah.

*Supervisor:* And this could turn out the same way. You don't know a lot about counseling, but you know enough to get started, and the client is going to be more worried about himself than about you.

*Trainee:* That's the hard part to remember!

*Supervisor:* Sure. You might remind yourself from time to time about how you didn't know much in that first teaching situation either, but you knew enough to get started, and you got better and better at it as you went along.

The supervisor acknowledged the trainee's anxiety. Then the supervisor explored a past successful early performance experience of the trainee and used it to build the trainee's confidence in the counseling situation in a realistic way.

## 11. Help the Trainee Define Personal Competencies and Areas for Growth

In the process of learning to be therapists and working with clients, trainees face themselves, sometimes in ways they have never done before. They help clients define their personal strengths and weaknesses in conducting their lives. This often precipitates awareness of their own strengths and weaknesses. As they begin to trust their supervisors, trainees often express these thoughts. The supervisor listen, affirms observations of strength, and supports the process of exploring areas for growth.

Affirming areas of strength includes acknowledging not only the strength, but also the fact that the trainee has developed it. In addition, it is important for the supervisor to ask questions about the process the trainee has gone through, so that the trainee continues to attend to process as well as outcome.

Exploring the areas in which growth is needed is a somewhat more complex process. If possible, the supervisor lets the trainee initiate discussion of a concern; however, often the supervisor must raise an issue of inadequate performance in some area of counseling responsibility. In either case, the supervisor encourages the trainee's exploration of the difficulty. Then the supervisor asks how the trainee wants to change. Finally, the trainee and supervisor work together to make a plan to achieve the desired change.

From time to time, trainees will also encounter personal strengths and weaknesses as a function of the demands of graduate training in general.

*To illustrate:*

*[In this situation, the trainee has a learning disability; he managed in under-graduate life by obtaining help from family and friends in a fashion charac-teristic of his culture, but he can no longer manage when faced with the pace and demanding individual performance standards of graduate school. When he fails to hand in case notes in a timely manner, the supervisor confronts him.]*

*Supervisor:* I am concerned that you have not yet handed in your case notes for the first session you observed, even though by now you should have handed in case notes for four sessions.

*Trainee:* Yes, I have them; I just keep forgetting to bring them in.

*Supervisor:* I am a bit confused by this. I have been reminding you for several weeks now, and you always say that you will bring them in—but then you don't.

*Trainee:* Well . . . I was hoping that I could get through this program without bringing this up, but I don't think I can . . . I have already talked it over with my testing instructor, but she is an outsider to this program . . . and anyway, she was pretty discouraging. Before I came here, I had a series of tests back in Colorado, and I was told that I had such a severe learning disability that I would not be able to make it in graduate school. I have been terrified ever since I got here that I wouldn't be able to make it—and this quarter it seems to be catching up with me. I took incompletes in two courses in the fall, and I managed to get the papers done over the break, but now I can't keep up, and I don't know what to do. I am wondering if the people who tested me were right. Maybe I don't belong here.

*Supervisor:* Wow . . . that's quite a burden you've been carrying around! I'm pleased that you have finally decided to talk about it with me.

*Trainee:* Yes . . . it's a relief just to talk about it.

*Supervisor:* How did you get through your rather successful undergradu-ate career?

*Trainee:* Well, you know, I lived at home, which is common in my culture . . . and you know, in our culture, families support and help one another with everything. My family has always been behind me and my success. My mother and my brother worked with me, so that I would talk through my ideas and they would help me with them. Then, when I wrote a paper, they would go over it and correct all the errors. The ideas were all mine, but they would help me. And on the semester system, we had more time to work these things out. I would start really early, and I would finish on time.

*Supervisor:* So you were able to compensate by planning ahead. But now you can't do that because quarters are so short.

*Trainee:* Yeah, and Dr. L, the instructor for the assessment course, says that so much of what psychologists do is reading and writing reports that I should reconsider my career before I go any further.

*Supervisor:* Gosh . . . it sounds as if you are getting discouraged.

*Trainee:* Yeah . . . and I haven't handed in my case notes because they seem so poorly written, but I don't know how to fix them.

*Supervisor:* Well, we can start with those. Bring them in, and we can work on some strategies for doing them. But what do you think you are going to do about the larger problem of handling the reading and writing required for graduate work?

*Trainee:* I don't know; I am really worried.

*Supervisor:* Perhaps you know that there is a learning disabilities center on campus. If you went there, and if you took your test results there, I'll bet they could give you some help. In that way, maybe you could learn some new strategies.

*Trainee:* I didn't know that. I'll go there today. But do you think it would hurt me if I were to tell my other instructors about this?

*Supervisor:* I think you are going to have to. I don't know if it will hurt you, but I think it will hurt you less than not turning in things without an explanation.

*Trainee:* Yeah. What if I really can't do graduate level work?

*Supervisor:* That is a concern. You don't know and I don't know what you can do with some help from the learning disabilities center. It doesn't sound as if you are in a position to make any decisions about that until you know more about how you can do with some help.

*Trainee:* Yeah.

*Supervisor:* So can I assume that you will address this by going to them before the week is out?

*Trainee:* Yes.

*Supervisor:* And will you bring me whatever case notes you've got in time for our next supervision session, so that we can address your difficulties with this assignment?

Trainee: Yes.

*Supervisor:* Good. Now that we've talked about that, let's look at the videotape of your role play. Your role play last week was very effective, so I'm looking forward to seeing this one.

In this vignette, the supervisor affirms the trainee's honesty about his difficulty, encourages him to express his feelings about his current situation, and aids him in finding campus support and training to further his graduate work. The supervisor indicates where he can be of assistance in this course and supports the areas of strength the trainee has demonstrated in previous role-plays. At the same time, the supervisor acknowledges the complexity of the issue and does not try to make a pronouncement about the trainee's future, which is beyond the competence of the supervisor to make.

## 12. Provide Opportunities for Trainee to Process His or Her Own Affect and Defenses

Psychotherapy is a very personal process and frequently stirs the counselor's personal feelings. A trainee, for instance, may work with a client who is extremely distressed and expresses strong affect. This experience will leave residual feelings to be explored in supervision.

As the trainee processes these feelings after a session, the supervisor supports this exploration. Questions are appropriate here, because the supervisor needs to understand the feeling as much as possible. And trainees can usually answer questions about feelings, especially when they have initiated the discussion; this is different from the cognitive questions with which trainees sometimes struggle.

Should the trainee become very emotional in expressing feelings, the supervisor remains calm and accepts the feelings. The supervisor neither argues with the feelings nor attempts to normalize them by saying that the supervisor also has these feelings. This is important because the trainee is learning from the supervisor how to behave when clients express strong feelings. In the unlikely event that the trainee expresses feelings inappropriately, for example, by banging on the wall, the supervisor sets suitable limits. In these ways the supervisor demonstrates effective counseling behaviors to the counselor trainee.

When exploring areas for growth (as for strategy 11) and providing opportunities for the expression of affect, the trainee and supervisor may realize that the trainee would profit from psychotherapy. The supervisor reminds the trainee that he or she cannot be the trainee's therapist, from either an ethical or educational perspective. The supervisor asks how the trainee plans to address this concern so that it will not interfere with his or her functioning as a counselor. If the trainee expresses the intention of pursuing psychotherapy, the supervisor supports that decision. If, on the other hand, the trainee reports that just talking to the supervisor has helped, the supervisor accepts that for the present. If the trainee expresses a desire to pursue therapy and a concern about cost, the supervisor should not start making suggestions about ways of affording it. The supervisor simply encourages the trainee to find a way to pursue what is needed in this area.

*To illustrate:*

*[In this situation, the trainee has experienced a very angry client.]*

*Trainee:* I'd like to show you a portion of a session where my client became extremely angry, because I felt very uncertain about what I was doing.

*Supervisor:* Good for you for bringing it to work on. Let's watch. [*They watch the tape.*] You looked rather calm. How were you feeling?

*Trainee:* Well, in all honesty, I got very anxious, and then I sort of shut down. I sort of blanked out, and I wasn't sure how I got out of the session until I saw the videotape. It was a strange experience.

*Supervisor:* Yes, you ended the session fairly quickly after that. I had the feeling that you were pretty overwhelmed—and maybe your client was too—because you brought things to an end so abruptly.

*Trainee:* Yeah . . . I can see that.

*Supervisor:* Tell me when you first became uncomfortable.

*Trainee:* Well, it was when he began raising his voice and gesturing.

*Supervisor:* Sure. And were you aware of this anywhere in your body?

*Trainee:* Yes. My chest got tight, and so did my jaw. I had a headache later.

*Supervisor:* So you had some pretty strong reactions, at least in your body. You've already said that you stopped being clear in your thinking. Can you recall your worst fear in the situation?

*Trainee:* Yes. I had the sense that he would get up and start swinging at me, even though he really wasn't mad at me. As I look at it now, I see how silly that was.

*Supervisor:* Is this a common set of feelings for you when people get angry?

*Trainee:* Yes . . . I know where it comes from, I think. You know, when I was a kid, my dad was an alcoholic. You never knew what he was going to be like when you came home. If he'd been drinking, he would take it out on whomever was around . . . So I think I just learned to look calm and try to make myself small and keep out of his way.

*Supervisor:* Sure. That makes sense for a child—it's a perceptive choice that makes the child safe. You were creative to figure that out and know how to take care of yourself in that situation.

*Trainee:* Yeah. I suppose so . . . but I can't have that happen as a counselor.

People get angry all the time, and I can't just blank out . . . I've been thinking that I should get some counseling for myself about this.

*Supervisor:* That makes sense . . . you would probably be more comfortable, and you would also be better able to tolerate strong feelings in professional situations.

*Trainee:* Is this something we could work on in supervision?

*Supervisor:* I am flattered that you think I could help you, but I have a different role with you. If I became your counselor, my ability to teach and evaluate you would be compromised, and so would my ability to be a dispassionate therapist for you.

*Trainee:* Yeah, I can see that. Well, I've thought about getting therapy before, but I just don't have the money right now.

*Supervisor:* Sure, grad students are perpetually poor, and therapy always involves sacrifices . . . but I have seen you be creative and resourceful in other situations around here. I'll bet you could find a way to get some therapy for yourself, if you really feel strongly about this.

*Trainee:* Well, it makes me pretty nervous, to tell you the truth. I'm not sure I want to explore all this stuff.

*Supervisor:* Sure; I can understand that. It's always hard to go digging around in old material. But if you can face that, I think you could work out a contract with a decent counselor and make some real progress . . . and it would surely help your work here too.

In this vignette, the supervisor allowed the trainee to explore the feelings aroused in the session. The supervisor encouraged the trainee's expressed interest in psychotherapy and supported the trainee's ability to get what the trainee needed to be more comfortable personally and professionally. The supervisor did not, however, serve as a counselor for the trainee.

## CONSULTANT FUNCTIONS

When the supervisor acts as a consultant, both supervisor and trainee focus discussion on the client. Questions include what the client is doing and why as well as what the interaction means. The supervisor encourages the trainee to state what he wants from the supervisor. This builds on the belief of educators (Copeland et al., 1993) that the learner has the best understanding of what the learner needs.

Supervisors most often function as consultants when they work with experienced therapists. Nonetheless, as beginners gain experience and knowledge, they can consider strategies from the perspective of theory, and they can consider not only the immediate outcome of an intervention but its long-term possibilities.

## 13. Provide Alternative Interventions or Conceptualizations for Trainee Use

The supervisor encourages the trainee to develop hypotheses about the client (see strategy 2) and adds some alternatives for consideration and asks the trainee to build on these.

Having explored hypotheses with the trainee, the supervisor moves the discussion to interventions. Continuing to encourage reflective process, the supervisor proposes that interventions can be designed to achieve particular outcomes. This is just another hypothesis, the supervisor explains—that one strategy might lead to one outcome. The trainee is invited to suggest interventions and speculate on their outcome with a particular client.

The supervisor follows this by asking the trainee to consider which counseling theory could explain the hypothesized outcome. As a result, the trainee is encouraged to have a theoretical basis for interventions.

*To illustrate:*

*[In this situation, the trainee has just shown a portion of videotape to the supervisor and explained what the trainee believes it means.]*

*Supervisor:* That is one possible explanation and makes sense. You know, though, I noticed that the client pulled back physically and closed her posture when you asked about her mother's reactions to the situation . . . I'm wondering what else might be going on.

*Trainee:* I'm not sure, but now that you've brought it up, it is very apparent that something is happening there.

*Supervisor:* Perhaps she gets anxious whenever she thinks about her mother. Or perhaps, in her culture, this is a gesture of filial respect. From what you know about the client, what do you think?

*Trainee:* You know, now that you mention it, although it could be a gesture of respect, I think her mother does make her pretty uneasy. She describes her mother as quite volatile, someone who gets mad or upset pretty easily. And she has said she didn't know what to do when that happened.

*Supervisor:* Well, what do you think that means in her life now?

*Trainee:* Well, you know, when I think about it, she has a pretty hard time doing anything adventurous because she is afraid of how her mother might react. Even though she is 27 years old, she doesn't know how to say things to her mother in an assertive manner that is still polite and respectful.

*Supervisor:* So how do you think you might approach this? You want to maintain the good relationship you have by being attentive to the cultural aspects of the task, whether or not you address them explicitly with the client.

*Trainee:* Well, you know, I think now might be the time to introduce some practice in being appropriately assertive. Then we could role–play her telling her mother that she is traveling to New York.

*Supervisor:* And how do you understand that theoretically?

*Trainee:* It's a behavior rehearsal.

*Supervisor:* Sure . . . and one of the things you may want to remember about behavior rehearsal is the concept of successive approximations. You might start with something a little easier than telling her mother she is doing something her mother wouldn't like. Can you think of something in another situation that might be easier?

*Trainee:* Yes, I can. I could have her practice being more assertive about things with her roommate, say, asking her to turn down her CD player or something . . . Then we could gradually work up to asking her professor for an extension on a paper. That gives her the opportunity to address something with an older authority figure. It might seem hard, but wouldn't be as hard for her as talking to her mother, and it's a chance to approach an older person respectfully, yet assertively.

*Supervisor:* Okay . . . that makes sense. Let's talk about the precise plans a little more carefully before you go to the next session.

The supervisor has made observations and interjected suggestions when appropriate, while continuing to solicit the trainee's thoughts about the strategy and the client. Cultural elements were addressed as part of the counseling relationship as well as possible components of the client's behavior with her mother.

## 14. Encourage Trainee Brainstorming of Strategies and Interventions

In this instance, the supervisor's goal is not to push the trainee to use particular interventions. Rather, the supervisor is encouraging the process of generating interventions. The focus is on creativity and theoretical reasoning. In brainstorming, the supervisor asks the trainee to come up with as many strategies or interventions as possible. The supervisor listens and writes them down. Neither evaluating the possibilities nor allowing the trainee to do so at this stage, the supervisor simply encourages the trainee to come up with more. Usually the trainee generates several and will stop. At that point, the supervisor encourages the trainee to produce more.

When the trainee has generated as many interventions as possible, the supervisor asks the trainee to group them by theory. Then the supervisor asks the trainee to consider the impact of these interventions on this client, based on personal style and history, gender, and the client's racial, ethnic, or religious background and socioeconomic status. Finally, the supervisor focuses the trainee's attention on the fit between the strategy and the client's personal history and style.

The trainee is then in a position to choose an intervention, based on theory and on knowing the client.

*To illustrate:*

*Supervisor:* You sound discouraged that your client never does her homework.

*Trainee:* Yes. I really don't know where to go next.

*Supervisor:* Well, given that you are a creative person, why don't you try thinking up as many ideas for what to do next as you can. Just come up with ideas; don't evaluate them. I'll write them down so that you can keep thinking.

*Trainee:* That's pretty hard. Well, okay . . . I could write things down for her. Or I could call her during the week to check upon her . . . better yet, I could have her call me on Wednesday and Friday to let me know what she has done. Then I could reinforce her accomplishments.

*Supervisor:* Okay, I've got those. Now give me some more.

*Trainee:* Well, instead of following up on her homework, I could say that I really don't want her to do homework this week because it seems too difficult for her. Nah, that won't work.

*Supervisor:* Just keep generating ideas; don't evaluate them. I'm writing that one down.

*Trainee:* Gee, I can't think of any more.

*Supervisor:* Stay with it. Can you think of a few more, however outlandish they might sound?

*Trainee:* Well, let's see . . . I could carry that last one a bit further . . . I could say that this week it is important that she not do any homework, that she not even think about homework.

*Supervisor:* Anything else?

*Trainee:* Well, you know, I could ask her what stops her from completing her homework. That could get into how her father always told her what to do, and I could make an interpretation about that.

*Supervisor:* Okay. That's a different tack altogether. Anything else?

*Trainee:* I could also explore what this particular assignment means to her . . . I mean, I'm not sure how she feels about regular exercise.

*Supervisor:* Sure. What about one last idea?

*Trainee:* You know, the reason I was suggesting she take walks every day is that she seems so depressed. But maybe she is too depressed even to walk. Perhaps it's time to refer her to our staff psychiatrist to do an evaluation for medication. Maybe she just can't get herself to do exercise.

*Supervisor:* Good . . . okay, let's look at each of these ideas from a theoretical point of view. When you consider calling her or having her call you for follow-up and reinforcement, what theory are you operating from?

*Trainee:* A behavioral approach.

*Supervisor:* All right. And suggesting that she not do the homework? You had two of those.

*Trainee:* Well, that's paradoxical, which is from Jay Haley; I guess that could be called, I don't know, Ericksonian.

*Supervisor:* Or strategic. And the interpretation?

*Trainee:* That's psychodynamic. And suggesting that she get a psychiatric evaluation for medication is clearly the medical model.

*Supervisor:* Good! You seem to have a good grasp of theory. Now let's look at this in terms of this client, including her gender and cultural background.

*Trainee:* Yeah, okay. Can I look at the list again? Okay, well, I don't think calling or having her call will help. This is too much like an order, and my giving her an order just reinforces gender stereotypes about dominance.

*Supervisor:* Ah, okay. And the paradox?

*Trainee:* You know, it could work, but I'm too uncomfortable with it. I feel as if I am tricking my client, and that's not consistent with how I see myself.

*Supervisor:* What about interpreting?

*Trainee:* You know, now that I think about it, I'm not sure whether it's a reaction to her father or to her mother or what. Or just something about exercise. Maybe it doesn't make much sense to her because she is glad to be out of a job where she did so much physical work—and exercise might seem like a step backward—well, I'm not sure. But I think she would be open to discussing an interpretation or two, because she is quite bright and articulate, and she seems to be sort of introspective. Interpretations have worked before to affect her attitudes.

*Supervisor:* And a referral for medication?

*Trainee:* You know, I have my doubts about that. She has the idea that seeing a psychiatrist means she is really crazy; I don't think she'd go for it. Besides, she is a Christian Scientist, and taking medication is inconsistent with her theology. And in reality, she isn't showing the signs of depression most amenable to medication; she sleeps okay and her appetite is fine. She's just upset about what has happened to her.

*Supervisor:* Okay, it sounds as if you know what you want to do. You seem to prefer the psychodynamic most of the time and it's consistent with what we've been doing in practicum; it's been working pretty well with this client. Perhaps the homework was too much of a deviation from that . . . In any event, you have a clear sense of what you want to do and why you want to do it . . . and it's nice to see how many ideas you can come up with if you try!

The supervisor has assisted the trainee to think through and settle on a strategy for working with the client while supporting the trainee's ability to generate possibilities.

## 15. Encourage Trainee Discussion of Client Problems and Motivations

This requires a rather simple invitation. As the trainee proceeds to describe the client, the supervisor can occasionally ask for more information to round out the picture. The supervisor also asks for some of the trainee's reasoning. The supervisor affirms the trainee's information gathering and thinking about the client with brief comments.

*To illustrate:*

*Supervisor:* Tell me about this client.

*Trainee:* He's a 38-year-old widower who raised two children. He comes from a rather strict Irish Catholic background and was the middle of five kids. He seems to be in some sort of transition, because his youngest child finished college this year, and he's not sure what he wants to do now that he no longer has to support everyone. He's contemplating everything from going back to school to marrying again and having a second family.

*Supervisor:* Okay . . . and what did his assessments show at the intake?

*Trainee:* His only elevated score on the symptom inventory was anxiety. And even that was just on the border. The diagnostic questionnaire confirmed that anxiety score. The intake interviewer was required to give him another test because of his course requirement in appraisal, so the client also completed a standard personality assessment, but nothing really showed up on that as problematic.

*Supervisor:* Gee, sounds like a good client for you to work with. Isn't it interesting that he got you as a counselor and you've returned to school after raising a family on your own?

*Trainee:* Yeah. But I haven't told him much about me because I don't want my experiences to influence him.

*Supervisor:* Good for you. Many beginning counselors think that what applies to them applies to their clients; I'm impressed that you are able to avoid that. So how do you plan to work with him?

*Trainee:* Well, I've thought a lot about it. He comes from a rather conservative background, and his religion is important to him, so I want to respect that. The thing is, I find it hard that he would even think of starting another family when the world population is growing. But I think I can manage those feelings and look at it from his point of view.

*Supervisor:* Great! It's hard to do that. It doesn't sound as if your value is so strong, though, that you would feel as if you lacked integrity if you didn't speak out on that.

*Trainee:* No, I have feelings about it, but it's not in the same league with the feelings I would have if he were beating up his kids or something. Then I would need to intervene, even if the law didn't require me to.

*Supervisor:* I can see you've reflected on this. That's great!

*Trainee:* He seems like a classic case of someone who wants to do some basic decision making. I thought I would use some of the career decision making theory proposed by Liz Yost [Yost & Corbishley, 1987] in her career-counseling model. That involves getting him to think about what things he has liked doing in the past and what he liked about those things, and then going from there. It provides a place for exploring his decisions in terms of his values too.

*Supervisor:* Good. It sounds as if you have thought this through very well.

In this vignette, the supervisor questioned the trainee about the client, elicited the theories underneath the trainee's responses, and validated the way the trainee thought about the client's problem and planned interventions.

## 16. Solicit and Attempt to Satisfy Trainee Needs During the Supervision Session

At the outset of the term and at the outset of each session, the supervisor asks the trainee what he or she wants from the supervisor. As long as the trainee's goal is consistent with general supervision goals and process, the supervisor attempts to fulfill the trainee's request during the session. Whenever possible, however, the supervisor encourages trainees to use their own resources to solve problems.

*To illustrate goal-setting for a single session:*

*Supervisor:* In addition to the things we had agreed to work on at the end of last time, which included your practicing some relaxation exercises, are there other things you want to work on today?

*Trainee:* Yeah, actually, something came up in the session that I didn't know what to do with. I think I handled it okay, but I'd like you to look at it.

*Supervisor:* Okay. Shall we start with the videotape?

*Trainee:* Yeah. *[Moves to begin the tape.]*

*Supervisor:* Before we start, tell me what you particularly want me to attend to as I watch.

In this brief segment, the supervisor has made it clear that she is willing to follow the trainee's lead and respond to the trainee's felt needs. The trainee apparently feels comfortable enough to begin by showing a segment where help is needed.

## 17. Allow the Trainee to Structure the Supervision Session

This occurs when the trainee is sufficiently experienced with both therapy and supervision that the supervisor is comfortable with letting the trainee set the direction. This is an elaboration of the preceding strategy, which allows the trainee to lay out plans for the entire session, without supervisor direction.

*To illustrate:*

*Supervisor:* Tell me what you have in mind for today.

*Trainee:* I want to show you part of my session with the family I am working with. I'm having trouble seeing what is going on.

*Supervisor:* Let's see. You've had the family therapy course, haven't you?

*Trainee:* Yes, and although I originally thought I'd just be working with the mother, I'm glad to have this opportunity to work with the whole family. I know you worked at Family Service Agency last year, so I'm glad you're supervising me. But I'm kind of lost here.

*Supervisor:* Okay . . . it sounds as if it is pretty hard for you to be an observer as well as do therapy right now.

*Trainee:* Yeah . . . they are such an active family that there is too much going on. I'd like help in figuring out what is happening and some suggestions about how to use what we see.

*Supervisor:* All right . . . And how much time do you want to spend on that?

*Trainee:* Let's see . . . I think about half the time. Then in the other half I can show you some segments and get you caught up on my other cases, which I think are going pretty well.

The supervisor has elicited the entire day's plan from the trainee and asked questions to clarify the trainee's plans for time usage during the session. The supervisor also verified that the trainee has the theoretical background to take on the challenge of family work.

◆

Because it is important to use strategies in supervision and know them well, it is best to stop here and practice the basic ones. Deliberate practice with these strategies offers the opportunity to integrate the theoretical knowledge into the supervisor's own practice and style with trainees. Until the initial strategies have been established in the supervisor's repertoire, there is no point in studying the advanced ones described in the next chapter.

CHAPTER 4

# ADVANCED SUPERVISION AND CASE CONCEPTUALIZATION

When supervisors have a good grasp of the basic strategies and can use them easily, they are ready for the advanced strategies listed in Table 2. These combine teaching, counseling, and consulting roles into single strategies. They require supervisors to attend to both the client and the therapist while holding the case conceptualization model and the therapist's theory of change in mind. Again, each strategy incorporates reflective inquiry in the context of the supervisory relationship. Before proceeding, we describe the case conceptualization model and the use of reflective inquiry to explore change theory. These concepts undergird the advanced strategies and fill out our picture of supervision. With a firm grasp of the case conceptualization model and the reflective inquiry process, supervisors can use the advanced strategies effectively.

## CASE CONCEPTUALIZATION MODEL

We have incorporated the work of Beutler and Clarkin (1990), Collins & Messer (1991), Mahoney (1991), Persons, Curtis, and Silberschatz (1991), and Vaillant (1977) into a comprehensive model for case conceptualization. It is designed to be used with a variety of theoretical orientations and in the variety of settings (mental health agencies, counseling centers, and schools) in which counselors and therapists are likely to work. The model has three major parts: develop valid information, set the problem, and develop change strategy. Table 3 presents an outline of the model.

### Develop Valid Information

In family systems theory, the person (or persons) who is distressed about the problem is considered to be the client (Satir, 1967). In our model, the client* may therefore be an individual who comes to a clinic for help with

*The word *client* will be used henceforth to mean one client or several individuals who make up a family or other client system.

**TABLE 2:** *Advanced Strategies for Supervision*

18. Encourage the trainee's exploration of change theory.
19. Help the trainee conceptualize a case.
    a. Develop valid information
    b. Set the problem
    c. Develop a change strategy.
20. Explore the trainee's feelings to facilitate understanding of the client.
21. Encourage the trainee's identification and use of cues in the client's and the therapist's behavior.
22. Explore the trainee's intentions in a session.
23. Help the trainee assess compatibility between in-session behavior and theory of change.
24. Present a developmental challenge.
25. Explore trainee-client boundary issues.
26. Use parallel process to model appropriate strategies for dealing with clients.
27. Reframe trainee ideas and behaviors in a positive manner and build on them.
28. Help the trainee to process feelings of distress aroused by the client's experience.

**TABLE 3:** *Outline of Case Conceptualization Model*

  I. Develop valid information
    A. Designation of client or clients
    B. Initial sources of information about client
      1. Interview with client
      2. Observation in important settings
      3. Formal assessments
      4. Impressions and reports of others
      5. Personal reactions of the therapist (feelings or hunches)
    C. Sources of information about setting in which client functions
      1. Direct observation
      2. Interviews with significant others (professionals, family members, and peers)
      3. Written materials—reports on the setting, relevant research, and others
  II. Set the problem
    A. The nature of the problem
      1. Present concern
        a. Client's description of problem
        b. What has precipitated the client's seeking assistance now?

*(continued)*

**TABLE 3:** *Outline of Case Conceptualization Model* (continued)

    2. What historical factors in this individual or family's life and in the institution have contributed to the problem?

    3. What cultural, social, and economic factors contribute to the problem?

       a. Cultural background

       b. History of social oppression

       c. Economic situation of individual (socioeconomic status) or institution

       d. Social value of person or institution in American society

    4. What client assumptions and patterns in behavior contribute to the problem?

    5. What personal resources does the client bring to bear on the problem?

       a. Usual coping strategies

       b. Personal strengths

       c. Life skills client has not mastered

    6. What institutional characteristics and patterns contribute to the problem?

    7. What institutional resources are available?

    8. Counselor's hypothesis about the nature of the problem(s) the client faces

  B. Nature of initial contract—bilateral (or multilateral) agreement

    1. Resolution among parties to address an issue that involves change at an agreed level

    2. Agreement among parties to work in a given setting in a way that is specified as clearly as possible at this point

    3. Agreement to work at a specified rate for a specified or open-ended period of time based on nature of concern, imminence of issue, client's availability, counselor's availability, constraints of the setting, and financial resources

III. Develop change strategy

  A. Change strategy

    1. Counselor's theory of human change (based on personal values, beliefs, and experiences as well as research on change)

    2. Match between client, setting, and change strategy

       a. Personality and cultural background of client

       b. Appropriateness of strategy for agreed goals

       c. Time and resource constraints

    3. Counselor or consultant's responsibilities, delineated by therapist

    4. Client's responsibilities, agreed to by client

    5. Expected challenges by client and institution

  B. Desired outcomes

    1. Insights and understanding

    2. Behaviors

a specific problem; the parents of an adolescent or child who are concerned about the behavior or feelings of that child; the school system with concerns about a given child or children; a school professional (teacher, counselor, school psychologist, or head teacher in an after-school program) who wants assistance with a child or children.

Initial sources of information vary by the standards of the setting in which counseling takes place. In some settings formal intakes are conducted by interviewers who are not counselors, and counselors get information about the intakes from the interviewer or from other sources. In our setting, trainees have access to videotapes of intake interviews, along with the client's responses to a life-history questionnaire and the results of formal assessments. Counselors may also have access to reports of others who know the client, such as parents, teachers, school counselors, physicians, or employers. Once they have met with their clients in the clinic or in the school setting or observed them personally, trainees can use their own feelings and intuitions about the client as additional important information. All of these are used, along with knowledge of the client's cultural background, to understand each client. As new information is obtained in the course of psychotherapy, the picture of the client can be modified.

Counselors have a variety of sources of information about the setting in which a client encounters problems. They may go into a school, for instance, and observe the client, talk with other professionals or with family members, or read written reports and records with permission from the client or parents of a minor. In this process, they pay attention not only to what they are told about the client but also what they learn about the school. Is this school a place in which teachers enjoy working, for instance? Are kids expected to learn in a passive or active manner? How does the principal feel about the usefulness of psychological interventions? Likewise, with the client's permission, a counselor may visit an office or factory where a client works. Goals of the employer, attitudes of supervisors, treatment of the client by others, and the client's responses to criticism can all be observed.

## Set the Problem

The client's problem is considered in a systematic fashion. Initially, attention is focused on whatever is going on in the present. How does the client describe the problem? This will be the basis for formulating goals for treatment that are acceptable to the client.

Why has the client come in now? This includes both the client's feelings about the problem and particular circumstances, such as an accumulation of stresses, a job change, or a change in family status. In an institutional or school setting, what else is going on? Has the business just been reorganized or have budget constraints in a school system meant that a child is in larger classes with little individual attention?

Next, the counselor focuses on historical factors in this person's life. What past experiences have contributed to the problem? The client's personal history is explored in a formal history-taking, which may include written documents along with the clinical interview. It includes information about the client's family of origin and current family status, social relationships, sexual history, educational and employment history, significant medical information, and significant life events. When taking a history, the therapist looks for patterns, such as a series of romantic relationships that ended when there was a demand for commitment or a series of jobs that were initially exciting and then disappointing to the client.

Cultural and social factors may contribute to the problem as well as to its solution. The counselor considers the client's cultural background to understand expectations for the client's current life and social functioning. Many Asian American adults, for instance, are expected to have close family ties and to consider their families when making personal decisions. European Americans, however, expect adult children to leave home and live in a fashion that is emotionally and physically independent of parental influence. When counselors of any cultural background fail to consider such differences, they may incorrectly label client's behavior as either disrespectful or immature. For instance, a client from a minority background may be faced with adapting to a work or school setting; in that case, the counselor's task is to help the client make necessary adaptations without giving up cultural values.

If the client belongs to a racial, ethnic, religious, sexual orientation, or gender group that has experienced social oppression, the client's history will have been shaped by it, and in determining the nature of the problem, one must take this into account. For example, what might seem to indicate a diagnosis of paranoia, for example, in the dominant culture, may be appropriate wariness in a member of a group that has experienced repeated discrimination.

How an institution is viewed by the society at large affects the problem's definition. Schools, for instance, are highly valued in some communities and generally dismissed in others. Mental hospitals may be seen as places to warehouse people or places where a person may be taught to live outside the hospital environment

To this point, understanding the problem has focused on problem descriptors. The client, however, brings assumptions and patterns of behavior that may contribute to the problem. In an adaptation of the Plan Formulation Method, described by Persons et al. (1991) and Collins and Messer (1991), counselors are encouraged to focus on patterns of traits and behaviors demonstrated by the client within and outside of counseling sessions.

The counselor's theoretical orientation determines the focal point, which might be the "hypothesized mechanism" used in a cognitive-behavioral formulation, the "obstructions" used in a psychodynamic formulation (Persons et al., 1991), or the "central conflicts" used in interpersonal process (Teyber, 1997).

Once they understand the nature of the problem, counselors can attend to the personal resources the client brings to bear on the problem. This includes an individual's usual manner of addressing problem situations and all solutions that the client has already used to resolve the current problem. In addition, all clients have personal strengths, which may include personality attributes such as perseverance or emotional openness, cognitive attributes such as a quick intelligence or a capacity to integrate information into insights, and social attributes such as an ability to form lasting friendships. Also included might be adaptive defenses (Vaillant, 1977), such as humor and suppression, which enable the client to get through difficult times. As well, clients may have strengths as a result of cultural background. A supportive family structure or a closely knit religious community might be cultural strengths.

At the same time, clients have limitations, such as a lack of specific living skills, or learned coping strategies that were adaptive at one time in the client's life but do not fit the current situation. These limitations may include personality attributes such as an inability to express feelings or a tendency to procrastinate, cognitive attributes such as impaired reading ability, and social deficits such as extreme shyness. They can also include the maladaptive things a client habitually does to avoid dealing with overwhelming feelings, such as daydreaming to the point of excluding reality.

Special attention needs to be paid to the institution in which the client is functioning. The client's personal characteristics and coping strategies interact with that system. A person from an argumentative, expressive family background may find life uncomfortable in a quiet, reserved family or community. A child who has developed learning strategies in a structured school setting may be lost in an alternative school that requires learner initiative. Institutions also have resources. Counselors are encouraged to explore the resources available to the client from a social or institutional system. These include support systems such as family and friends, institutional benefits such as an employer-paid insurance plan, and time limitations, such as the length of the school year or a limited number of counseling sessions covered by insurance.

Based on the preceding information collected from a variety of resources, what patterns does the counselor see in the client's history and current experience? How does the counselor define the problem? What is the nature of the change needed? With an initial picture of the problem, the counselor is able to make a contract with the client.

Clients and therapists make contracts of varied specificity at both an explicit and implicit level. In general, a contract for counseling is a resolution among parties to address an issue that involves change at an agreed level that can be realistically accomplished within the available time or a given number of sessions. This includes the level at which the client and therapist have agreed to conduct their work. Mahoney (1991) described a first-order focus and a second-order focus for work. Agreement on a first-order focus, he suggested, involves commitment to relatively minor changes in parts of a system, which tend to be goal-oriented and instrumental in emphasis, such as overcoming a fear of public speaking. Agreement on a second-order focus, on the other hand, involves a commitment to transforming the entire personal system, structurally and functionally; an example might be changing the way one relates to the opposite sex, which involves friendly, romantic, filial, and employment relationships. A second-order focus typically involves exploration of deeper meanings and longer work.

The contract also includes an agreement to meet at specified times and to work to address the selected problem through methods described to the client for a specified or open-ended period of time. These include the need for immediate resolution (e.g., the client is on a 2-month probation at work), the client's availability for treatment (including the client's work schedule, whether the client can easily get to the clinic, and whether the client can be seen in the institutional setting), the counselor's availability, limits of the setting (e.g., an inability to provide weekend services, a limit of six sessions in a counseling center or managed care facility, or need for reports to a school official or probation officer), and the financial capacity of the client or the system to pay for treatment.

Therapists must clearly delineate, to themselves and to their clients, what they will and won't do as a part of therapy. By the same token, therapists must make clear what they expect clients to do for work to proceed effectively. As clients and therapists make contracts, the work to be done during the session, such as goal setting, behavioral rehearsal, or free association, is specified. Likewise, the behavior expected outside of sessions, such as trying out new behaviors or remembering dreams, is specified.

## Develop a Change Strategy

Treatment planning begins with a theory of change. In general, how does this counselor think people change? What are the theoretical underpinnings of her or his approach to clients in this situation? In training programs such as ours, a theory of change is specified and trainees work to integrate their personal theories of change with the specified counseling approach.

More advanced therapists can explore the match between the client, setting, problem, and change strategy. What client characteristics might influence change? Both personality and cultural factors contribute to the appropriateness of a change strategy for a particular client. In a systematic approach to treatment selection, Beutler and Clarkin (1990) emphasized the importance of matching psychotherapeutic treatments to the client's personality; they suggested, for instance, that a highly resistant client would do well with guided bibliotherapy but poorly in a strict behavioral approach. With reference to cultural background, Ivey, Ivey, and Simek-Morgan (1993) pointed out that clients from some non-European cultures prefer a structured approach focused on a specific problem.

In addition, some treatments have proven effective for the treatment of certain disorders; relaxation strategies have historically been effective in addressing phobias, for instance. Case planning must also take into account the depth of focus to which the client and therapist have committed. Clients who have contracted to change their social skills, for instance, are not well served by strategies that encourage regression and deep processing. When the time available for therapy is limited, by either client or therapist constraints, some treatment approaches are inappropriate. An effort to dismantle the defense structure can be destructive, for instance, in a treatment program limited to six sessions.

The therapist must be prepared for the erratic nature of change; it is seldom, if ever, a linear process. Persons et al. (1991) pointed out that some difficulties during therapy can be predicted, based on the personality, history, and current circumstances of the client. In addition, there may be difficulties within the institutional setting when the client begins to change. It is wise for therapists to consider these problems in advance, so that when they arise, they can be understood and dealt with in context.

Finally, there needs to be a sense of what constitutes success in counseling. How do the client and therapist know when it is time to terminate? The number of sessions may be specified in some managed care or agency limitations, but this is not a criterion for successful termination. Usually counselors and clients have some sense of what they are working toward and they have identified their goals with greater or lesser degrees of specificity. In some cases, learning a method to help oneself process feelings or events is desirable. This might mean incorporation of a cognitive-behavioral strategy or development of a capacity to be introspective and produce one's own insights. In other cases a behavioral change is the goal. Behavioral changes can include in-session and out-of-session changes. In all cases, therapists are encouraged to assess their effectiveness with each client in some systematic manner.

The model for case conceptualization is provided to help counselors plan their cases. Clearly the nature of clients, settings, and institutional or financial limitations influences the planning process.

# THEORY-BASED REFLECTIVE INQUIRY

Argyris and Schön (1974) emphasized the importance of understanding the theoretical basis for professional action. Likewise, counselors-in-training are encouraged to articulate a theoretical orientation for their work with clients. What Argyris and Schön observed, however, is that professionals' descriptions of the theoretical basis for their actions (their espoused theories) often bear little relationship to their actual behavior. The procedures they use to work with others do not match their verbal declarations. Norman Kagan (1983) described gathering prominent counseling supervisors together, who had written out their theories of supervision and brought along videotapes of themselves interacting with supervisees. The participants "were surprised to observe how different the written description by each supervisor often was from that person's actual supervisory behavior. In fact, it seemed that in most instances the written theory was, in effect, a self-admonition" (p. 69).

Argyris and Schön (1974), along with many educators, suggested that professional actions are based on a practical theory of what works with people. Most of their seminars were focused on looking for professionals' practical theories, which the authors referred to as their theories-in-use. Counselors, for instance, might espouse the idea that clients know what they need to do because they know themselves and their own situations better than anyone, but in session the same counselors give a great deal of advice. Advice giving seems to be predicated on the practical theory that clients really do not know what is best for them, and it is incumbent on therapists to tell them what to do.

Once counselors can articulate a theory of action, it is possible for them and their supervisors to look at what they've done to see whether their espoused theory and their practical theory match. If they do not, we encourage supervisors to help their trainees sort out what must be adapted to bring the two theories into line. In some cases, therapists may decide that they need to adapt their actions to match their espoused theories, but in other cases, they may decide on the basis of their experience that the theory needs to be changed. In this way, supervision facilitates the reflective practice described in chapter 1. Figure 2, which draws on the work of Argyris and Schön (1974), illustrates the role of supervision in development of a congruent theory of practice.

Without the framework for examination of counseling sessions based on case conceptualization and change theory, supervision is a rather haphazard affair, dependent on what a particular supervisor happens to think would work with a given client. The counselor is left to follow the supervisor's advice without fitting it into a larger picture of the whole process of psychotherapy and, as Rønnestad and Skovholt (1993) pointed out, coun-

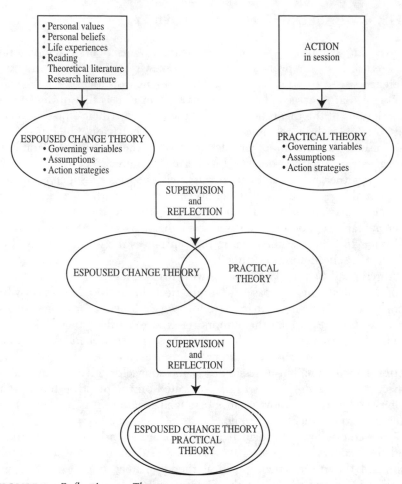

**FIGURE 2:** *Reflection on Theory*

selors become focused on what others think they should be doing instead of developing their own reflective skills. We have incorporated both the case conceptualization model and the reflections on theory into the advanced strategies that follow.

## ADVANCED SUPERVISION STRATEGIES

Now that supervisors have learned the basic strategies, they are prepared to combine teaching, counseling, and consulting functions in their use of the advanced strategies. At this level, supervisors can attend to the client, the counselor, and the relationship between them in the counseling session. Simultaneously the supervisor attends to the counselor trainee, the supervisor's own thoughts and feelings, and the relationship between the trainee and the supervisor in the supervision session. While attentive to all of this, supervisors hold the counselor's case conceptualization and theory of change in mind and ask the trainee to reflect on the events of the counseling session in that context. The initial advanced strategies are used to explore trainees' theories of change and case conceptualization so that the rest becomes possible.

The strategies can be applied effectively within many theoretical orientations. In our examples, we have continued to emphasize the interpersonal process therapy (Teyber, 1997) approach as the theory of change. In some cases we have used the behavioral orientation included in Hill and O'Brien's (1999) three-stage approach. The strategies can also be used with Gestalt theory, a person-centered approach, or other approaches.

## 18. Encourage the Trainee's Exploration of Change Theory

This strategy is designed to help trainees develop their own theories of change. Supervisors ask trainees to tell how they think people change. They label this the trainee's espoused theory of human change. If desired, the supervisor can also ask the trainee to indicate where his or her theory of change fits with an established theoretical orientation in counseling.

Following this, the supervisor investigates the trainee's experiences of change in his or her own life. The supervisor asks the trainee to describe an occasion when he or she changed in some significant way. The supervisor asks about details of the situation to discern just how the change came about. From this analysis of actual life events, the supervisor encourages the trainee's understanding of his or her practical theory of change and so labels it. Then the supervisor asks the trainee to look at ways in which the espoused theory, frequently based on declarative knowledge, and the practical theory, which demonstrates procedural knowledge, overlap and ways in which they differ.

Until trainees understand the idea of espoused theory and practical theory, they will be unable to take a good look at what they are doing in terms of theoritical orientation.

*To illustrate:*

*Supervisor:* Much of what we do in counseling involves helping people to change something in their lives. How do you think people change?

*Trainee:* Well, I suppose people have to be ready to change.

*Supervisor:* So part of your theory of change involves a readiness to change. Is that simply an attitude on the part of clients?

*Trainee:* Well, partly. It also seems to me that people are most likely to change when they are in a lot of pain and don't want to go on the way they are.

*Supervisor:* Okay. So readiness for change is important. Then how do people actually go about changing?

*Trainee:* Well, I think that they have to analyze what's wrong and how they are contributing to the situation before they can figure out what to do to change it.

*Supervisor:* So they need to be somewhat objective about their situation.

*Trainee:* Yes. If they're just governed by their emotions, they can't think straight. So they have to calm down and become more objective.

*Supervisor:* Okay . . . and then what happens?

*Trainee:* Well then they figure out what's going on and what they're doing. Where do things go wrong and why? And what's their part of that?

*Supervisor:* And is that understanding sufficient for change?

*Trainee:* I don't think so. They or some other people who know them and their situations have to come up with some ideas about how they can change what they're doing—or thinking. Then *[laughs]* they actually have to do those things.

*Supervisor:* So you think people change by taking a long, analytical look at their situation, devising a way to act differently or think differently, and then doing that.

*Trainee:* Yeah . . . that's pretty much it, I guess.

*Supervisor:* Well that's what I would call your espoused theory, your description of your theory of change. Do you have a sense of where that theory of change would fit with a theoretical orientation in counseling?

*Trainee:* Sure, that's why I'm a behaviorist. In fact, that's probably why my advisor was interested in my coming into this program.

*Supervisor:* Perhaps so. . . . Now I'd like to shift our focus a bit. I'd like to spend some time thinking about a significant event in your own life where you felt that you really changed. Can you think of a time like that? I know we've talked about some important times, and maybe you want to use one of those—or maybe something new comes to mind.

*Trainee:* Well, you know, it's been a year since I moved back here, and I was thinking this morning about how that came about.

*Supervisor:* Mmm-hmm . . . tell me about it.

*Trainee:* Well, you know, I was living up in Idaho. I moved there for a job.

*Supervisor:* Yeah, I remember that you came here from Idaho, but I didn't realize you'd lived here before.

*Trainee:* Well, not right here, but in New York.

*Supervisor:* Oh, okay. And you were a graphic designer then, weren't you?

*Trainee:* Yeah. I didn't think I'd like to live in Idaho forever; that was a planned adventure. And I got this job offer to go to L.A. and work for a big advertising agency.

*Supervisor:* That must have been exciting.

*Trainee:* Yeah, it was; everyone kept telling me to go for it, that now was my big chance. It sounded pretty good, but I couldn't figure out why I wasn't more excited about it. Then one night I had this dream, and in the dream I was walking around with my best friend; he's a psychologist in New York. And I was saying to him that I really envied him, that he did work that helped people and he got to live where he wanted. . . . When I woke up, I felt really sad. I knew the last place I wanted to go was to L.A. I never have liked driving much, although I could cope with Idaho. The idea of driving on those endless L.A. freeways terrified me; that's not my idea of urban life at all. And I knew I didn't want to work for an ad agency and just encourage people to buy a lot of stuff they didn't need. I got sick of that even with the low-level promotional stuff I was doing. So I moped around all day, and then I decided not to go. I called them up and turned down the job. It wasn't too long before I moved to Boston and not much longer after that before I applied to go to graduate school. And here I am.

*Supervisor:* Wow! That's quite a story! And are you glad you made these changes?

*Trainee:* Oh yeah . . . I'm much happier now.

*Supervisor:* My therapist brother says "Dreams never lie," and this sounds like a case where that was true.

*Trainee:* Yeah, I guess so.

*Supervisor:* So let's think about this. What do you think made you change, when you reflect on it?

*Trainee:* Well, I guess my dream told me about how I really felt, instead of what would make me rich and famous or something, and then I knew what to do.

*Supervisor:* So you're saying that dreams are important indicators of what's going on inside a person.

*Trainee:* Sure. And how you feel when you awaken—

*Supervisor:* And that you can use them to take a look at what you're doing.

*Trainee:* Yeah. And then make changes if that's what's called for.

*Supervisor:* So this, what you actually did—paying attention to your dreams and your feelings about them and then acting—is what we call your practical theory, the theory you act on in daily life, even though you don't think about it as a theory.

*Trainee:* Yeah, I guess you could say that.

*Supervisor:* Well, let's go back to where we were earlier. Your espoused theory said that you take an objective look at a situation, figure out your part in it, devise plans for action, and then act on them. And your practical theory involves listening to your dreams for clues and then taking action. . . . How do you think they overlap?

*Trainee:* Well, they both call for taking a look at the situation [*laughs*], but looking at dreams isn't what I usually think of as objective analysis! Once past that point, I think that there is some similarity in that action follows and that's where the change is.

*Supervisor:* Yeah, I think you're right. I think you understand the idea of practical theory and espoused theory pretty well.

In this vignette, which is clearly an abbreviated version of a complex story, the supervisor first worked in the cognitive domain as an inquiring teacher. Following that, the supervisor elicited an experience that had meaning for the trainee, and then worked as a counselor in the affective domain. At the appropriate moment, the supervisor drew from the trainee's experience to describe an underlying practical theory and then encouraged the trainee to compare the two theories. This strategy requires an ability to shift skillfully between the teacher and counselor roles where appropriate.

## 19. Help the Trainee Conceptualize a Case

Trainees have been presented with a model for case conceptualization and case formulation. Each time a new case is assigned, supervision is focused on an initial conceptualization of the case. The supervisor begins by helping the trainee to look at as much information as possible to get a valid picture of the client and the client's concerns. The supervisor asks the trainee about the intake interview, any formal assessments made at intake, and information gleaned from the personal history provided by the client. The supervisor follows by asking the trainee to give impressions of the case and reactions to the client.

More than a description of the client is needed, however, and the supervisor moves on to determine the nature of the problem. The supervisor questions the trainee closely about the client's description of the problem, the reasons for seeking help now, the client's background, and other factors that may influence the existence or maintenance of the problem. After asking the trainee about the client's personal resources, including a support system, financial resources, and time to resolve the issue, the supervisor inquires about the initial contract the trainee has made with the client.

At this point, the supervisor elicits the goals and the level of focus agreed to by the trainee and the client. With that in mind, the supervisor proceeds to explore the case in depth. This includes questioning the trainee about the proposed strategy for change and predictions for the course of therapy.

*To illustrate:*

*[The following dialogue is about a client who is a college student unable to make classroom presentations because of her fear of public speaking.]*

*Supervisor:* So tell me how you plan to work with this client. You say that this client wants to address her problem of public speaking before she takes a seminar next semester when she will need to make presentations. What is the depth at which you expect to be working?

*Trainee:* Well, this is a first-order focus, and involves just minor changes. We could have worked on her anxiety about performance and her family's expectations for success, but in this amount of time, it seems important just to help her reduce her anxiety about public speaking.

*Supervisor:* Okay, that makes sense. . . . Tell me what characteristics she has that produce this problem?

*Trainee:* Well, as I said, she has high expectations for herself. And that makes her anxious when she has to perform.

*Supervisor:* Are there cultural factors in her anxiety?

*Trainee:* Yes, she comes from an Asian American family, and she said that they have very high expectations for her. Her parents are first-generation immigrants, and they have spoken with her about not bringing shame on the family with poor academic performance.

*Supervisor:* Oh. That's quite a lot of pressure. At the same time, her family's support and expectations are important assets; they have helped her achieve up until now

*Trainee:* Sure.

*Supervisor:* Have any things happened in the past that particularly contributed to the problem?

*Trainee:* Yes. She was always quite anxious, but she did well in school and was praised often for her written work. Then, when she was in the 12th grade, she took a public speaking class. When she gave her first talk, she was so nervous, she sweated clear through her clothes, and the kids commented on it. She was ultimately so embarrassed that she dropped the course.

*Supervisor:* So that made things a lot worse. Has she spoken before a group since?

*Trainee:* No. She says she has always been able to get around it, and she studies hard and writes very well, so she has a very high academic average. But next semester she will be in a senior seminar where the students must present their work to the class.

*Supervisor:* So that's why she came in for counseling now. Okay, how do you think you might approach this?

*Trainee:* Well, I thought I'd teach her some relaxation techniques and do a basic desensitization and rehearsal approach.

*Supervisor:* Tell me how you decided on that with this client.

*Trainee:* Well, she doesn't have much time, and this strategy has been used a lot. She told me she is an athlete and has done some visualization training, so I think she could learn to lessen her anxiety through relaxation training.

*Supervisor:* And do you think that would be enough?

*Trainee:* No, I don't think that will be enough for her. She said she didn't really learn to use her athletic visualizations until she went out to the track and tried them. So I'd want to have her try to relax in different places, like in our session and then in a class when she wouldn't have to speak and then in a situation where she would ask a question in a large class. Then I'd encourage her to give short speeches, first to me, and then when she had mastered that, to a group of friends.

*Supervisor:* Those all sound like good ideas. Do you anticipate any setbacks?

*Trainee:* Well, I think it will be hard for her to get over the hump and speak up in class.

*Supervisor:* How do you think you and the client might address this?

In this way, the supervisor walks the trainee through the formulation of the case. At the end of the session, the supervisor reminds the trainee that as therapy proceeds, understanding of the client and the strategy for therapy may be modified.

◆

Strategies 20, 21, and 22, which follow, are drawn from the work of Kagan (1983), and amplified by Elliott (1984). Supervisors have already learned to evaluate observed counseling session interactions (strategy 1) in the teacher role, and to explore trainee feelings during the counseling session (strategy 7) in the counselor role. Strategies 20, 21, and 22 are expansions of those skills, to be used as ways to revise the trainees' understanding of their clients as they work. The use of the three strategies enables trainees to process their feelings and thoughts to examine both their relationships to clients and their in-session behavior in light of their treatment plans and espoused theories.

✦

### 20. Explore the Trainee's Feelings to Facilitate Understanding of the Client

Trainees are often unaware of their own feelings and intentions in a session. Their feelings can assist them in "detecting clients' subtle but important issues and . . . responding effectively to clients" (Gelso & Carter, 1985, p. 181). The trainee's videotape of a counseling session may be stopped at any point during a supervision session. The supervisor begins by asking about the trainee's feelings at that place in the counseling session. When the trainee responds, the supervisor asks where the trainee thinks the feelings may be coming from. Most trainees identify something within themselves, and the supervisor acknowledges that. The supervisor moves on to ask what client characteristics or behaviors may have stimulated that particular feeling. After the trainee responds, the supervisor asks whether other people in the client's life have reacted in the same way the trainee did. Regardless of the counselor's theoretical orientation, the supervisor can discuss the client's behavior as a learned adaptation. This encourages the therapist's respect for the client's behavior when it may seem illogical or counterproductive. The important point here is that the counselor's feelings can provide valid information about a client and then can be used within a therapist's own orientation for further understanding.

*To illustrate:*

*[In this situation the trainee espouses an interpersonal approach.]*

*Supervisor:* Let's stop for a minute. . . . Now tell me how you were feeling right then in the session.

*Trainee:* Well, I was feeling pretty bored . . . and I was feeling guilty because I'm not supposed to be bored.

*Supervisor:* So you were feeling bored and guilty while you were listening to her. . . . And why do you think you had those feelings?

*Trainee:* Hmmm . . . well, she was talking and talking, telling me one story after another of what her roommate said and what her boyfriend did, and I just don't really care about those things . . . I guess I got turned off by that gossip stuff pretty early—my dad used to say, "Superior people talk about ideas, mediocre people talk about events, and little people talk about people," and maybe I've internalized that.

*Supervisor:* That's interesting. . . . Do you find yourself turning off a lot of conversation and getting bored with a lot of people?

*Trainee:* No—just when they start talking on and on about people I don't know.

*Supervisor:* So her talking about people you don't know is the turnoff?

*Trainee:* Yeah, and the way she does it—I mean, she didn't really leave any openings for me to say anything.

*Supervisor:* Do you think she does that with other people?

*Trainee:* Oh yeah, I'm sure, because she complains a lot that people don't listen to her. . . . You know, I like her, but now that you call my attention to it, I realize she just goes off on these tangents and then I lose interest.

*Supervisor:* Are there particular times when she goes off "on these tangents?"

*Trainee:* Again, now that I think about it, I guess it happens a lot just when we begin to talk about things that are emotional for her, especially when she is talking about things that might make her angry.

*Supervisor:* So she goes into this way of talking when she might be emotional and maybe angry. . . . It sounds like a pattern. How do you think she learned this pattern?

*Trainee:* Well, she grew up in a family that fought a lot—and her brother was always getting hit. I wonder if she just tried to distract everyone and keep them from getting excited or mad at each other by talking about things that were removed from the immediate situation.

*Supervisor:* That's possible . . . and if that's true, what worked for her then isn't working now to help her develop and maintain adult relationships. . . . Within the interpersonal process orientation you employ, how will you understand and use this?

*Trainee:* Well, it seems to me that I need to explore it when it happens in our relationships—you know, something like, "What just happened there? I asked you about your feelings and then you began to tell me a whole story and the whole tone of the conversation changed."

*Supervisor:* Yeah, that's a good start, brings it right into the room and allows her to notice and explore this.

In this example, the supervisor inquires about the trainee's own feelings and then facilitates the trainee's understanding that feelings can provide information about the client's pattern of operating with people. From there, the supervisor can help the trainee to build a strategy for dealing with the issues, within the trainee's theory of change.

## 21. Encourage the Trainee's Identification and Use of Cues in the Client's and the Therapist's Behavior

Prior supervision strategies have emphasized the trainee's recognition of counseling events as they were observed on videotape or experienced by the trainee during the supervision session. This supervision strategy focuses on teaching the trainee to make observations during the counseling session itself. The supervisor focuses the trainee's attention on an event that has occurred in the counseling session they have just observed. Following this, the supervisor encourages the trainee to identify cues (i.e., client behaviors or counselor feelings) that might signal an important counseling event. Once these have been identified, the supervisor suggests that the trainee anticipate their recurrence in counseling and plan to respond to that in session.

*To illustrate:*

*[In this situation, the supervisor and trainee have just viewed a session and decided that the client was angry with the trainee but not expressing it directly.]*

*Supervisor:* So now that you have looked at this again, you think Mary was pretty angry with you?

*Trainee:* Oh, yeah! I'm surprised that I didn't really notice it when it was happening!

*Supervisor:* I'm not completely sure you didn't notice it at some level. Were you feeling anything while you were sitting there?

*Trainee:* Oh, I was pretty uncomfortable. In fact, I remember looking at the clock and noticing that it was only 10 past the hour and thinking that this session was taking forever!

*Supervisor:* So a cue for you that something important was transpiring was your discomfort and impatience for the session to be over?

*Trainee:* Yeah. I hadn't thought about it that way, but you're right. That could have been a cue for me.

*Supervisor:* Okay. Anything else you were aware of in yourself?

*Trainee:* Hmm . . . no, not particularly.

*Supervisor:* Now, as you think about it, what did you notice about Mary when we were watching the tape just now?

*Trainee:* Could we look at that part again?

*Supervisor:* Sure. . . . Pay particular attention to anything about her that is different from her usual demeanor.

*[They watch the segment again.]*

*Trainee:* Well, she was looking around a lot and not making good eye contact—and usually she looks right at me!

*Supervisor:* Sure. Her pattern changed. And what else did you notice?

*Trainee:* She was sitting in a pretty closed position. And you know, her lips, well, her lips were kind of tight, like in a line.

*Supervisor:* So that's another nonverbal cue. So far you've suggested that when you noticed you felt uncomfortable, you could have looked at her pretty carefully and you would have seen some nonverbal signs that she was angry.

*Trainee:* Yeah.

*Supervisor:* And did she say anything then or earlier that could have alerted you?

*Trainee:* Well, when she first came in, she said something odd. . . . You know, because I'd been away, I'd been looking forward to talking with her. And then when she came in, she made a remark about the license plate of my car, you know, how "California" it was to have a license plate that says "Cheer up."

*Supervisor:* Ah—so you had warning right from the beginning that something was up.

*Trainee:* Yeah, you know, I did. But I didn't think about it that way because I got defensive about my license plate!

*Supervisor:* Sure. . . . Now I don't suppose that will be the last time she'll be angry at you. So what have you learned to attend to so that you can notice it in the session and respond to it?

*Trainee:* Well, my own feelings first. And then when I notice those, I can look to see what she is saying or what she is conveying nonverbally—and how that differs from her usual pattern.

*Supervisor:* Yeah, you've got it. . . . Now let's talk about how you will want to work with her next time you notice some cues that suggest she might be angry.

In this vignette, the trainee brought up her own feelings first, so the supervisor asked the trainee to continue to explore those feelings as data about the session. Then the supervisor encouraged her to look at the client's behavior. After the supervisor summarized the trainee's observations as verbal and nonverbal, the supervisor suggested that in the future the trainee could use those observations in the counseling session, and the supervisor began to explore ways to do so.

## 22. Explore the Trainee's Intentions in a Session

Clara Hill and her colleagues (Hill et. al., 1988; Hill & O'Grady, 1985) have studied the effect of therapist intentions on the course of a psychotherapy session and on the outcome of therapy. They described stopping the videotape of a counseling session after a therapist statement and asking the therapist for the rationale for each statement. The strategy she and her colleagues used to study therapist intentions is a useful supervision technique for exploring a trainee's intentions and is similar to the strategy used by Henry, Schacht, et al.'s (1993) most effective supervisor. In this way the supervisor can also initiate a discussion of any discrepancies between espoused theory and practical theory. Hill and her colleagues (1988; Hill & O'Grady, 1985) elicited therapists' responses with a prepared list of intentions; in our strategy supervisors ask open-ended questions to stimulate trainees' own thoughts. Once a trainee has explained a rationale for statements or actions, the supervisor and trainee can continue to watch the tape to see if the intervention achieved the desired result.

*To illustrate:*

*[In this situation, the trainee has made an interpretation to the client by saying, "Each time you tell me about wanting to be taken care of by a woman, you look away as you talk, and I'm imagining that you are embarrassed because you don't think you should want anything from a woman," and the supervisor is asking about it.]*

*Supervisor:* Please stop here. . . . Now, when you said that, what did you want to happen here?

*Trainee:* I was thinking that he has a terrible time talking about what he wants from women, and I wanted to help him explore and make sense of his feelings.

*Supervisor:* So you wanted to provoke his self-exploration. . . . How did you happen to hit on that particular way of approaching it?

*Trainee:* I've been wondering about why he presents such a strong persona and yet seems so lost and lonely, and I thought that this provided a good opportunity to explore this.

*Supervisor:* So you made this interpretation. . . . Let's look and see what happened when you did that.

*[They look at the tape, and the client indicates that he was embarrassed to admit*

*he wanted anything, and goes on to say that he was ridiculed as a child by his father for being a "baby" and a "mama's boy."]*

*Supervisor:* As you looked at that segment, did you think your intention was met?

*Trainee:* Yes. I wasn't completely accurate with my interpretation, but it led to his noticing his own embarrassment and connecting it with some history.

The supervisor explored the trainee's intentions for the interpretation and then examined whether the intervention elicited the desired result. In this case, it did. If it had not, the supervisor and the trainee could have explored some alternatives to achieve the same goal.

## 23. Help the Trainee Assess Compatibility Between In-Session Behavior and Theory of Change

In describing this strategy, we are assuming that the supervisor has used strategy 18 (encourage trainee's exploration of change theory) and already knows the trainee's theory of change. Use of this strategy may come after the use of strategy 22 (explore the trainee's intentions in a session) but will not always do so. After viewing a videotape, the supervisor proceeds to explore the trainee's in-session behavior in terms of the trainee's theory of change. This strategy draws on teaching, counseling, and consulting roles.

The supervisor asks the trainee about the interaction between the trainee and client in a somewhat open-ended way. As the supervisor gets a sense of what was happening, he or she questions the trainee about how the trainee decided to proceed in that way at that particular time. Then the supervisor explores the discrepancies between the trainee's espoused theory and apparent practical theory, and they work together to modify one theory or the other or both.

*To illustrate:*

*[In this situation, the trainee has shown a portion of a counseling session in which the trainee has advised the client to go to her child's school, report what has happened in her child's classroom, and ask that her child be transferred to another teacher.]*

*Supervisor:* Tell me a little bit about what was happening there.

*Trainee:* Well, she came in extremely upset. She said that the boys in the class had her daughter down under the desks in the back of the room during recess, and they had pulled down her panties. The daughter was crying. When the teacher came into the room, he apparently said something like, "Now everyone take their seats; recess is over," and seemed to ignore the incident.

*Supervisor:* And so what happened with you?

*Trainee:* I just got enraged! I've been a teacher, and I know that you have to deal directly with sexual harassment. . . . I have a daughter in junior high, and I know something about what goes on there. But this is in an elementary school classroom and it's happening right under the eyes of the teacher and he's not doing anything!

*Supervisor:* So your feelings dictated what you should do here. . . . What would your counseling theory say you should do?

*Trainee:* Well, I suppose I could have asked the client what all this meant to her. And I could ask if something about the way that the teacher ignored her child reflected what she felt was happening between us.

*Supervisor:* Sure. And do you wish you had done that?

*Trainee:* No! I mean, it might be important to get to that at some point, but she told me this near the end of the session, and I believed it was a serious situation for her as a parent and for her child. Because she's an immigrant, I think she is hesitant to make waves at the school, and I felt I needed to show her how to respond and give her permission to do so. I didn't think we could wait until the next session, because situations like that tend to repeat themselves once kids get the idea they can get away with it. . . . I suppose I could have checked the accuracy of her story a little more before swinging into action, but my experience with this client is that she makes light of events rather than exaggerating them, and so does her daughter. So I believed the facts as she told them.

*Supervisor:* So what does this mean for your theory of change?

*Trainee:* I think I need to change the theory a little to accommodate emergency situations.

*Supervisor:* Okay, I can follow that. In an emergency, you respond to that situation and become more directive. . . . Is there a way you can do that and still work within your theoretical model?

*Trainee:* Well, let's see. I suppose I could frame it somewhat differently. For instance, before I rush in to offer her advice, I could check with her by saying something like, "It sounds as if you want some advice from me about this."

*Supervisor:* Yeah, and what would she do?

*Trainee:* She'd say yes right away, I think.

*Supervisor:* And then what?

*Trainee:* I could explain why I was being so directive in this situation without disempowering her, I think. I've talked with her before about feeling unsure how to adapt to life in the U.S., because she immigrated only 2 years ago. I could say, "Since you are new to this country, you might feel unsure about what is considered appropriate childish play in an American school and what is appropriate for you to do as a parent." My guess is that she would agree, and then I could proceed as I did. Then after I gave her my advice, I could ask her not only how she would feel carrying it out but also how she felt about my telling her what to do.

*Supervisor:* Yeah, I think that's good. You've found a way to modify your espoused theory to accommodate emergencies and your practical theory to integrate your theoretical beliefs about counseling.

In this example the supervisor inquired about the trainee's use of advice and encouraged the trainee to modify espoused theory and practical theory in a way that integrated the trainee's experience with this particular client.

## 24. Present a Developmental Challenge

A developmental challenge is designed to promote change (accommodation) in the trainee's usual ways of thinking to process (assimilate) the new information. There are a number of appropriate points for a developmental challenge. Some of these include hearing only the surface content of a client's statements and missing the underlying meaning, viewing a client from another culture through the lens of the trainee's own culture, or inaccurately assuming that what has helped the trainee to change is also what will help the client.

A common place for trainees to founder is when they first meet client resistance. They often see resistance as a negative event in therapy rather than as information and communication, which can be used in the therapeutic process in a manner consistent with a theoretical orientation.

*To illustrate:*

*[In this situation, a trainee's understanding of the meaning of client resistance is challenged.]*

*Supervisor:* Tell me about how therapy is going with Jane.

*Trainee:* Actually, it's pretty frustrating. She always comes late to sessions, and she doesn't think about what we've talked about between sessions, or hardly ever.

*Supervisor:* Has that always been a pattern with her?

*Trainee:* No. . . . It's just been in the past 2 or 3 weeks.

*Supervisor:* And what's been happening in therapy in the past two or three weeks?

*Trainee:* About 3 weeks ago, she brought in her journal, and she read some things to me about what happened in the first grade, how she failed first grade and how her mother cried every night trying to teach her to read. She suddenly seemed to understand that her mother had not supported her very much in those hard times and had, in fact, made her feel pretty bad about herself. And she was sort of relieved to think that she might not have been such a failure all the time.

*Supervisor:* Yes . . . and what happened next?

*Trainee:* Well, we were both pretty excited about this, and I suggested that she think more about what happened in 1966 and how that shaped her view of herself. And she said she would. But she hasn't done it. She's been coming late to sessions and she talks the whole time about the problems she is facing at work.

*Supervisor:* And do the problems seem important?

*Trainee:* Yes and no. I mean, that work situation is pretty bad, but it hasn't changed much, and she doesn't think she can find a new job that pays as well or gives as much vacation, so it's sort of a waste of time to talk about it. . . . I'm pretty frustrated with her. I don't see that we're getting anywhere right now, and she doesn't seem to care much about therapy.

*Supervisor:* So what do you think she's telling you by coming late and talking about her job and not continuing with the work you began several sessions ago?

*Trainee:* Telling me?

*Supervisor:* Yes. I mean, she is talking about her job, but what is she communicating to you about herself?

*Trainee:* Well, she is saying, I guess, that she doesn't want to do what I asked her to do or that it's not very important or something. . . . You know, I really thought we were getting somewhere, but now I'm pretty discouraged.

*Supervisor:* Let's stay with this a little longer. Where did you think you were getting when you were getting somewhere?

*Trainee:* I thought she was going to discover that she was really an okay person and that it was her mother who made her feel that she wasn't.

*Supervisor:* And what is she saying to you now by her behavior?

*Trainee:* Oh—I see what you mean. She's saying she doesn't want to talk about that

*Supervisor:* Yes, probably. . . . And that's telling you a lot about her. What do you think it means to her to talk about those things?

*Trainee:* I don't know. Maybe it's scary or maybe she feels disloyal or something.

*Supervisor:* And if that were true, what would that tell you?

*Trainee:* I'm not sure . . . maybe that she doesn't want to think about her mother like that.

*Supervisor:* Yes, or perhaps that she doesn't want to think about that right now. How can you explore her resistance and find out more about what she's telling you about herself?

The supervisor can proceed from here to help the trainee devise appropriate strategies that incorporate the information the client has communicated by "resisting." The client, for instance, might have lived a lot of her life protecting her mother and not saying anything bad about her, and in a psychodynamic model, the therapist can explore that with the client. Or the client may be communicating that she is a reactive person who doesn't like to be told what to do, and the therapist can take this into account and avoid giving directives. But the challenge forces the trainee to think about resistance in a different way, as information about a client in the continuing therapeutic process rather than as something that is stopping the therapy. The trainee is forced to hear the music instead of the words, and to expand his or her ability to understand clients. Other challenges expand the trainee's thinking in different ways.

✦

The next two strategies provide two different ways for the supervisor to educate the trainee based on what has happened in the counseling session. Again, teaching, counseling, and consulting functions are involved.

✦

## 25. Explore Trainee-Client Boundary Issues

A frequently occurring problem in psychotherapy is the testing of limits and boundaries. The beginning trainee, who wants to seem like a kind and responsive therapist, is often particularly vulnerable to a client's unreasonable requests. It is important for the trainee to learn how to set appropriate limits. Although psychodynamic theorists might refer to this as "establishing the frame," and behaviorists as "reinforcement of appropriate therapy behavior," both would agree that limits must be set.

We will assume that beginning trainees have already been taught to start and end promptly, to collect fees at the end of each session, to hold the fee at the amount set by the agency for this client, and to limit contacts with the client outside of therapy sessions. Nonetheless, in some circumstances, trainees find this difficult.

*To illustrate:*

*Trainee:* The supervisor on duty has interrupted my session each of the last two times to tell me that someone else needed the room. . . . I was wondering if some arrangement could be made so that when a client becomes very emotional at the end of a session, I could keep working with her, and maybe the supervisor could arrange for another room for the next case. . . . Two weeks ago, for instance, she was a little late for the session and she spent a lot of it telling me about her weekend . . . and then right at the end, she started talking about how angry she is with her parents because they never listen to her and always cut her off, and she started crying.

*Supervisor:* And so what were you feeling then?

*Trainee:* I didn't want her to feel cut off by me too, and I started to let her talk it through, but then John knocked on my door after a few minutes and said I had to end. It was very difficult.

*Supervisor:* So you wanted to let her know that you cared about her, and that's why you let her go on?

*Trainee:* Yeah.

*Supervisor:* And what happened in the next session?

*Trainee:* Well, she cancelled the next session. Then this week she did exactly the same thing—she talked about a lot of unimportant stuff and then she got really emotional at the end.

*Supervisor:* Okay, I see. It's becoming a pattern. As you know, we have to begin and end on time because other clients are scheduled to use the room. Even when there is another room available, clients often prefer to keep meeting in a room that is familiar to them, and we make every effort to respect that client's wishes when it is time for their appointment, just as we respect your client's wishes during her scheduled time. However, this interaction can be looked at in a couple of ways. . . . Let's begin by trying to understand the client's pattern, not only in the context of your sessions but in the context of her history.

*Trainee:* Okay. But where do we start?

*Supervisor:* Refresh me a little about this client. What did she come in for?

*Trainee:* She came in saying that she was having trouble getting along with her roommates, that this was the third set who couldn't get along with her. She said she had had some pretty big arguments with them, and the arguments reminded her of some of the arguments she'd had with her parents.

*Supervisor:* And what were the arguments like with her parents?

*Trainee:* Well, so far as I can tell, her parents, who never had much money and had to work all the time, didn't pay very much attention to her. They didn't have a lot of time to listen to her, and she still doesn't think they are very interested in her. What she did as an adolescent to get their attention was to stay out late and not do well in school, but they really didn't seem to notice. The only way she could get their attention was to get really upset and either blow up or start crying hysterically; then, I guess because they really did care about her, they'd pay attention.

*Supervisor:* So what do you think she learned from that about relating to other people?

*Trainee:* Gee, I don't know. . . . Well, maybe she's afraid that people don't really care much about her and don't care what she does, but if she gets upset, she can find out if they do care about her.

*Supervisor:* That's possible. And if that were true, what do you think would be happening in her relationship with you in therapy?

*Trainee:* Oh! *[laughs]* I see. She sort of bores me for a long time with her chit chat and then she gets really emotional.

*Supervisor:* And how are you feeling in this process?

*Trainee:* I get pretty irritated, actually, by the fact that she shows up late. And then I feel bad that I have those feelings, so when she starts getting emotional, I am glad to be able to be caring toward her.

*Supervisor:* So what does the client learn from this pattern of yours with her?

*Trainee:* She learns that I don't care what she does in the beginning of the session, even if I don't like it, and then I respond to her emotional behavior.

*Supervisor:* Yeah. . . . And do you think she is like this with other people, like her roommates?

*Trainee:* Oh, probably.

*Supervisor:* And what do you think happens in those relationships?

*Trainee:* Well, eventually people probably get pretty burned out if she disregards what they ask, the way she disregards our starting time and then gets really dramatic at other times.

*Supervisor:* It makes sense. Now this is just our idea about the client. It might change a lot as you see her longer. But how could you begin to work with these ideas in therapy?

*Trainee:* I guess I could talk to her about it.

*Supervisor:* And how would you do that?

*Trainee:* Well, I could tell her that I've noticed that she often comes late and then brings up the important stuff at the end.

*Supervisor:* Sure. That would be a good confrontation if you said it as gently and straightforwardly as you just said it to me. And then where would you go?

*Trainee:* I could explore further how she feels in our relationship and how she interprets the way that I respond. Later I could tell her what feelings are stirred up in me when she does that.

*Supervisor:* Yeah, or you could do that when you first point out what she does, but you need to find a way to do it that breaks the pattern of her experience and lets her know you won't abandon her the way that everyone else does, that you want to understand what goes on for her. How might you frame your remarks?

The supervisor begins by explaining the agency reasons for not complying with the trainee's request for more time in the room at the end of a session. Then the supervisor quickly moves to help the trainee use this experience to understand the client and expand the trainee's conceptualization of the case.

Sometimes a trainee does not explicitly describe the ways a client is pushing the boundaries; instead, the trainee communicates by acting out the client's role, by pushing the boundaries with her supervisor. In that event, the parallel process strategy might be used before the supervisor begins to address the issues presented by the client.

## 26. Use Parallel Process to Model Appropriate Strategies for Dealing With Clients

Parallel process is described in Schön's (1987) *Educating the Reflective Practitioner* as the "Hall of Mirrors" approach to educating an apprentice therapist. According to parallel process theory (Friedlander, Siegel, & Brenock, 1989; Glickauf-Hughes & Campbell, 1991; McNeill and Worthen, 1989), the trainee experiences the relationship with the client in a way that is then represented in the interactions with the supervisor; that is, the trainee acts like the client when he or she is with the supervisor. This is considered to be an unconscious process by the psychodynamic theorists who first described it, a way to show the supervisor what it is like to work with this client. A behavioral explanation of the supervision strategy for working with parallel process, on the other hand, might describe it as modeling. In supervision, parallel process is suspected when trainees act in a way that is somewhat frustrating and significantly different from their usual pattern of functioning in supervision.

Although the supervisor may plan in advance to implement supervision skills such as the exploration of trainee feelings or intentions in a given session, the opportunity to use parallel process in a supervision session occurs serendipitously (Glickhauf-Hughes & Campbell, 1991). The supervisor must be aware that parallel process could occur at any time and should be prepared to address it.

Psychodynamic supervisors of advanced trainees or practicing therapists ordinarily point out and interpret parallel process when it occurs in supervision. Unfortunately, this direct approach can create confusion and excessive defensiveness when trainees are just beginning. It is also less effective with them, as McNeill and Worthen (1989) have pointed out. Instead, in the strategy for supervising trainees during their first practicum experience, we recommend that supervisors recognize the parallel process as a metaphor and respond in a metaphorical manner. They respond to trainees as they intend trainees to respond to clients. In effect, the supervisor teaches by modeling but offers no interpretation of trainee behavior or explanation of supervisor behavior.

*To illustrate:*

*[In this rather complex situation, a trainee has come to supervision expressing a great deal of embarrassment about showing her videotape. The trainee has not cued the tape and states some discomfort with this client. The trainee explains that she is uncomfortable with showing her tape because she is afraid her impatience with the client's complaint is apparent. Nonetheless, the trainee proceeds. In the videotape, the client has described similar embarrassment about displaying her own feelings and joked about turning the video cameras off in the training clinic's consulting room.]*

*Supervisor:* Tell me a little about being uncomfortable with showing me this segment.

*Trainee:* Well, I don't think I should be judgmental about the client.

*Supervisor:* Let's back up a little. Tell me just how you were feeling in the session with her.

*Trainee:* Well, I was annoyed with her, actually. It seems to me that she should just be glad she's got a boyfriend who has a good job and is making money. It's pretty hard to make a living here, and he's doing it. . . . So I was thinking about that instead of being aware of her feelings. That's why I was a little abrupt in asking her why she felt that way, and then I felt bad because she seemed embarrassed, so I changed the subject pretty quickly.

*Supervisor:* And you were kind of embarrassed about having those feelings and about showing me the part where you were abrupt?

*Trainee:* Yeah.

*Supervisor:* Because you think you shouldn't have those feelings.

*Trainee:* Yeah.

*Supervisor:* Are you still a little embarrassed?

*Trainee:* A little, but it's not quite so bad. You don't seem to be judging me; you seem more curious about my feelings.

*Supervisor:* So you were uneasy and hoped I wouldn't spend much time on these feelings, but now that I did, you feel a little more comfortable?

*Trainee:* Yeah.

In this vignette, the supervisor gave the trainee the experience of exploring her feelings. She was able to see that even though she really wanted to skip over her feelings of embarrassment in this segment, she actually became less embarrassed and more understanding of herself as she talked about them. The supervisor, however, did not explicitly draw the parallel to her work with the client; the supervisor simply modeled it. The expectation, supported by Friedlander, Siegel, and Brenock's (1989) case study of parallel process, is that the trainee will now act with the client as the supervisor has acted with the trainee.

◆

The final two strategies are focused more on the interaction in supervision than on consultation about the client. Strategy 27 combines teaching with attention to the trainee's feelings, and strategy 28 uses counseling skills to assist the trainee in processing what has come up for the trainee in hearing the client's story.

◆

## 27. Reframe Trainee Ideas and Behaviors in a Positive Manner and Build on Them

Much of supervision takes place in groups in which a skillful supervisor questions group members about a case. This allows everyone to become involved and everyone can practice case conceptualization skills and analysis of counselor behavior in terms of espoused change theory. This skill is especially helpful in group supervision when one trainee makes observations about a colleague's case. When new trainees make observations, they often do not have the skill to make thorough and accurate observations of their fellows. The supervisor must find a way to validate one trainee for making an observation and yet refine the observation so that another trainee can use it. Following an observation by a trainee, the supervisor agrees with a specific aspect of the trainee's statement and then adds an additional observation. It is particularly important for the supervisor to follow the trainee's observation with the word "and" before giving the refined observation. Too often instructors give a "yes, but" response, which invalidates the prior speaker. Using "yes, and" includes the prior speaker's observation as a part of the useful feedback. In individual supervision, the supervisor can agree with some of the individual trainee's comments about the trainee's own case and then add an observation.

*To illustrate:*

*Trainee 1:* Boy, that guy really seems out of touch with his feelings. Maybe you could ask him what is so upsetting about this situation.

*Supervisor:* You are right about his not being in touch with his feelings, and it's interesting to think about how that is useful for him right now. Is it helpful to him to repress those emotions while he looks for a job or does he need to address them now?

In this case, the supervisor agreed with Trainee 1's observation about the client and then instead of agreeing that amplification of feelings was needed, began to explore the meaning of the client's behavior.

*To illustrate further:*

*Trainee 2:* You were so quiet there. I kept wanting you to say something!

*Supervisor:* Good observation, Trainee 2! It must have been hard for you to keep silent while all that was going on, Trainee 3; just like Trainee 2, you must have been feeling impatient. . . . You were able to remain quiet in spite of your feelings, and the client got there on his own.

The supervisor validates Trainee 2's feelings about the slowness of the session and builds on them to validate the counselor's behavior in session. This skill is actually quite difficult to practice and requires the supervisor to proceed very deliberately to facilitate the group and simultaneously provide useful feedback for use in counseling sessions.

## 28. Help the Trainee to Process Feelings of Distress Aroused by the Client's Experience

This is a version of supervision strategy 7 (explore trainee feelings during the counseling session) that is focused on the experience of a therapist's encounter with the reality of traumatic events or of humans' inhumanity to humans. In the process of conducting psychotherapy, even sophisticated therapists are sometimes overwhelmed by feelings of distress about their clients' experiences. Sometimes therapists' emotional reactions occur because events in the clients' lives echo events in their own lives, and sometimes the feelings are simply their very human responses to a tale of trauma, pain, or degradation. In working with trainees, the supervisor's task is to help trainees sort out their own feelings so that they can go on to work effectively with their clients. It is important to give trainees a chance to process their feelings before asking them to focus on their work as therapists. This strategy is placed last because it is somewhat outside the usual focus (enhancing the trainee's professional development). Nonetheless, it is an important strategy because it allows trainees to consider some consequences of professional experiences for their personal development. This strategy falls within the ethical guidelines for exploration of feelings described by Neufeldt and Nelson (in press).

*To illustrate:*

*[In this situation the trainee is reacting to a client experience that is connected to an experience of her own. In reality, it would take longer to process such a situation than is represented by the example, but the example shows the likely progression of such work.]*

*Supervisor:* Tell me a little about your impressions of this case before we look at the videotape.

*Trainee:* Okay. Actually, I wanted to talk about it. . . . You know, I've been seeing this client for a while, and she's pretty volatile.

*Supervisor:* Yes.

*Trainee:* And you know, she's had a very difficult relationship with her mother. They have fought a lot in a rather dramatic style.

*Supervisor:* Yes.

*Trainee:* Well, this week she told me about a fight she had with her mother, where she yelled at her mother that she hoped she'd never see her mother again, and she didn't. Because her mother shot herself that night.

*Supervisor:* Oh! How awful! That must have been overwhelming to hear!

*Trainee:* Yes. *[Begins to cry.]*

*Supervisor:* *[Waits before talking]* Tell me what you're feeling.

*Trainee:* Well, there are some things I haven't told you about my family. But my father committed suicide last year.

*Supervisor:* Oh. . . . That must have been awful for you.

*Trainee:* *[Continues crying]* You know, when my father killed himself, I had just written him a letter because we were coming down to visit him the next week, and I told him how glad I was that we were going to see him. I know he got the letter because I found it in the wastebasket.

*Supervisor:* So you must have felt pretty abandoned when he didn't wait to see you.

*Trainee:* Yes. *[Continues crying.]*

*Supervisor:* It sounds as if you still are struggling with your feelings about this.

*Trainee:* Yes. I'm seeing a therapist myself.

*Supervisor:* Good. I'm glad that you have found someone to talk with and work through these feelings.

*Trainee:* But when this client brought this up, I was pretty overwhelmed. And then when she had shouted at her mother—well, that was pretty different from my experience of writing to my father.

*Supervisor:* Yes. I can imagine that that would create a lot of feelings in you . . . and yet, you are a pretty different person from your client.

*Trainee:* Oh, yes. *[Wipes eyes, seems calmer.]* I would never tell anyone I didn't want to see them again. But she is pretty histrionic and she says extreme things all the time.

*Supervisor:* And how do you think she feels about having said this, which is usual for her, and then having her mother kill herself?

The supervisor responds in a therapeutic manner to the trainee until the supervisor feels the trainee is ready to go on, and then the supervisor shifts the discussion back to the client. If the trainee had not had a therapist of her own, the supervisor might have asked how she was working out her feelings and encouraged her to find an appropriate way to do so. Nonetheless, the supervisor eventually would have moved from working with the trainee's own feelings to looking at the client.

◆

The manual to this point can be used by supervisors of therapists at any level. Strategies described for use with beginners can be modified for advanced trainees and practicing therapists. Part III, which follows, outlines a beginning practicum course that includes individual and group supervision sessions designed to supplement classroom presentations.

# PART III

# PRACTICUM COURSE OUTLINE AND SUPERVISION MODULES

To this point, the manual can be used by both beginning and advanced supervisors in a variety of situations. In part III, chapters 5 and 6 outline a basic practicum course for beginning counselors in which the supervision strategies are embedded. The course and supervision are designed to teach trainees to develop a relationship with clients in the first term and to conceptualize cases in the second. Although 15 weeks are outlined for each term, the materials can be used for terms of 10 weeks simply by dropping five lessons, as we have done in our program. (Lessons 10 through 14 and 25 through 29 are those that can be dropped most easily without sacrificing the structure of the course.)

We assume that the practicum course consists of a weekly class conducted by the course instructor, followed by a group or individual supervision session conducted by the supervisor-in-training. The classes include teaching and student case presentations. Because we have designed this manual to foster effective supervision rather than to detail classroom instruction, we simply outline the lessons. We recommend that the instructor assign appropriate texts so that students can read about the concepts under discussion whenever possible.

Supervision sessions for each week are described in detail with vignettes to illustrate them; use of specific supervision strategies from the previous chapters is noted. The weekly supervision meetings are conducted by one student supervisor working with one or more trainees. Supervision sessions in the first term involve two or more trainees, because role-playing and instruction are highlighted. During the first term, when students are engaged in structured role-plays with one another followed by brief counseling with undergraduate volunteer clients, the supervisory vignettes are tied closely to the lessons, although they may vary at times because of material presented by peer or volunteer clients. In the second term, when trainees begin to meet with community clients, supervisors meet with their trainees individually during some weeks and together during others. Joint supervision sessions are expected to last 3 hours; individual sessions may vary from 1 to 1 1/2 hours each. When trainees begin to see community clients in the second term, supervision sessions are focused almost entirely on case presentations. Vignettes for the second term illustrate the concepts under discussion, but actual supervision sessions may differ greatly. Although we continue to use an interactional process approach for counseling, we have included some examples from other approaches. In truth, both relationship building and case conceptualization are skills necessary for all counselors and therapists, regardless of their theoretical orientations.

**TABLE 4:** *Practicum Course*

| *Term A*<br>*Relationship Building* | *Term B*<br>*Case Conceptualization* |
| --- | --- |
| **Week A-1**<br>Introducing relationship concepts<br>Building relationships within class | **Week B-1**<br>Developing change theory: espoused<br>theory and practical theory |
| **Week A-2**<br>Establishing a collaborative<br>relationship: setting the tone and<br>understanding the client's story | **Week B-2**<br>Introducing the case conceptualization<br>model:<br>   Gathering valid information<br>   Building relationship with a<br>      structured intake |
| **Week A-3**<br>Building a collaborative relationship:<br>acknowledging the client's experience<br>in the moment | **Week B-3**<br>Learning intake procedures that<br>facilitate gathering valid information:<br>using structured intake, assessments,<br>and clinical interview |
| **Week A-4**<br>Building a collaborative relationship<br>with children | **Week B-4**<br>Gathering valid information in school<br>or other institutional setting |
| **Week A-5**<br>Building a collaborative relationship<br>with institutions (schools, agencies,<br>family members) | **Week B-5**<br>Setting the problem with individual<br>clients and in school or agency settings |
| **Week A-6**<br>Identifying patterns and formulating<br>working hypothesis | **Week B-6**<br>Developing change theory and goals<br>for a client |
| **Week A-7**<br>Identifying resistance, working with it,<br>and learning from it | **Week B-7**<br>Using the relationship to effect change<br>*(continued)* |

We have developed our lessons and supervision modules around the reflective model described in chapter 1 and elaborated in the supervision strategies presented in chapters 2 and 3. We continue to assume that students come with strengths and ideas on which we can build. In the manner of Paulo Freire (1993), we envision supervisors as "teacher-students" who learn with "student-teachers" to construct a way of working that fits the client and the counselor and meets the standards of good practice. Students bring some skills and knowledge to supervision, but supervisors, by definition, bring significantly more knowledge and practical experience.

More important than development of any particular skill is the counselor's development of a reflective process to be used throughout her or his professional career.

Table 4 provides a brief description of the practicum course.

**TABLE 4:** *Practicum Course* (continued)

| *Term A*<br>*Relationship Building* | *Term B*<br>*Case Conceptualization* |
|---|---|
| **Week A-8**<br>Establishing focus for change | **Week B-8**<br>Understanding the course of change for clients |
| **Week A-9**<br>Facing clients' emotions and working with them | **Week B-9**<br>Terminating: preparation and completion |
| **Week A-10**<br>Identifying counselor factors that interfere with responding to clients | **Week B-10**<br>Conceptualizing and counseling for social skills needs |
| **Week A-11**<br>Exploring multicultural elements that may enhance or interfere with the relationship | **Week B-11**<br>Learning conceptualization and counseling for social skills needs |
| **Week A-12**<br>Working on problems requiring action: clients who are a danger to themselves and others | **Week B-12**<br>Conceptualizing and counseling for depression in adults, children, and adolescents |
| **Week A-13**<br>Reporting child abuse: working with families and protective agencies | **Week B-13**<br>Learning conceptualization and counseling for anxiety in adults and children |
| **Week A-14**<br>Intervening in institutions on the client's behalf (schools, after-school programs, agencies) | **Week B-14**<br>Introducing family counseling |
| **Week A-15**<br>Reviewing the term and evaluating the trainee | **Week B-15**<br>Reviewing the course and terminating supervision |

CHAPTER 5

# FIRST-TERM SESSIONS DESIGNED TO HELP TRAINEES BUILD COUNSELING RELATIONSHIPS

During the first term, trainees concentrate on relationship building. Beginning trainees are generally very anxious (Skovholt & Rønnestad, 1995). By and large, they enter graduate programs with skill at "doing school" and some confidence in their academic ability. They do not, however, know how they will perform as counselors and therapists. We have tried a range of approaches to facilitate trainee's early performance with clients in ways that ease their anxiety enough to allow them to focus on the clients in front of them.

In our first edition, we recommended a constructivist approach, in which we encouraged counselors-in-training to figure out just what conveyed focused listening. I have rejected that approach in this edition for two reasons. First, we found that educators had responses in mind when asking trainees to "discover" what made people feel "listened to." It is inappropriate for educators to ask students questions for which we already have answers; this is manipulative and only encourages students to watch us to ascertain what we want rather than to reflect on their own ideas. If we want them to do something, we should simply let them know what it is and reserve our questions for those occasions when we want to discover what they think.

Second, Grace, Kivlighan, and Kunce's (1995) study showed that early training of novice counselors to attend to nonverbal behaviors significantly improved their working alliances with clients. These alliances were significantly better than the working alliances developed by counselors without this training. This finding convinced us that specific training in nonverbal behaviors, along with some basic listening responses to keep the client going, belonged right in the beginning of our practicum course. We have used this approach successfully for the past 3 years with our students, and it is included here.

We encourage beginning counselors to focus on each other and try to understand one another's experience. We provide opportunities for novice counselors to listen to others and attend to their nonverbal behavior. Then counselors respond in a way that conveys understanding. We believe that clients want to be understood more than they want to be reassured. Counselors must demonstrate that they understand their clients to build relationships and work with them to promote change in their lives.

In our program, trainees work for the first few weeks in role-play sessions with one another as clients. Following this practice, they see undergraduates who have volunteered to be clients for three sessions. The undergraduates learn something about the counseling process, and the trainees can begin with clients who talk about developmental issues such as roommate problems. Until trainees see clients who are not their classmates, they are encouraged not to formulate hypotheses about their clients, because such formulations would be intrusive and inappropriate if done with their peers.

In this chapter, we describe lessons and supervision sessions for each week of the first semester of a practicum course. The weekly lecture topics and goals are described briefly so that instructors can develop more elaborate lessons based on the level of understanding and particular needs of their own students. Because this is a supervision manual, however, the objectives for each supervision session are followed by an outline of material to be addressed. Much of the first term's supervision is conducted from the teaching role, because beginning counselors and therapists need and want structure. This also avoids their guessing what we might want, as addressed above. As the term progresses, however, supervision moves from specific instruction to responding to a wider range of counseling sessions conducted with undergraduate volunteers or, in some programs, real clients who present real problems.

# WEEK A-1. INTRODUCING RELATIONSHIP CONCEPTS

## Class

*Objectives:*
1. *Introduce the class members, supervisors, and instructor to one another.*
2. *Explain the idea of working together as teacher-student and students-teachers in an interactive process.*
3. *Outline the basic requirements for the course and evaluation procedures.*
4. *Explain the working alliance and facilitate discussion of it as it applies to a variety of relationships.*

The class begins with student and instructor introductions. This is especially important for this practicum course because of the emphasis on interactive process as well as the potential personal nature of group supervision.

As the instructor introduces him- or herself, he or she describes his or her own ethnicity, culture, sexual orientation, or socioeconomic origins, all of which are important aspects of identity. To invite discussion of these elements immediately, the instructor states something to this effect: "In one or more ways I am likely to match you, and in other ways I probably differ from you. Please identify whichever characteristics you wish to in your introduction. Let me know, now or at any time, if I am not sensitive to cultural issues, or when our differences seem to interfere with our relationship." This approach was recommended by a student supervisor whose supervisor used a similar introduction with her (Maria Alvarez Chamorro, personal communication, November 1998).

After introductions, the instructor explains that he or she and the students will be working together to develop ways to build relationships between therapists and clients. The instructor has a sophisticated knowledge base and clinical experience, and the students have considerable history in forming relationships with others. Some students may possess a theoretical knowledge base as well.

Following that, the instructor explains the outline of the term's work. Included is an explanation that the first term emphasizes building the counseling relationship, and the second term emphasizes case conceptualization. Consistent with the ethical principles elaborated in chapter 2, students are then told exactly how they will be evaluated at the end of the course. Each student receives a list of required competencies, a copy of the final evaluation form, and a statement that explains the requirements for videotaping supervision and counseling. The instructor encourages students to ask questions about all three documents. At the end of the discussion, the instructor asks students to sign the statement indicating that they understand the course requirements. Then trainees are assigned to supervisors and encouraged to set times for their regular weekly meetings.

The instructor facilitates a discussion about relationship development, based on the working alliance as articulated by Gelso and Carter (1985, 1994). Emphasis is on drawing out the trainee's general ideas about relationships and identifying the elements that make up different kinds of relationships. Trainees are asked for examples of transference, working alliance, and real aspects of relationships from their personal lives. In addition, the instructor elicits discussion of the effects of gender, ethnicity, religion, and sexual orientation on the working alliance. Trainees are encouraged to think about the potential working alliance they will form with the instructor and their supervisors. The importance of a strong working alliance for successful counseling (Beutler et al., 1994) is explicitly emphasized. Throughout the term, new skills and information will be presented in relation to this core concept.

In the last 30 minutes, the instructor introduces basic listening skills to enable students to keep discussion going in their first role-plays.

## Supervision

*Objectives:*
1. *Develop a relationship with the trainees.*
2. *Assist the trainees to understand the relationship concepts further.*
3. *Practice basic listening skills along with open questions and restatements.*
4. *Review the basic mechanics of site procedures.*

In the first part of the session (75 minutes), the supervisor explains the way in which supervision will be conducted, learns about each trainee, and shares some personal and professional history in a way that is similar to the instructor's self-introduction in the first class. The supervisor asks questions to explore trainees' reasons for entering the field. Questions may emphasize personal and cultural factors, along with the trainees' sense of suitability for this work, academic and professional history, and long-term professional goals as they see them. Supervision strategy 8 (explore trainee feelings during supervision session) is used.

*To illustrate:*

*Supervisor:* I'm looking forward to our working together. I know in class Dr. N explained that she is supervising my supervision of you. As part of that, I am required to videotape our sessions. The videotapes will be seen only by Dr. N and the other student supervisors. They will be evaluating my supervisory skills more than your performance in those sessions.

*Trainee 1:* I'm a little uncomfortable about it. Will the supervisors talk about me?

*Supervisor:* We will talk about you in terms of your needs for supervision and my competence in responding to your needs. The emphasis will be on my ability to help strengthen your counseling behavior. You also need to know that we will keep confidential anything that we discuss. We will not discuss it among ourselves or with anyone else outside of the supervision seminar time.

*Trainee 1:* I guess I can live with that.

*Supervisor:* How are you feeling about this, Trainee 2?

*Trainee 2:* I am really uneasy about it. I don't see how we can have a trusting relationship with you if whatever we say or do will be seen by Dr. N and the other supervisors. What if I get into my personal issues?

I'm not convinced that displaying my personal feelings won't affect my evaluation.

*Supervisor:* I can understand how that might feel to you. It is, however, important for your development and your client's protection, so that my supervision is as useful as possible for you as you work with clients. This is part of the way we maintain our ethical commitment to provide you with the best supervision and your client with the best counseling possible. Nonetheless, I know that you will not want to talk about things that you do not want anyone else to hear, and I will not press you to do so. You have control over what you say here.

*Trainee 2:* I can see I don't have much choice about this, but I think it will affect what I say.

*Supervisor:* Sure. Only you can decide how much you can trust Trainee 1, me, and the supervision seminar group. . . . We need to clarify a few things about our meetings now. We will continue to meet at this time throughout the term unless an emergency arises, and we have to reschedule. During the sessions we will review and elaborate on lecture material, we will talk about your work, and you will show videotapes of what you have done in counseling. How does this sound to you?

*Trainee 2:* It sounds okay, but I'm worried about bringing tapes in for both of you to watch.

*Supervisor:* Are you concerned that your work will be too closely scrutinized or criticized?

*Trainee 2:* Well . . . I just feel uncomfortable. . . .

*Trainee 1:* Yeah. Me, too. I've never had to do anything like that before.

*Supervisor:* Well, I know it's uncomfortable. I had a hard time getting used to it at first. I think you'll find that as you work to develop your skills, you'll want feedback more than you'll be afraid of it!

*Trainee 2:* Okay. We'll see. But what if in our role-playing sessions, the person who is acting as the client reveals personal material?

*Supervisor:* Again, when you play a client, you will need to decide what topics you are willing to discuss on videotape. As you know, you have the option of inventing a problem, but you must let the counselor know. It is more difficult to practice counseling with an imaginary problem. It will be important when you are the counselor and when you see videotapes of your colleagues with Trainee 1 or in class, that you do not talk about what was said to others outside of supervision. It is our commitment to one another that nothing that is said by a student in a counseling role-play or in supervision becomes material for gossip. Can you both commit to confidentiality about these things?

*Trainee 1 and Trainee 2:* Yes.

*Supervisor:* Good. . . . We will be working together for the rest of the year, and I would like to begin by getting to know you a little bit and helping you to know me. Are you comfortable with that?

*Trainee 2:* Sure.

*Supervisor:* Perhaps you could begin by telling me how you decided that you wanted to enter this field of counseling.

*Trainee 2:* Well, somehow I've always been a person that people talked to about their problems. Even my parents would come and ask my advice about my little brother. In college, whenever anyone in the dorm had a problem, they'd come and talk to me.

*Supervisor:* Did you enjoy that?

*Trainee 2:* Yes. I like being able to help people. But I felt lots of times that I didn't know what I was doing, so I finally decided to go back to school.

*Supervisor:* And how did you decide to come to this particular graduate program?

*Trainee 2:* When I was an undergraduate, I started reading books about psychotherapy. I read a book by Dr. B, and I got really interested in what he had to say. It made a lot of sense to me. And then my undergraduate advisor told me that he had worked with Dr. B at one time and that I should apply to this program. So here I am.

*Supervisor:* Gosh! Not many people are that organized when they make that decision. You must be pleased to have followed it through.

*Trainee 2:* Yes, although my first term here wasn't really the way I expected.

*Supervisor:* Oh?

*Trainee 2:* I thought I'd be learning right away from Dr. B about doing therapy. Instead, he's got me involved in a research project, and I won't take a counseling course from him until next year.

*Supervisor:* I can imagine that is disappointing for you. . . . Tell me something about your background. You told me that you studied psychology and that your friends have confided in you. Have you had any other counseling or counseling-like experiences?

*[Supervisor engages in a similar dialogue with the other trainee.]*

In this illustration, the supervisor has attended to the concerns of the trainees, reflected the trainees' feelings of anxiety with the first-term experience, and confirmed the commitment between the trainees and the supervisor to confidentiality. Then the supervisor moved forward to the next task, and neither joined in criticism of the program nor defended the program. Keeping discussion on task and away from discussing the merits of the academic program is a constant challenge for supervisors who work in an academic setting.

In the second portion of the session (1 hour), the supervisor discusses building a relationship with a client. Trainees are given an introduction to the basic listening skills of minimal verbal responses, restatements of verbal content, open-ended questions, and silence. These behaviors convey understanding to clients and enable them to continue talking. Often a brief handout with examples facilitates the discussion. Then trainees are invited to listen to one another talk about an interesting personal experience in a 15-minute role-play. Each trainee plays the counselor once and practices conveying understanding of the client's experience with the basic responses. Counselors are directed to ask no more than three questions during the 15-minute interview. Afterward, each is asked to talk about the experience as counselor and as client.

*To illustrate:*

*Supervisor:* Tell me about your experience as a listener.

*Trainee 1:* I was so anxious at first that I had a hard time even paying attention to Trainee 2 when he was talking.

*Trainee 2:* Yeah, I had that problem too when I was listening to you. But after a while I got interested in what you were saying and stopped worrying so much about what I was doing.

*Supervisor:* So you began to notice her and what the experience was like for her.

*Trainee 2:* Yeah.

*Supervisor:* And did that happen for you, Trainee 1?

*Trainee 1:* It took me a while, but yes, when Trainee 2 started talking about how being in that accident had made him think about what he was doing in his life, I was pretty riveted. At the same time, I was thinking about what that sort of experience would have meant to me.

*Supervisor:* Yes, that shows that you are listening. Thinking about the meaning of it in your life helps you develop empathy. At the same time you need to be careful that you continue to pay attention to the unique meaning of the experience in the client's life and not get it confused with your own.

*Trainee 1:* Yeah, I could see that I was so sure I knew what he meant for a minute that I stopped listening. But then I went back to him and his experience.

*Supervisor:* Great! Now tell me, both of you, what you paid attention to as a listener. What did you use to understand the person who was talking to you?

*Trainee 2:* Well, Trainee 1 was talking about a lot of different things, and I tried to figure out just what had happened. I kept trying to put the whole story together.

*Trainee 1:* Yeah, I did that too. I found myself trying to understand just what went wrong so that Trainee 2 crashed when he did.

*Supervisor:* And did that help you understand his experience further?

*Trainee 1:* Well, a little. But the important part turned out to be what he experienced when he was in the hospital afterwards.

*Supervisor:* And what did you get out of that?

*Trainee 1:* Well, Trainee 2 said that all of a sudden he stopped to think about what was important to him in life.

*Supervisor:* How did you decide that this was an important experience for him?

*Trainee 1:* Well, he said it was.

*Supervisor:* Was there anything else besides what he said that helped you to know that?

*Trainee 1:* Oh, I see what you mean. Yeah, he got much quieter and talked more slowly when he was describing that. He seemed to look at me a lot, as if to check out whether I got what he meant.

*Trainee 2:* Yeah, you know, all of a sudden Trainee 1 got a little teary when she was talking. I knew right away that this was the important stuff.

*Supervisor:* Good. *[Discussion continues in this vein for a while.]* Let's talk a bit about your experiences as speakers. What seemed to keep you talking and what interfered?

*Trainee 1:* I know that when I was talking, it helped me when Trainee 2 asked me what it was like for me.

*Supervisor:* So an open-ended question helped you to continue. Were there any questions that got in the way of your story?

*Trainee 2:* When Trainee 1 asked which hospital I was in, I got off the track for a while.

*Supervisor:* Yeah, a closed question, or one that just calls for unimportant information, can stop exploration and make the person turn to the counselor for direction. It can also get speakers away from their own difficult or important experiences because it's often easier to talk about unimportant details than about what matters. . . . Trainee 2, what helped you keep going?

*Trainee 2:* Well, most of the time Trainee 1 didn't question me much. She just seemed to listen, nod occasionally, and let me keep going. And then every so often she'd repeat back to me what she thought I'd said.

*Supervisor:* So nonverbal encouragers helped you keep exploring, because you had the sense that she was listening and following what you were saying. And then when she summarized what you had said, you realized that she really did hear you.

*Trainee 2:* Yeah.

In this vignette, the supervisor explored the trainees' experiences as counselors first. Then the supervisor questioned their experiences as clients to show the effects of counselor activities.

During the third segment (30 minutes), the trainees tour the training facility with the supervisor. The supervisor demonstrates each procedure for client contact and record keeping, and explains how to keep track of time during a session.

At the end of this and every week's supervision, trainees are invited to express any feelings or concerns; following this, the supervision session is closed.

## WEEK A-2. ESTABLISHING A COLLABORATIVE RELATIONSHIP: SETTING THE TONE AND UNDERSTANDING THE CLIENT'S STORY

### Class

*Objectives*
1. *Explain basic procedures for opening and closing sessions and provide practice.*
2. *Present concept of empathic understanding and discuss.*
3. *Teach tracking of nonverbal behavior.*
4. *Provide trainees with practice in tracking.*

Before beginning the class, the instructor asks students for feedback about their experiences in the course to date. Any questions are answered, and complaints are considered. This will be repeated in each class so that students can feel understood by the instructor and the instructor can respond to any concerns that students may have. This allows the students to develop an investment in the class and keeps the instructor apprised of what needs to be addressed in a timely fashion.

Then the instructor teaches skills for opening and closing sessions. Opening statements include a greeting and an invitation to the client to speak. Closing skills involve warning the client that the session is about to end and then ending the session on time. Students are then directed to practice with each other both opening and closing statements. This takes approximately 30 minutes. Students are told that they will practice these skills and others more extensively in supervision.

The instructor then presents the concept of empathic understanding of the client's description of the problems they face outside counseling. The instructor explains that it is very important to communicate that the counselor understands the client's feelings and the meaning of the client's experience. Discussion follows, with an emphasis on how careful listening and responding can convey understanding of the client's story.

Then the concept of tracking, "the skill of following the flow of the other's present experiences . . . the constant seeing and listening in order to keep track of what is happening for the other" (Kurtz, 1990, p. 75) is introduced. Attention to nonverbal behavior is described as a means of understanding the client's experience at a deeper level. Students are asked to contribute to a list of important nonverbal behaviors to which they might attend while listening to a client. Instructors may add to the list.

In this way, the instructor shifts attention to nonverbal client behavior and away from counselor behavior. This emphasizes the importance of attending to the client instead of to oneself. Novice counselors' anxiety about their own performance can be alleviated by this focus on the client.

Students are divided into groups of three to practice listening and tracking for at least 45 minutes. In each triad, one student is the counselor, one is the client, and one is an observer. Those in the role of client are asked to talk about something real, so that their nonverbal behaviors will be congruent with the content of their talk, but they do not need to talk about a problem. Those in the role of counselor pay very close attention to the student client's nonverbal behaviors to track their experience. Counselors use the basic listening responses learned in supervision to keep the discussion going and allow the client to feel heard and understood. After approximately 10 minutes, the student counselor and observer discuss their observations of the student client's nonverbal behaviors. All three discuss their feelings during the experience. Then the exercise is repeated until each student has played every role. When all have completed the role-plays, the class members discuss their experiences with the instructor.

At the end of class, the instructor explains that all students will be asked to work with a partner from the class, who will act as a client, in a counseling role-play that will last 30 minutes. The role-play is to be completed before the next class and must be videotaped. Students who will be clients are invited to talk about a problem that is real but not so personal that it cannot comfortably be viewed in supervision. Some students, however, may be uneasy about talking about a real experience, and they need to feel free not to do so. Instead, these students are encouraged to invent a problem to present. They are asked to let the student counselor know at the beginning of the role-play that it is an invented and not a real problem.

## Supervision

*Objectives for check-in for this and subsequent supervision sessions*
*1. Assess supervisee's readiness to work.*
*2. Facilitate relationships among supervisors and supervisees.*

In this supervision session and those that follow, the supervisor always checks in with the students. Because both supervision and counseling are based on complex interactions between people, we believe that each person must understand the general well-being and concerns of others in the group for supervision to proceed smoothly. Normally check-ins are brief; this is not intended to promote group therapy but rather to establish a basis for relating in any given supervisory hour. The explanation and initial check-in take about 20 minutes.

*To illustrate*

*Supervisor:* Before we start, I want us to let one another know how we are feeling and tell each other about any ideas that are important to us this week. I will start. I am feeling excited about what we are beginning here and at the same time a little anxious about how we are all going to work together. I have also been a bit distracted this week because my mother just moved to town. Also, I've been reading Parker Palmer's *The Courage to Teach* (1998a), and that's affecting the way I'm thinking about teaching and supervision. I may be stumbling around a bit today, since I'm trying to integrate some of his ideas into what I do as a supervisor. . . . Who would like to go next?

*Trainee 2:* Well, I'll go. I am totally overwhelmed by all the work we have to do in this program.

*Supervisor:* Sure.

*Trainee 2:* At the same time, my family called to say that my sister is really sick and in the hospital. I don't know whether to go home and see her or what, and I think about it a lot.

*Trainee 1:* Gee! That seems pretty hard.

*Supervisor:* Yes, I'm impressed that you're continuing to carry out all your responsibilities when you have so many concerns and are feeling anxious as well.

*Trainee 2:* Well, it's distracting too, and sometimes that helps.

*Supervisor:* Trainee 1?

*Trainee 1:* Well, nothing that dramatic is happening in my life. I've just been working a lot, struggling with statistics—I've never been that good at math. I want to get started counseling, even in role-plays, but at the same time I'm pretty scared that I'll screw up.

*Supervisor:* Of course! If you weren't at all anxious, you wouldn't be paying attention to what's going on! Is there anything else that may affect what you're doing here today?

*Trainee 1 and Trainee 2:* No, not really.

*Supervisor:* Okay. Then let's move on.

In this check-in vignette, the supervisor explained the reasons for it and then modeled check-in behavior. This allowed the trainees to see what was expected. In future sessions, instead of starting, the supervisor would ask who wanted to begin.

## Objectives for supervision session:

1. *Explain procedures specific to initial counseling sessions and practice.*
2. *Enhance understanding of tracking nonverbal behaviors, and discuss how tracking fits into the overall goal of understanding clients.*
3. *Facilitate practice in understanding clients and tracking through role-play.*
4. *Explain the role-play assignment in greater detail.*

In this supervision session, the supervisor models talking on the telephone with a client and then greeting the client in the lobby and beginning and ending an initial counseling session. Supervision strategy 5 (explain the rationale behind specific strategies and interventions) is used. Procedures are demonstrated for calling the client on the phone, greeting the client in the clinic, making appropriate opening statements, presenting limits to confidentiality, ending the first session and setting a time for the next session, and appropriate in-lobby behavior (e.g., not talking about the client's issues in the lobby). Trainees practice with one another in turn as the supervisor observes and gives feedback (45 minutes). A break is often appropriate here.

Supervisors discuss the concept of tracking with trainees. Then they ask students to take turns talking to one another about something meaningful. While keeping the conversation going with appropriate minimal verbal responses, nods, restatements, naming of feelings, silence, and occasional open-ended questions, the listener's task is to track one particular nonverbal behavior of the other that arouses his or her curiosity. At the end of the conversation, the listener simply shares what he or she has observed and tracked. Speakers may or may not respond to that or tell what the nonverbal behavior means to them. Supervisors check with trainees to see how they experienced the exercise. The entire exercise takes 45 minutes.

*To illustrate: [In this situation, the supervisor is checking in with the trainee after tracking exercise.]*

*Supervisor:* Tell me what it was like for you to practice the tracking exercise when you were in the role of counselor.

*Trainee 1:* Well, it was harder than I thought. I'm not used to watching another person so closely.

*Trainee 2:* Actually, I know that I do watch closely, but I usually am not so conscious of it.

*Supervisor:* What do you mean?

*Trainee 2:* Well, at some level I am pretty aware of what is going on with someone else, but I don't acknowledge it, even to myself. But, you know, I grew up in a big city, and I got into the habit of being pretty aware of what was going on when I was talking to people, just for my own safety. At the same time, I learned to act pretty casual about it, as if I weren't doing that, so people didn't notice, and I got so used to it that even I didn't notice anymore.

*Supervisor:* But when you pay attention to it, you realize you've been aware all along?

*Trainee 2:* Yeah, sort of like when there's a faint hum in the background and you forget about it, but then someone calls your attention to it and you are conscious of it again.

*Trainee 1:* That's interesting. Maybe because I'm male, I may not have had to pay such close attention. In fact, when I'm talking to women, I generally try not to stare, and that might be part of what made it hard today.

*Supervisor:* Good point. Women and minorities are often more tuned in to nonverbals because they have to be . . . Tell me what it was like for you to be the client and be observed so closely.

*Trainee 1:* Well, I liked it that you, Trainee 2, seemed to be paying such close attention to me. At the same time, when you told me that you had noticed me looking away every time I talked about becoming a counselor, that made me a little uneasy . . . like I don't really want to be scrutinized and having people try to read me. And I didn't think it meant that I didn't like talking about that.

*Trainee 2:* No, I know. I was glad you told me that, really.

*Supervisor:* That was good. How was it for you to be observed closely, Trainee 2?

*Trainee 2:* Well, at first I felt uneasy too, especially when Trainee 1 said I put my hand to my face when I was talking about being a good runner. On the other hand, I know I have a hard time talking about being good at anything, and that's why I decided to talk about that, just to see if I could. It wasn't surprising that you noticed that I was a little embarrassed. So even though I felt uneasy, I felt as if you were pretty accurate about me.

*Supervisor:* Good. That's what we're looking for. But even if you aren't accurate in what you see, the client can tell you, the way Trainee 1 did.

In this vignette, the supervisor elicited the trainees' experience with the exercise and facilitated their discussion.

Toward the end of the session, the supervisor explains the mechanics involved in arranging and videotaping a role-play with another student during the week. Trainees are asked to practice their new counseling skills during the role-play. Questions about the process are solicited before the meeting is closed.

## WEEK A-3. BUILDING A COLLABORATIVE RELATIONSHIP: ACKNOWLEDGING THE CLIENT'S EXPERIENCE IN THE MOMENT

### Class

*Objectives*
1. *Review and clarify responses to convey understanding of the client's story.*
2. *Practice contact statements.*
3. *Learn to use nonverbal behaviors to gain information about the client's emotional state.*

The instructor checks in to see how role-plays went and responds to other current questions. Then the instructor asks students which responses they found useful to convey their understanding of a client's story. At this point, the instructor explains that although it is important to let the clients know their story is understood, it is even more important to demonstrate comprehension of the client's present feelings about their experience.

The instructor then explains that tracking nonverbal behavior is a key to grasping clients' emotional experiences. Counselors, the instructor explains, can deepen the counseling relationship by making contact with clients on the basis of their nonverbal behaviors. Counselors can demonstrate that they "are aware of and attending to [the client's] present, in-the-moment experiences, including those little things that are happening on the edge of communication" (Grace et al., 1995, p. 549).

A contact statement is described as a single brief phrase to clients that lets them know the counselor has observed them closely and come to conclusions about their current experience. The instructor demonstrates with a class member or shows a videotape to illustrate the use of contact statements. Then someone volunteers to speak (it can be the instructor) and students make contact statements. Then the class is divided up into groups of three: a client, a counselor, and a consultant. After the client has talked for a few minutes, the client pauses. The consultant assists the counselor to assess the affective component conveyed by nonverbal behaviors and design contact statements to use with the client. Then the counselor makes a contact statement, and the client responds.

During the latter part of the class, the instructor explains how to present a videotape for discussion in class or in supervision. The presentation should include a brief history of each case, something about this session and this segment, and requests for particular feedback.

## Supervision

*Objectives:*
1. *View the taped role-plays and discuss.*
2. *Practice role-playing contact statements within counseling dialogue.*

After a brief check-in, trainees show their role–plays and share feedback with each other about the first interviews in which they acted as counselors for their peers. The supervisors use strategies 1 (evaluate observed counseling session interactions), 7 (explore trainee feelings during the counseling session), and 9 (explore trainee feelings concerning specific techniques or interventions). Allow 30 minutes for the opening discussion and 35 minutes for each trainee's role play.

*To illustrate:*

*Supervisor:* Before we look at the videotape, tell me how you experienced the role-play.

*Trainee 1:* When we talked about it in supervision last week, it seemed as if it would be very easy, but I felt anxious when I started. When I was actually doing it, I had a hard time paying attention to Millie because I was so worried about what I was going to say next.

*Supervisor:* Sure . . . and did you get to the point of attending to her?

*Trainee 1:* Yes. When she began to talk about her family's lack of support for her in graduate school, I began to focus on her.

*Supervisor:* In general, how did you feel about your ability to listen and convey your comprehension to her?

*Trainee 1:* After we got rolling, I felt better, but it still seemed like an awfully long 30 minutes!

*Trainee 2:* Amen! It seemed like a long time when I was the counselor too. And I kept wondering if I were boring him.

*Supervisor:* How did you get past that?

*Trainee 2:* Well, when I played the client, I was impressed with how good it felt when Trainee 1 was listening to me. I liked being attended to so closely. And when I thought about that, I decided to pay good attention and see what happened.

*Supervisor:* What did you two pay attention to in the client?

*Trainee 2:* Well, first, just what he said. I wanted to follow closely.

*Supervisor:* And how did you let him know you were listening?

*Trainee 2:* Well, I nodded a lot, and then from time to time I restated what he was saying.

*Supervisor:* Good. And you, Trainee 1? Was there anything else besides words that you used to understand her?

*Trainee 1:* Yes. She was talking pretty rapidly at first, but then she slowed down, and I realized that her upper lip was trembling and her eyes were all wet.

*Supervisor:* And how did you let her know that you had noticed a change?

*Trainee 1:* I just said, "You must be sad about that."

*Supervisor:* Good.

*Trainee 2:* You know, I didn't notice the nonverbal things so much. I got so caught up in the story that I neglected to watch him as carefully as I might.

*Supervisor:* Sure; that often happens in the beginning, and that's what we'll be working on later today. Okay. Let's get to the tapes. Who wants to go first? [*Trainee 2 volunteers.*] Good. Now, we can assume that your purpose in this first role-play is simply to understand the client's story and convey that. Would you show us a part where you felt really capable of showing your understanding and then another part where you were struggling a bit?

*Trainee 2:* Okay. That's what Dr. N suggested we prepare.

[*They watch the videotape. The supervisor stops the videotape from time to time and talks with the trainee about the segments. It is best to stop first after a portion in which the trainee conveyed responsiveness and acknowledge what the trainee did well and why.]*

*Supervisor:* Let's stop here for a minute. You did a nice job of easily reflecting his body posture with yours. It looked as if you made the client feel very comfortable. This is a subtle skill that not everyone does well.

*Trainee 2:* Thanks. I never thought of that as a way of building a relationship, but it makes sense.

*[They watch more and then stop again.]*

*Supervisor:* That was a good example of a restatement. How do you feel about it now that you see it on tape?

*Trainee 2:* I thought it was kind of awkward.

*Trainee 1:* I thought it was really good. I was kind of rambling there when I was playing the client, and I remember feeling that you were tracking with me.

*Trainee 2:* Well. Thanks for the feedback. I guess it's not as bad as it felt at the time.

*Supervisor:* Now that you have the time to stop and consider your restatement, would you do it differently?

*Trainee 2:* Hmmm. Well, actually I really wouldn't change it.

*Supervisor:* Great.

*[They proceed to watch Trainee 2's tape.]*

*Supervisor:* Okay, stop for a minute. Is this where you were having trouble?

*Trainee 2:* Yeah. I was really confused by what he was saying —he kept changing what he was talking about.

*Supervisor:* I suspect that happened because you were just listening to the words. Now that you watch it again, what do you see happening?

*Trainee 2:* Oh, I see what you mean! He is looking around a lot.

*Supervisor:* Yeah. And you were right the first time. He is changing the topic frequently, and that must mean something too. How could you have responded to what you saw?

*Trainee 2:* I don't know, maybe I could have mentioned that he's changing the subject a lot.

*Supervisor:* Sure.

*Trainee 2:* But that seems so rude!

*Supervisor:* I know. We have to unlearn a lot of our polite conversational skills when we go into counseling. It helps to remember that if people just wanted polite conversation, they could talk to their friends. Would it have seemed rude to you, Trainee 1?

*Trainee 1:* No. I might have been startled, but I would have stopped to consider why I was doing that.

*[They watch the remainder of the tape.]*

*Supervisor:* Okay. Now that we've seen the whole tape, Trainee 2, why don't you tell me how you feel about it?

*[After Trainee 2 responds, supervisor solicits feedback from Trainee 1.]*

After viewing the videotapes and taking a break, the supervisor asks students to describe what they learned about contact statements in class. The supervisor reminds the trainees that it is important to base contact statements on nonverbal and paraverbal behavior in session. Contact statements communicate to the client that the counselor is attending to his or her experience during the session itself. Then the supervisor asks trainees for examples. If trainees still seem to be confused, the supervisor demonstrates the use of contact statements in a role-play with a trainee.

The supervisor proceeds to ask trainees to conduct brief role-plays with one another. Each trainee acts as a counselor once. The counselor attends to the client and makes a contact statement after a few minutes. At this point, the supervisor gives feedback to the counselor, sometimes with assistance from the other trainee.

*To illustrate:*

*[This represents the counselor's attempt to give a contact statement and the supervisor's feedback.]*

*Trainee 1 (the client):* And so then I just gave up and went home.

*Trainee 2 (the counselor):* You really didn't like her response, and you gave up.

*Supervisor:* Let's stop here and look at that.

*Trainee 2:* Okay.

*Supervisor:* You did a good job of summarizing the story she was telling you about her discussion with her boss the other day.

*Trainee 2:* Thanks.

*Supervisor:* A good summary of past events can be helpful, but right now I want you to make contact with her immediate experience in the session with you. What nonverbal behaviors did you notice?

*Trainee 2:* Oh, okay. Well, she kind of shrugged her shoulders and looked down.

*Supervisor:* And what did you notice about her voice?

*Trainee 2:* Let's see . . . it got sort of low and trailed off.

*Supervisor:* Yes. What does that mean to you that she is experiencing right now when she's talking to you?

*Trainee 2:* Oh. That she's pretty discouraged.

*Supervisor:* Is that right, Trainee 1?

*Trainee 1:* Yes.

*Supervisor:* So that's what you can say to make contact. Try it now.

*Trainee 2 (to Trainee 1):* Pretty discouraged, aren't you?

*Supervisor:* That's it! Now you've got it!

In this vignette, the supervisor praised the trainee's accurate summary and then explained that a contact statement was a statement about a client's feelings during the session itself. This is really the crucial distinction between restatements or summaries and contact statements, and difficult for trainees to grasp. Once the trainee focused on the nonverbal behaviors of the client, the trainee was able to develop an appropriate contact statement.

The practice with contact statements takes about an hour. Afterward, the supervisor checks in with trainees to see if any questions remain. The supervisor also reminds students that they begin their counseling sessions with volunteer clients in the following week. Then trainees are encouraged to make two or three contact statements to facilitate the counseling relationship in the upcoming sessions.

## WEEK A-4. BUILDING A COLLABORATIVE RELATIONSHIP WITH CHILDREN

### Class

*Objectives:*
1. *Familiarize students with the basic developmental stages of childhood that influence interviewing.*
2. *Present and demonstrate the establishment of rapport and interviewing style with children.*
3. *Present structured intake interview format for use with children.*

The instructor presents a brief summary of developmental information relevant to interviewing children. Included is a summary of self and social concepts along with a synopsis of language skills. Students are referred to appropriate literature to elaborate their understanding. Rapport-building strategies using age-appropriate language, tone of voice, nonverbal behavior, and contact statements are explained, followed by a demonstration (live or on video) of an interview with a child that displays their use.

In the second half of class, the instructor provides materials for a structured clinical interview with a child and explains how one is conducted. Students pair up and conduct two 10-minute role-plays. For the first role-play, one person plays a child between the ages of 4 and 8 years, and the other is a counselor who builds rapport and begins a structured interview with the child. After discussing the experience, they trade places, and the previous counselor plays a child between 10 and 12 years for the other student to interview. The role-play experience serves as the focus for subsequent class discussion, and there is no student video presentation.

## Supervision

*Objectives:*
1. *Brainstorm common skill issues with respect to interviewing children.*
2. *Facilitate the practice of child-interviewing skills in a role-play exercise.*
3. *Observe portions of interviews with volunteer clients and provide feedback in terms of basic relationship skills.*

The session will be divided so that half the time is devoted to child-interviewing skills and the other half is devoted to supervision of current counseling with volunteer clients. After a brief check-in, the supervisor spends about 20 minutes discussing the relationship skills with the trainees, including making contact statements, which they can adapt for use with children. Supervisors will use strategies 4 (teach, demonstrate, or model intervention techniques) and 5 (explain the rationale behind specific strategies and interventions). Effort should be made to tap into the experiences the trainees have had with children in work, family, or social settings. Although many students have not had formal training to work with children (for example, in the schools) most have had some type of interaction with kids, and all have been children themselves. The supervisor also focuses the discussion on the differences between building relationships with children and building relationships with adults in an initial interview. The supervisor uses supervision strategies 5 (explain the rationale behind specific strategies and interventions) and 9 (explore trainee feelings concerning specific techniques or interventions).

During the next half hour of supervision, trainees do a role-play with each other that will allow them to practice the use of language appropriate for children at different levels of development. The supervisor then encourages trainees to provide both challenging and supportive feedback to one another for the next half-hour and adds observations, using strategies 1 (evaluate observed counseling session interactions) and 9 (explore trainee feelings concerning specific techniques or interactions).

*To illustrate:*

*Supervisor:* So, Trainee 1, what were your thoughts about your own performance as a counselor with a child?

*Trainee 1:* I thought I did a good job of asking her questions, but I really had some trouble when she changed the subject and kept playing with the doll when I wanted to talk more about school.

*Supervisor:* You were a good model of a child, Trainee 2!

*Trainee 2:* Yeah, you know I taught elementary school before I came to graduate school.

*Supervisor:* Did you have any thoughts about how Trainee 1 could have kept you talking?

*Trainee 2:* Well, you know, I was supposed to be 5 years old. When I talked, she nodded a lot, but kids don't get that.

*Trainee 1:* What do you mean?

*Trainee 2:* Well, remember how in class Dr. M talked about how kids need more responses than adults? Well, you needed to say more when I talked. If I were a child, I wouldn't know that you liked what I said or were interested if you just said "mmm-hmm" or nodded your head.

*Trainee 1:* Oh, I see.

*Supervisor:* Good observation. Do you see what you need to do, Trainee 1?

*Trainee 1:* Yeah.

*Supervisor:* Okay, let's do that portion of the role-play over, and this time you can be more effusive in responding. Before we start, tell us how doing this feels to you.

*Trainee 1:* Well, really, it feels kind of stupid. I mean, I feel so phony responding in that excessive way that elementary teachers sometimes do.

*Supervisor:* Yes, I can imagine. And every teacher doesn't talk to kids the same way. The way we talk to children has to be genuine and fit us, and yet fit them. This means getting down at their level and talking in their language and showing more enthusiasm in speech, but it doesn't mean becoming silly. Have you ever watched *Sesame Street?*

*Trainee 1:* Sure . . . Oh, I see. I don't have to be Mr. Rogers, but I could be like some of the people on *Sesame Street.*

*Supervisor:* Exactly! Now, can you visualize one of the adults on *Sesame Street?*

*Trainee 1:* Yeah. I can imagine being like Luis.

*Supervisor:* Okay. Now imagine that you are Luis and you are interviewing a 5 year old, and let's do the role-play again.

In this way the supervisor elicits feedback from the trainee who played a child and builds on it. Clearly, if the other trainee doesn't offer useful feedback, the supervisor will need to do so. Redoing a role-play is an effective way to make sure that the trainee has incorporated the feedback in a useful way.

Supervision of the volunteer student cases in the last half of the supervision session proceeds in a fashion similar to that described previously, with an emphasis on contact statements. Supervisors use strategies 1 (evaluate observed counseling session interactions), 8 (explore trainee feelings during the supervision session), and 10 (encourage trainee self-exploration of confidence and worries in the counseling session). Inclusion of supervision strategy 7 (explore of trainee feelings during the counseling session) allows the trainees to begin paying attention to their own internal experience and using it as information about their sessions and their clients.

## WEEK A-5. BUILDING A COLLABORATIVE RELATIONSHIP WITH INSTITUTIONS

### Class

*Objectives:*
1. *Introduce elements of effective collaboration with institutions.*
2. *Discuss ways in which the structures and priorities of these settings can influence the development of a collaborative relationship.*
3. *Foster peer supervision.*

The instructor introduces the elements of effective collaboration with institutions such as schools, agencies, and families. These elements include forming a partnership with the institution (or a representative) in which both partners believe in a shared purpose or goal, agree to share relevant knowledge, have equal status and shared ownership of ideas and services, and trust and respect the other. Additional information can be found in Lippitt and Lippitt (1986).

The instructor also acknowledges and discusses the fact that institutions often have priorities and political needs that differ from those of individual counselors. Ways in which this dynamic can affect the formation of a collaborative relationship are discussed, and trainees are asked to generate their ideas about how they might work with agencies to serve their clients.

Finally, group supervision and discussion are conducted with videotapes of counseling sessions with volunteer clients. The instructor encourages other students to offer support and feedback to those who present cases.

## Supervision

*Objectives:*
1. *View videotapes of trainees' counseling experiences.*
2. *Discuss techniques for establishing a collaborative relationship with an agency.*
3. *Provide an opportunity to practice these techniques.*

After checking in, 45 minutes is alloted for each trainee's presentation of the first counseling session. Supervision of this first individual session, conducted before the week's lecture, precedes the discussion of working within an institution. Appropriate for this portion of supervision are strategies 1 (evaluate observed counseling session interactions), 6 (interpret significant events in the counseling session), and 7 (explore trainee feelings during the counseling session). The supervisor encourages each trainee to share feelings about both the material on the tape and the experience of watching it in the group. The supervisor also solicits feedback from the observing trainee.

*To illustrate:*

*Supervisor:* Who wants to present their tape first?

*Trainee 1:* I know we're both ready because we were talking about it before supervision. We flipped, and I get to go first.

*Supervisor: [Laughs]* Great. What do you have cued up?

*Trainee 1:* Well, I just want to show you what happened at the beginning here. . . .

*Supervisor:* Okay.

*[They watch the tape for 5 minutes. The supervisor stops the tape.]*

*Supervisor:* That was a good opening. What specifically would you like us to give you feedback on?

*Trainee 1:* Well, at the time, I wasn't really sure if I understood what she wanted from counseling. I felt as if I were missing the boat.

*Trainee 2:* It sounded to me as if you were following her, and you responded really well to what she was saying.

*Supervisor:* Yes, I'd agree with that. Your response to her initial statements indicated that you grasped her experience, and I think you communicated that in a way that helped her feel understood as well. But I wonder . . . what might be a way for you to check that out for yourself, during the counseling session?

*Trainee 1:* Hmm . . . well, I could ask her if she felt as if I understood what she was saying. Or I could just be quiet for a few minutes and see if what she added confirmed what I was thinking. I could even let her know that I wasn't sure about my understanding and help her find ways to clarify what she was saying. I guess there are a few things I could have done right there.

*Supervisor:* Good! It seems as if you are able to be quite reflective as you think about your work with a client, and that's important. It's also important to point out that what you did do in the session was fine. I'm glad that you can think of these options now, but it takes practice and experience to think of them during the actual session. You did a good job here and you seemed very composed and competent, which is important to help the client feel more comfortable.

*Trainee 1:* Thanks. I felt really nervous, but I look better than I thought I would! But this next section I'm not sure about *[starts tape.]*

*Supervisor: [After several minutes, talks during the tape]* Is there something specific in this segment that you're concerned about?

*Trainee 1:* No. Not really. I just wanted to see what you thought.

*Supervisor: [Asks trainee to stop the tape.]* I'd like to be able to watch your whole session, but we don't really have enough time to do that in our meetings. For you to make the best use of supervision, it's important to narrow down the areas you'd like me to see, so that I can provide the feedback you really need. How does that sound to you?

*Trainee 1:* Oh, yeah, I guess that makes sense. Let me think a minute . . . there was a section about 20 minutes into the session where I felt as if I missed something important. Let me find that *[cues up and plays tape.]*

*Supervisor:* Okay. I really appreciate your willingness to share things that were difficult for you. Risk taking is a good way to learn new skills, and it can be scary. What are you uncomfortable with here?

*Trainee 1:* Well, right after I paraphrased what she had been saying, it seemed as if she got uncomfortable. She sort of looked away, and then just agreed with me. But I felt as if I missed the mark, and maybe she was just trying to be nice.

*Supervisor:* Hmm. What do you think that might be about?

*Trainee 1:* Well, this is just a hypothesis, but I wondered if it might be happening because I'm a man. She had said earlier that one of her concerns was her relationship with her husband, and that sometimes she goes along with him even if she doesn't want to. I was just thinking, maybe she went along with my perception of what she was saying, even if it wasn't accurate.

*Supervisor:* That's a hypothesis worth checking out, Trainee 1. Let's talk about ways that you might go about doing that.

After viewing the segments the trainee has prepared, the supervisor randomly picks two more and views them. Again, the supervisor asks the trainee for impressions before giving feedback. This process is then repeated with the other trainee.

Following a short break, the last $1\frac{1}{2}$ hours of the supervision session are focused on ways to form relationships with agencies and institutions. Supervision strategies to emphasize during this segment are 4 (teach, demonstrate, or model intervention techniques) and 14 (encourage trainee brainstorming of strategies or interventions). During the first half hour, the supervisor elaborates on the material presented in class, and describes the skills necessary for building a positive collaborative relationship. These include improving problem-solving skills, learning to convey an attitude of trust and respect to colleagues in other specializations, and acknowledging the value of the institution's role in the client's life. The supervisor also emphasizes the importance of knowing as much as possible about the characteristics of the setting, to help trainees understand possible barriers that can arise.

When both trainees seem to have a beginning understanding of collaboration with institutions, the supervisor asks them to do short role-plays in which one trainee is a counselor who wants to establish a relationship with an institution and the other trainee is a representative of that institution. The supervisor provides feedback on the trainee's ability to integrate the characteristics of effective collaboration as described above, and the process is repeated with the trainees switching roles.

## WEEK A-6. IDENTIFYING PATTERNS AND FORMULATING WORKING HYPOTHESES

### Class

*Objectives:*
1. *Introduce and illustrate construction of a working hypothesis.*
2. *Introduce and illustrate discernment of client patterns.*

The instructor presents the idea of working hypotheses and asks students for examples from their daily lives. Typical examples might include moment-to-moment hypotheses that one makes while driving a car on the highway or speaking in class.

In the latter part of class, one or two students talk about their clients and show videotape segments. Class members are asked to look for patterns in clients feelings and behaviors as they listen to the case presentations. These patterns are integrated into working hypotheses. Students are encouraged to describe how these might be tested.

## Supervision

*Objectives:*

1. *Assist trainees to identify patterns of feelings and behavior in their clients.*
2. *Assist trainees to formulate their ideas in hypothetical terms.*
3. *Assist trainees to develop ways to test their hypotheses in session.*

After checking in, the supervisor asks each student in turn to show a videotape of portions of a counseling session with a volunteer client. After some discussion about relationship behavior in the session (30 minutes), trainees are asked to develop hypotheses about the client's patterns of behavior and feelings (45 minutes). Both trainees are encouraged to participate in the process with each client. Supervision strategies 2 (ask counselor to provide a hypothesis about the client) and 14 (encourage trainee brainstorming of strategies and interventions) are employed. The supervisor then asks trainees how they might test their hypotheses in session and what they would understand from various potential responses from the client. The supervisor may use strategy 13 (provide alternative interventions or conceptualizations for trainee use) in the process. The following vignette exemplifies the application of this process to one client's feeling patterns.

*To illustrate:*

*[In this situation, which exemplifies the application of this process to one client's feeling patterns, the supervisor and trainees have just watched the first trainee's videotape, and the supervisor and second trainee have provided feedback on the first trainee's use of relationship skills.]*

*Supervisor:* Now that we've responded to your efforts to build a relationship with him, Trainee 1, let's all think about Steve for a minute. What are some patterns that you think might run through his life? What feelings recur over and over, and how do they show up?

*Trainee 1:* He sounds angry most of the time.

*Supervisor:* Yeah. What else? Trainee 2?

*Trainee 2:* I agree. He seems like an angry young man.

*Supervisor:* And how might you, Trainee 1, test this hypothesis?

*Trainee 1:* Well, I've already reflected his anger several times.

*Supervisor:* And how does he respond?

*Trainee 1:* He always says, "No, I'm just frustrated."

*Supervisor:* What do you make of that?

*Trainee 1:* I think he is angry but has a hard time saying it. He doesn't seem to want to see himself as angry.

*Trainee 2:* Yeah.

*Supervisor:* So that's a second hypothesis, that Steve dislikes the expression of anger or at least finds it difficult to acknowledge. How might Trainee 1 test that?

*Trainee 2:* Well, I would want to ask him about this, but I'm not sure that would work if he doesn't like to see himself as angry.

*Trainee 1:* Yeah, I think it involves more subtlety than that. . . . Maybe I could just say to him that I've noticed that he doesn't seem to want to be angry.

*Supervisor:* You're on the right track here; keep developing that idea. Remember that you're looking for a pattern that has occurred over time.

*Trainee 2:* Well, you know, you could ask him about his past, I mean, what his family did around anger.

*Supervisor:* Good; keep going. That's one way to check for a pattern.

*Trainee 1:* Well, I know his father blew up all the time and frightened Steve's mother and all the kids. So maybe I could start with that. But I'm not sure how to do that.

*Supervisor:* Well, what if you just tell him what you know.

*Trainee:* Yeah, I guess I could just say, "Steve, you said that your father blew up at all of you a lot," and if he agreed, then I could say something like, "I know you've said you don't want to be like your father. . . . That must make it hard for you to get angry."

*Supervisor:* That sounds good. And how might Steve respond?

*Trainee 1:* Well [*laughs*] he could say, "Trainee 1, you're right. I never thought of that before!"

*Trainee 2:* Actually, he could.

*Supervisor:* Then your working hypothesis would be verified. But what would you discover if he said in an angry tone, "I'm nothing like my father; I just don't get angry!"

*Trainee 1:* Well, then I'd figure that this was a hot topic for him. I mean, everyone gets angry once in a while, and if he claims he doesn't, then I'd think he wasn't ready to acknowledge it.

*Supervisor:* That makes sense. Any other possibilities?

*Trainee 1:* I'd think he was upset with me for bringing that up. That might mean that he understands a question about his feelings as an attack.

*Supervisor:* Yeah.

The trainees and supervisor would continue in this vein about feelings that emerge in patterns of behavior. Of greatest interest would be client patterns that occur with a variety of people or in a number of situations. Only when one client's patterns have been explored does the supervisor move on to view the second trainee's videotape and develop hypotheses about the second client. They close with a summary of hypotheses about patterns to test in the next counseling session.

## WEEK A-7. IDENTIFYING RESISTANCE, WORKING WITH IT, AND LEARNING FROM IT

### Class

*Objectives:*
1. *Explore the concept of resistance.*
2. *Elicit appropriate responses.*
3. *Introduce skills of confrontation (challenge) and interpretation.*

This lesson looks at resistance in terms of the interpersonal process model and may not be appropriate for courses that focus on other theoretical orientations. The instructor asks the class for examples of resistance from their own lives and from their initial experiences with clients. Students explore the manifestations of resistance and consider them with respect. Resistance, like other defenses, is described as an adaptive response that clients have learned early in life to protect themselves in a difficult environment. Following discussion of resistance, the instructor asks the class to develop appropriate counselor responses to one or two of the examples presented. When trainees show videotapes during the latter part of class, the students are asked to identify resistance and explore its meaning when it appears.

At the end of class, the instructor gives the trainees an outline for future case presentations in class and supervision during this term. The outline appears in Table 5.

---

**TABLE 5.**  *Outline for First-Term Case Presentations*

1. Brief history of case to date
2. Assessment of the relationship, particularly in terms of the working alliance
3. Working hypotheses about client patterns
4. Demonstrated resistance and ways in which it has been addressed
5. Focus for change

---

## Supervision

*Objectives:*
1. *Explore the idea of resistance further.*
2. *Provide feedback on trainees' counseling.*

The supervisor asks the trainees about their understanding of resistance from reading and class instruction and elicits examples from their own cases. Methods for approaching resistance are briefly discussed. Most of the supervision time is used to show videotapes of each trainee's counseling sessions and discuss them. Working hypotheses and client resistance are highlighted along with the trainee's ability to convey understanding to the client and make contact statements. Many supervision strategies are appropriate here, especially strategies 1 (evaluate observed counseling session interactions), 2 (ask counselor to provide a hypothesis about the client), 14 (encourage trainee brainstorming of strategies and interventions), and 13 (provide alternative interventions and conceptualizations for trainee use).

*To illustrate:*

*Supervisor:* Let's stop the tape for a minute. . . . What do you see the client doing there?

*Trainee 1:* She changed the subject. I mean, I asked her whether she was angry that her roommate went out with friends and didn't take her, and she said she wasn't. Then she immediately began talking about how helpful her roommate had been with her calculus assignment.

*Supervisor:* And as the two of you think about it, how do you understand what happened?

*Trainee 2:* Maybe she really wasn't angry at her roommate.

*Trainee 1:* That's possible, but her voice was pretty angry when she talked about the roommate going out. I think she was mad but didn't want to talk about it.

*Supervisor:* So what do you think that means, Trainee 1? You have seen this client a couple of times; what's your hypothesis?

*Trainee 1:* Well, you know, she seems awfully nice when she comes in. She always asks how I am and even complimented me on what I was wearing.

*Trainee 2:* So she must like to seem nice.

*Supervisor:* Do you imagine it's hard for her to see herself as the kind of person who gets mad?

*Trainee 1:* Oh, yeah. In fact, she's criticized her mother for being crabby so much and yelling at the kids.

*Supervisor:* So you've got working hypotheses that she has a pattern of avoiding anger by changing the subject because she doesn't like to see herself as an angry person like her mother.

*Trainee 1:* Yeah.

*Supervisor:* Trainee 2, does that make sense to you?

*Trainee 2:* Sure, but I don't see what to do then. I mean, do you just say all that to her? That seems pretty overwhelming.

*Supervisor:* I think you're right about that—it would be overwhelming. So Trainee 1 needs to start to address the issue gently, perhaps just with a simple observation of her behavior. Later, when she knows this client better, she could make an interpretation based on these ideas.

*Trainee 2:* Like a comment that the client changed the subject after Trainee 1 asked if she were angry?

*Supervisor:* Yeah. What do you think, Trainee 1?

*Trainee 1:* I could do that . . . But what if she says she was through talking about her roommate's going out without her?

*Supervisor:* Let's think about this. What are some possibilities?

*Trainee 2:* [*to Trainee 1*] Maybe you could make a challenge and say that her voice sounded angry even though she stated that she was not, and that makes you wonder if she were finished with the subject.

*Supervisor:* Keep going, both of you. Come up with as many possibilities as you can.

*Trainee 1:* Well, I could point out that she shifted from what sounded like a complaint about her roommate to praise.

*Supervisor:* Yeah. What else?

*Trainee 2:* She could ask if it's hard for her to get angry.

*Trainee 1:* Yeah.

*Supervisor:* As you think over these ideas, what seems best to to you?

*Trainee 1:* Well, I like the idea of asking her if she has trouble getting angry, but that seems abrupt.

*Supervisor:* Perhaps you could ask the same question in a hypothetical way. You could say, "Suppose you were mad at her for going off and leaving you behind. Could you talk to me about it?"

*Trainee 1:* Oh, I like that better. That seems much less threatening.

*Supervisor:* What do you think, Trainee 2?

*Trainee 2:* I like that too. That way you could explore it without arguing about what she actually felt.

*Supervisor:* It's helpful to remember that she might not have been upset in the first place. It's still a chance to explore her feelings about anger.

In this vignette, the supervisor has called attention to the client's potentially resistant behavior, explored its possible meaning and origin, identified the trainees' ideas as working hypotheses, encouraged the trainees to brainstorm possible responses, and offered a way to reword the selected response. The trainees were invited to reflect on the situation and develop ideas, and the supervisor offered expertise when it was needed but not so early that it cut off the discussion. This allowed the work to proceed in a collaborative way and built on the trainees' developing skills.

## WEEK A-8. ESTABLISHING FOCUS FOR CHANGE

### Class

*Objectives:*
1. *Present the focus of change as the clients' feelings, thoughts, or behavior.*
2. *Develop with the class ways to center the client's discussion on him or herself rather than on others in his or her life.*

The instructor talks briefly about focusing change on the client and then divides the class into groups and presents several counseling scenarios that show the client's description of a problem. The instructor encourages the class to suggest appropriate foci for change and to advance ways to direct the client's attention to themselves. Note that the identified target may be the client's thoughts, feelings, or behaviors, and the lesson may be adapted to accommodate whatever theoretical orientation the class may be using.

As students present cases to the group later in the class, the supervisor encourages them to provide the information called for in the presentation outline provided the previous week. They are directed to identify the focus for change with each client.

### Supervision

*Objectives:*
1. *Expand on the idea of a focus for change.*
2. *View videotapes with particular attention to ways to center the client's attention on him or herself.*

After check-in, the supervisor elicits any questions or ideas about the concept of focusing on the client. The group moves then to case presentations, and trainees use the outlines given in class and show videotaped segments. At this point, the supervisor has a number of concepts to attend to with each case: trainees' ability to understand the client and convey that with nonverbal and verbal responses including contact statements, trainees' working hypotheses, identification of and responses to resistance, and the skill of directing clients to talk about themselves rather than others. Although attention to any of these may vary when the trainees present videotapes, the supervisor should encourage trainees to develop ways to facilitate clients' discussion of their own issues. Supervision strategies 6 (interpret significant events in the counseling session), 2 (ask counselor to provide a hypothesis about the client), and 14 (encourage trainee brainstorming of strategies and interventions) are used.

*To illustrate:*

*Trainee 1:* Since we're talking about this, I'd like to show a part where this client would not stop talking about everything his mother does and says until I was ready to scream. It was nonstop.

*Supervisor:* Let's watch. Was this the first time you had seen him?

*Trainee 1:* No, and he did the same thing last time.

*[They all watch the videotape.]*

*Trainee 2:* Wow! I see what you mean! It's a bombardment!

*Trainee 1:* Yeah. And then, as you can see, he stopped and just looked at me.

*Supervisor:* You asked him if there were anything else. Is there something you would rather have said, now that we've talked about focus on the client rather than on other people?

*Trainee 1:* Well, I could have said, "How does that make you feel?" but the trouble is, last time I asked him that, he said, "I feel that my father shouldn't call me so much."

*Trainee 2:* Oh, that's not exactly focusing on his own feelings.

*Supervisor:* Let's brainstorm for a bit and see what we can come up with that might have shifted his direction. Since he's done this for two sessions already, you can guess that you'll have some opportunity to use whatever we develop. Trainee 2?

*Trainee 2:* You could ask him what upsets him the most out of all he described.

*Trainee 1:* Or what he thinks his father's trying to tell him — no, that's getting him to think about his father rather than himself. Let's see. . . . I could observe that he seems to find his father's behavior upsetting.

*Supervisor:* Sure. What else?

*Trainee 1:* I could just point out that he sounds really angry about this or make a contact statement, such as, "Angry, huh?"

*Trainee 2:* Yeah. And somehow move in the direction of what it's like for him to be away at college and have his father call him up all the time to give advice.

*Trainee 1:* I like that.

*Supervisor:* And you can always check with him about what he experiences in his body when he's talking with his father and maybe even when he's talking to you about his father.

*Trainee 1:* Thanks. Those ideas help. But what if he refuses to respond with anything about himself, no matter what I say?

*Supervisor:* Well, you can always point out that he seems to find it easier to talk about his father than about himself.

*Trainee 1:* You're right. I guess that gives me enough to go with.

In this vignette, the trainee presented the situation to find ways to shift the client's focus. The same strategy could have been followed if either the supervisor or the other trainee had noticed that the client was talking about his father rather than himself. Again, the supervisor elicits responses from the trainees and only adds suggestions after the trainees have developed some of their own.

## WEEK A-9. FACING CLIENT'S EMOTIONS AND WORKING WITH THEM

### Class

*Objectives:*
1. *Expand ways to observe and draw out a client's feelings.*
2. *Discuss the difficulty of experiencing emotions for both the client and the counselor who hears them.*

The instructor builds on the trainees' personal experiences as well as their experience with clients to develop new ways of eliciting client emotions. Attention is paid to emotions that may be underneath the apparent sentiments. Working hypotheses are encouraged. The instructor then asks students to talk about which feelings they find difficult to experience themselves and what it is like for them when clients express the same ones. Ways to bear clients' expression of strong affect are developed.

When students present cases and videotapes, the instructor and class attend to the expression of emotion and ways to facilitate it.

## Supervision

*Objectives:*
1. *Explore issues surrounding the expression of client affect in discussion and during case presentations.*

In the early part of the session (30–45 minutes), supervisors ask trainees what they experienced in class during the discussion of client emotions. They encourage further discussion of emotions trainees find difficult to tolerate and respond to questions trainees may have. Frequently a trainee questions the value of eliciting feelings, and the supervisor can facilitate exploration of this question within the context of both the primary theoretical orientation of the course and other theoretical frameworks.

Supervisors invite trainees to present their cases according to the outline provided in class in a previous week, and as they watch session videotapes, they all attend to issues surrounding the expression of emotion. (If trainees have not seen a client in the past week, they can use videotapes of previous sessions to present either expression or avoidance of feelings.) Supervisors use supervision strategies 15 (encourage trainee discussion of client problems and motivations), 7 (explore trainee feelings during the counseling session), 13 (provide alternative interventions or conceptualizations for trainee use), and 9 (explore trainee feelings concerning specific techniques or interventions).

*To illustrate:*

*[In this situation, the trainee has just presented a case where the client talked about difficult issues in an unemotional way.]*

*Trainee 1:* And so, you see, even though he says that his girlfriend dropped him and took up with his best friend, he doesn't show much.

*Trainee 2:* Boy, I'll say! He could be talking about the weather.

*Supervisor:* Yes. I notice he even wears a hat, so it's hard to see his face. . . . What were you experiencing during this, Trainee 1?

*Trainee 1:* His story made me sad, but the way he talked made me feel distant from him.

*Trainee 2:* Yeah . . . that's probably why his girlfriend left him!

*Supervisor:* That's a reasonable hypothesis, Trainee 2. . . . Let's think a little more about what was happening in this session so we can develop some ideas about where Trainee 1 could go next.

*Trainee 2:* Well, he must be afraid to show his feelings.

*Trainee 1:* I agree, but more than that, I wonder if he can stand to feel them.

*Supervisor:* And how does that affect you?

*Trainee 1:* I'm a little afraid to push.

*Supervisor:* What do you imagine might happen if you did?

*Trainee 1:* When I think about it, probably nothing. He seems pretty practiced in avoiding feelings. But if he did show how hurt he was, I don't know what it would be like. I'd be afraid that he'd get so upset he'd either get furious or desperately sad.

*Supervisor:* And if he got furious, what would that be like for you?

*Trainee 1:* I'd be frightened.

*Supervisor:* What do you imagine?

*Trainee 1:* Well, I think he could start shouting or pounding on the chair, and I would just want to crawl away.

*Supervisor:* So you may be as afraid of his anger as he is.

*Trainee 1:* That's a good point. I might be picking that up from him. Even though Dr. N said in class that beginning counselors often have trouble with clients' anger, I'm not usually bothered much when people get mad. I come from a family where people expressed all kinds of feelings, including anger, and we were all pretty used to it. So you're right. I'm feeling his fear about expressing feelings. And probably nothing terrible would happen if he got upset. He told me earlier that he hasn't hit anyone or gotten into a fight since junior high.

*Trainee 2:* That's interesting. Now that you mention it, I realize I've learned to stay away from subjects people don't want to talk about.

*Supervisor:* Yes, that's a time when a couselor needs to challenge the client and calibrate the challenge to the client's readiness for it. . . . So, Trainee 1, now that you think you want to encourage him to express more emotion, what might you do?

*Trainee 1:* Well, I asked him what it was like for him when all this happened, and he said he didn't like it but it didn't "bother" him.

*Supervisor:* Let's all think together about this. What could help him experience his feelings and express them?

*Trainee 2:* You know, it seems to me that you could get more specific, like you could say, "When you first heard that X was going out with Y, what did you feel?"

*Supervisor:* Good. Getting more specific about the experience helps. What else?

*Trainee 1:* I could also ask what he feels when he talks about it.

*Trainee 2:* And whatever he says when you ask him one of those things, you could ask him where he experiences his feelings in his body.

*Supervisor:* Nice. That can intensify the feelings. Keep going.

*Trainee 1:* I could reflect that he must feel betrayed.

*Trainee 2:* Or, if he denies that, you could ask him if anything like that has ever happened before and what he felt like then.

*Supervisor:* Yeah. These are all good ideas. And as you said, Trainee 1, he might not react anyway. Then what?

*Trainee 1:* Well, then I guess I explore what makes it so difficult to express feelings.

*Supervisor:* Sure. When a person is really reluctant to express feelings, you can explore the reluctance rather than the feeling. It's less threatening and you can learn quite a lot.

In this vignette, the supervisor explored the trainees' feelings about client anger before pursuing approaches to the client. In this way, the supervisor was able to teach each trainee to use his or her own feelings as a guide to the client's emotions. In addition, once trainees have examined their own feelings, they are more comfortable considering approaches to the client.

## WEEK A-10. IDENTIFYING COUNSELOR FACTORS THAT MAY INTERFERE

### Class

*Objectives:*
1. *Explore counselor factors that might interfere with responding to clients.*
2. *Provide modeling of risk-taking behavior by the instructor with a presentation of a countertransference issue from his or her work with clients.*

The instructor explores the relationship in counseling with special attention to countertransference in the therapy relationship in terms of the variety of theoretical orientations described by Gelso and Carter (1985, 1994). Working together, the class members should generate as many sources of countertransference as possible, that is, unmet needs and unresolved issues that may reside in the therapist. Students will be encouraged to reflect privately on areas that may potentially activate their own countertransference. Finally, the instructor facilitates a discussion of techniques for becoming aware of countertransference dynamics as they unfold in therapy and ways to use them to advance the therapy.

Group supervision will focus on viewing counseling tapes of the master supervisor or other experienced therapists with accompanying therapist disclosure that demonstrates countertransference issues. This is important modeling at this point in the year, as the students are being asked to take greater and greater risks in supervision.

## Supervision

*Objectives:*
1. *View and critique counseling session tapes with special focus on the development of the working alliance and the countertransference relationship.*

The supervisor may want to provide extra time for check-in, because the trainees will be asked to take somewhat greater risks in this supervision session. The supervisor should remind the trainees that countertransference is ubiquitous and that it can be used to promote client growth when the therapist is aware of its occurrence.

After the check-in, the supervisor invites trainees to present a client who evokes a strong feeling in the trainee. Working gently, all participants in the supervision session should help the counselor determine the source of the countertransference, explore how the countertransference reaction may provide information about the client, and formulate some ideas about how this could be used in session with the client. Supervision strategies 7 (explore trainee feelings during the counseling session) and 12 (provide opportunities for trainees to process their own affect and defenses) may be used.

*To illustrate:*

*[In this situation, a trainee is struggling with attending to the trainee's inner experience of a client.]*

*Supervisor:* I appreciate your agreeing to go first, Trainee 2. Which client do you wish to present today?

*Trainee 2:* Well, I'm not sure about this—in terms of whether or not what I'm experiencing is countertransference—but I want to talk about a client that I'm having a strange reaction to. This is the 30-year-old male client I talked about several weeks ago. I've seen him for 6 weeks and for some reason I don't seem to be able to remember things about him. . . . He's married with a couple of kids, but the details tend to slip my mind. I find myself spending time in session trying to dredge up these facts . . . his wife's name, the age and gender of his kids, what we talked about last week. . . .

*Trainee 1:* I have a hard time remembering all the details about my clients, too, sometimes.

*Trainee 2:* This feels different to me.

*Supervisor:* It's unusual for you to have such a pervasive memory lapse when working with a client, isn't it?

*Trainee 2:* Yeah. I usually have kind of a picture of their life and what their issues are. With this guy, I just don't know.

*Supervisor:* Can you take a moment and explore your feelings about this client?

*Trainee 2:* Well . . . he's very verbal and bright and seems capable of making good use of therapy.

*Trainee 1:* Do you like him?

*Trainee 2:* Do I like him? Yeah. He's not my favorite client right now, but I like him. I can't figure out what's going on.

*Supervisor:* Something that I find to be helpful when I am confused by my reaction to a client is to give myself permission to engage in a little fantasy about the client. You know—what you might imagine you'd like to do with this client.

*Trainee 2: [Laughs]* I have thought about snorting in session sometimes when he starts off on one of his tales.

*[Trainee 1 laughs, too.]*

*Supervisor:* Good. Now exaggerate that—what would you really like to do?

*Trainee 2:* I'd like to stand up in the middle of the session and yell at him.

*Supervisor:* What would you yell?

*Trainee 2:* Oh, shut up! Talk about what's really going on with you and stop trying to impress me. I don't want to know how many cars you own or what private school your kids attend. I want to know what has brought you into counseling!

*Supervisor:* Yes. That's exactly what I meant. Now what does your fantasy tell us?

*Trainee 1:* Well . . . clients that tell stories and try to impress me tend to irritate me sometimes, too.

*Supervisor:* So part of what Trainee 2 is experiencing is what many people may experience with this client?

*Trainee 2:* Yeah. He has mentioned that he doesn't have any close friends. But, I don't know, something tells me that this is more than simply reacting to a client's behavior.

*Trainee 1:* In what way?

*Trainee 2:* I'm not sure. I think it's how much he gets to me. Part of me really does want to stand up and shout at him in session.

*Supervisor:* Sure. As we learned in class this week, being aware of strong feelings about a client is very important. It does sound as if you are describing countertransference associated with this client. There are a couple of options available to you now. If you are willing, we can explore this further today or we can meet individually to discuss this.

In this vignette, the supervisor acknowledges the courage needed to face and inspect countertransference issues and provides the trainee with several ways to explore this issue. During discussion of any client, the supervisor may suspect that the trainee's reaction to the client is related to the trainee's own issues. If the trainee's reaction seems to interfere with his or her therapeutic effectiveness, the supervisor needs to point this out to the trainee. At the same time, the supervisor avoids taking on the dual role of therapist to the trainee, and continues to focus on the therapist's feelings toward this client only as they illuminate the therapist's interaction with the client.

After trainees have presented and worked on their reactions to a client, the supervisor might want to use strategy 4 (teach, demonstrate, or model intervention techniques) and model the use of therapist reaction to clients with an example or two from the supervisor's own experience. This will lay the groundwork for more extensive use of advanced supervision strategy 20 (explore the trainee's feelings to facilitate understanding of the client) during the next term.

It is recommended that supervisors end the session using strategy 8 (explore trainee feelings during the supervision session).

## WEEK A-11. EXPLORING MULTICULTURAL FACTORS THAT MAY ENHANCE OR INTERFERE

### Class

*Objectives:*
1. *Explore multicultural factors that might influence responses to clients.*
2. *Provide group supervision of client tapes, paying special attention to any potential cross-cultural situations.*

This class is designed to provide students with the opportunity to reflect on the impact of diversity on the counseling process and is not designed to be didactic in nature. It is expected that trainees will have had extensive course work in the area of diversity before this class session. If that is not the case, students should be referred to appropriate resource material (e.g., Atkinson, Morten, & Sue, 1998; Pedersen, 1994; Sue & Sue, 1990). It is particularly useful to discuss the importance of attending to common factors that affect counseling relationships while making adjustments consistent with clients' cultural experiences (Fischer et al., 1998).

The instructor facilitates the students' reflection on their training, reading, and experience with cross-cultural issues and discusses ways cultural differences may influence the working alliance. The students are reminded to look for cross-cultural factors that enhance or interfere with the developing therapeutic relationship. The ACA (1995) and APA (1993) guidelines for providing services to culturally diverse populations should be reviewed.

Students who present cases in class are asked to show segments that illustrate cross-cultural counseling.

## Supervision

*Objectives:*
1. *Continue the process of reflecting on issues of diversity.*
1. *View and critique a counseling session tape with emphasis on how culture may influence the relationship between the therapist and the client.*

After a brief check-in, the supervisor encourages the trainees to continue the discussion from the class meeting and attends to their specific knowledge and concerns. Using strategy 11 (help the trainee define personal competencies and areas for growth), the supervisor helps the trainees assess their skills in this critical area. He or she reminds trainees that building cross-cultural competency is a lengthy process, and reassures them that this topic will be revisited again and again during their training.

The remainder of supervision is focused on client tapes. Trainees are encouraged to view each counseling session as a cross-cultural experience, because they will never be culturally identical to their clients. Supervision strategy 13 (provide alternative interventions and conceptualizations for trainee use) may be helpful in assisting the trainee to explore the subtle or overt cultural differences in the counseling relationship. Using supervision strategy 7 (explore trainee feelings during the counseling session), the supervisor can encourage the trainee to process how it feels to acknowledge that cultural differences affect the working alliance.

*To illustrate:*

*Supervisor:* Okay, Trainee 1, what have you cued up for us to watch today, and what do you need from us in terms of feedback?

*Trainee 1:* I've been thinking a lot about cultural issues since the last class, and I think I have a situation with one of my clients that shows some insensitivity on my part.

*[They watch a segment of tape.]*

*Supervisor:* What are your concerns here, Trainee 1?

*Trainee 1:* Well, this client and I have been getting along really well. We have a lot in common . . . like our coloring. We have been able to laugh together about how difficult it is to be a student on this campus and not be tan and blonde! But lately she has seemed more depressed and during that segment she seemed to pull back from me.

*Supervisor:* Do you have a sense of why that was?

*Trainee 1: [Sadly]* Yeah. It was after I mentioned the Christmas holidays coming up. I'm really excited about going home for Christmas this year and I also want to prepare the client for our break. Anyway, I think I've mentioned the break a few times over the last several weeks. This time when I watched the tape, I realized how the client almost flinched when I used the term *Christmas holidays.* Now I remember that she is Jewish and I feel awful about my blithe use of the term. I wish I had had the wits to use the term *winter holidays* instead.

*Supervisor:* You are very upset with yourself about this.

*Trainee 1:* Yeah. I've had lots of course work on diversity and I try very hard to be aware of these issues. And we were developing such a great therapeutic relationship.

*Trainee 2:* Do you feel as if you've ruined it?

*Trainee 1:* No, not ruined it, I guess. But I feel thoughtless and sad.

*Supervisor:* How would your client react if you shared those feelings with her?

*Trainee 1:* I don't know. She is already so sad herself right now . . .

*Supervisor:* You're afraid your sharing your regrets might make her feel more sad?

*Trainee 1:* No. Well, yes. That's what I thought at first. But when I think about it more, I think she would be pleased by my sharing that with her.

*Supervisor:* Good point. Linehan [1993] described the value of admitting errors to clients. She said that clients really appreciated it, and the alliance was strengthened.

*Trainee 2:* Yeah, but why is your client so sad, Trainee 1? I can't believe it's all because you said the word *Christmas*, and I don't remember her presenting problem.

*Trainee 1:* She and her boyfriend broke up after an attempt to maintain a long-distance relationship.

*Trainee 2:* So maybe it really isn't your use of the word *Christmas* that upset her.

*Trainee 1:* You mean that it's also my joy about going home for the holidays?

*Trainee 2:* Yeah.

*Trainee 1:* Hmmm. But I think they're both important. . . . I am starting to visualize how she would react if I brought up my sadness at being insensitive to her. I think it might help her get into her whole reaction to the upcoming holidays, being home without her boyfriend and such Yeah. I think that would be good.

*Supervisor:* I'm impressed, Trainee 1. You reflected on your feelings and your work with this client quite effectively.

## WEEK A-12. WORKING ON PROBLEMS REQUIRING ACTION

### Class

*Objectives:*
1. *Teach crisis intervention procedures.*
2. *Cover the limits to confidentiality raised when clients present as a danger to others (Corey et al., 1998).*
3. *Provide group supervision of ongoing cases.*

Trainees receive the nuts and bolts of crisis assessment in lecture, including the following: warning signs of client crisis that a trainee should learn to recognize, steps that need to be taken in a formal crisis assessment, and follow-up steps when the counselor determines that this is a crisis. It is especially important that the counselor seek help from a supervisor when he or she suspects a crisis situation is emerging (Smith, 1994). Although this may seem early for such instruction, we find that increasing numbers of clients in all settings, including college student volunteers, present serious problems and crisis situations (Neufeldt, 1994a). The instructor provides written material, covering the ethical and legal guidelines involved in cases in which a client presents a danger to others (Monahan, 1993), to accompany the lecture.

The instructor supervises one or two cases at the end of the class period. Students briefly describe their cases and then ask for assistance from the group in an explicit fashion; that is, they explain what they were trying to do and ask for feedback on their effectiveness.

### Supervision

*Objectives:*
1. *Learn about crisis management through role-playing a crisis situation.*
2. *Discuss several vignettes with respect to the potential need to break confidentiality to protect the client's welfare or warn a possible victim.*
3. *Supervise counseling tapes and assist the trainee to continue to attend to building the relationship with the client.*

Drawing on the general crisis information provided in class, one trainee plays a counselor in a crisis situation with the other, who plays a suicidal client. If needed, the supervisor can provide prepared vignettes to the trainee who plays the client.

Each role-play situation should take about 20 minutes (5 minutes to prepare and allow trainees to ask questions and 15 minutes of actual role-playing time). The supervisor takes notes during the role-plays. As the trainees conduct the session, the supervisor jots down observations on the counselor's ability to recognize a potential crisis, conduct a thorough crisis assessment, maintain the relationship during crisis, and develop a plan for intervention.

Following each role-play, the supervisor asks the trainees what they experienced, both as clients and as counselors. They are asked to provide feedback, both supportive and challenging, to each other, about their crisis-management procedures. Then the supervisor provides feedback using supervision strategy 1 (evaluate observed counseling session interactions). Included in the feedback is a determination of the level of severity of the client crisis using supervision strategy 6 (interpret significant events in the counseling session). The supervisor asks the trainee what led to crisis assessment and how action was taken. Specific comments are provided to trainees regarding their skills, conclusions, and consequent interventions. The supervisor discusses the impact of crisis on the therapy process, and asks what possible options exist for the next session (or for follow-up between sessions, if necessary).

Feedback needs to be specific and should include the following:

1. *Adequacy of assessment (commenting on strengths, as well as possible weaknesses);*
2. *Counselor's affective response, possible impact on the relationship;*
3. *Alternative methods of handling the situation; and*
4. *General observations, and comments.*

The supervisor explores the trainees' feelings about handling crisis situations and acknowledges that counselors may experience a wide range of emotions when dealing with such circumstances, which relies on supervision strategy 7 (explore trainee feelings during the counseling session). Trainees are asked to imagine how they would feel if this were a real crisis situation.

During the second part of the session, the supervisor focuses on situations in which the client may be harmful to someone else and in which the counselor must decide when to warn a potential victim — both a legal and ethical decision. The supervisor should have several different vignettes that illustrate the potential for a client to be a danger to others. Discussion or role-play can be used to help trainees familiarize themselves with this limit to confidentiality. Supervision strategies 10 (facilitate trainee self-exploration of confidence and worries in the counseling session), 13 (provide alternative interventions or conceptualizations for trainee use), and 14 (encourage trainee brainstorming of strategies and interventions), are used during this section of supervision.

The final portion of the session should be focused on the ongoing cases of the trainees. If possible, of course, supervisors attend to issues that are salient to the weekly topic.

*To illustrate:*

*[In this situation, a female trainee and a male client were involved, and issues associated with depression and danger to others are addressed.]*

*Supervisor:* I know you were anxious to meet today, Trainee 1, and talk about your client. Now that we have looked at that videotape segment, what are your thoughts about it?

*Trainee 1:* It made me very nervous to hear Alan say that he had fantasies about going over to his parents' house and shooting them both, especially when he talked about having a gun.

*Trainee 2:* Yes, I agree. And I noticed that you didn't say much when he was through talking about that.

*Trainee 1:* No. I was really anxious in there; I didn't know what to do. I just wanted to get out of there. I was glad that I knew Megan [another student supervisor] was on duty and observing the session while it was happening.

*Trainee 2:* Yeah. That's what you said to me that night.

*Supervisor:* Yet, as uneasy as you were, you didn't contact me . . . you waited until today to tell me about it.

*Trainee 1:* Yeah, I think I was just nervous. I talked to Megan at the time, and we agreed that he really wasn't very likely to go over and actually shoot his parents. In fact, he said he wouldn't. So we were sure that *Tarasoff* (Corey et al., 1998) didn't come into it. It was late when the session was over, and I didn't want to bother you, and you know, he's so depressed that I don't think he could even get up the energy to go out and kill someone.

*Supervisor:* And you probably didn't want to talk about it anymore that evening. Nonetheless, you know you're supposed to let me know if there is any talk of homicide or suicide. Next time you should go ahead and call me, even if it is late. . . . But let's talk about what happened in the session.

*Trainee 1:* Okay.

*Trainee 2:* Why do you think he told you that?

*Trainee 1:* Well, I'm not sure. I know he's really depressed because he thinks no one cares about him, and he thinks it's because his parents were so critical that it's hard for him to get along with other people.

*Trainee 2:* So he must want you to care about him.

*Trainee 1:* Oh yes, I know he does. That's one reason I decided not to make a big deal of his saying that . . . I mean, I didn't want to seem critical of his fantasy!

*Supervisor:* Sure. As you think about it, though, he told you something pretty serious about himself, that he thinks about killing his parents somctimes. And you know that he has a gun.

*Trainee:* Yeah. But I didn't want to act as if I thought he would be likely to kill someone.

*Supervisor:* No. But you had an alternative. You could let him know that you take his telling you about a fantasy like that seriously.

*Trainee 2:* What do you mean?

*Trainee 1:* Yeah, how do I do that?

*Supervisor:* Well, if he told you those feelings, he might have wanted you to care for him and respond to his fear that he could do something like that some day. I agree with you that he is pretty depressed and that very depressed people don't usually act out, but I believe that you should always take homicidal or suicidal remarks seriously and respond to them. It's a case of making the client feel heard and setting firm boundaries.

*Trainee 1:* I'm not sure what that means.

*Supervisor:* When Alan says that he thinks about going over to shoot his parents, you need to say, "I don't think of you as the impulsive sort of person who would go out and shoot someone, but I do think there is a reason you brought that up here today and that this fantasy worries you a little bit. So let's talk about it for a minute." Then you could proceed to ask the usual questions: How often does he think about this? How carefully has he planned it in fantasy? Does he have ammunition for his gun? Does he ever carry it when he goes out for anything other than gun club shoots? Does he think he should keep the gun with someone else? Would he call you if he had a fantasy like that?

*Trainee 1:* But that seems so insulting! I'd be afraid he'd never come back or never tell me anything important again.

*Supervisor:* To the contrary. You're not criticizing him. You're acting as if you know he wants you to help him maintain control, and you're responding to that need. You are caring for him.

*Trainee 2:* Hmm. So there are times when it is better to act as if a person could be dangerous?

*Supervisor:* Yes, especially if that person thinks he or she is dangerous. A person wants to be seen for who he is more than he wants to be liked but unseen.

*Trainee:* Yeah, I guess that's right. I'd prefer that you tell me that I should have called you when I was afraid rather than act as if I handled it completely. If you had just let it go by, I'd think you didn't really want to be bothered.

*Supervisor:* Sure. Not that you couldn't handle the situation, but you want me to respond to your fear that you might not. And it's likely to be the same with Alan. He wants you to help him with this fantasy that scares him. He wants you to take charge and set a boundary for him.

*Trainee:* So one thing I could have done after questioning him was to make some sort of contract with him to help him feel more in control?

*Supervisor:* Yes. And then you could have called to notify me of what you had done.

In this situation, the supervisor pointed out the need to establish boundaries with the client and then helped the trainee to see that this was also a form of caring for the client, even though it might have felt like criticism at first. This created a challenge to the trainee's concept of caring that promoted her development as a counselor.

## WEEK A-13. REPORTING CHILD ABUSE

### Class

*Objectives:*
1. *Present procedures for assessing the occurrence of child abuse and for reporting the abuse.*
2. *Provide supervision of ongoing clinic cases.*

The instructor presents materials for the assessment and reporting of child abuse. As information about abusive situations often becomes apparent in the first interview, the trainees will be reminded to review the structured child intake procedure from week 4.

Although crucial didactic material is presented during this class, there should still be time for the instructor to supervise one or two case presentations. Again, attention should be paid to the trainees' behavior and responses in session that facilitate relationship building. Any indications of child abuse are explored.

## Supervision

*Objectives:*
1. *Practice skills for assessment of child abuse, as presented in the class session.*
2. *Provide feedback on sessions with volunteer clients that emphasizes the trainees' acquisition and demonstration of the basic relationship skills developed during the term.*

The supervisor opens the session by checking in with trainees, both in terms of their current feelings about their work and in terms of their reactions to the presentations on child abuse assessment (1–20 minutes). The trainees each role-play an interview that includes child abuse assessment. Again, the supervisor may need to provide vignettes for the trainee who plays the client. Following each role-play, the supervisor encourages discussion of the specific ethical considerations involved in each vignette. Supervision strategy 13 (provide alternative interventions or conceptualization for trainee use) is employed. After each trainee has played the role of the counselor, the supervisor facilitates an exploration of the trainees' feelings about the material. Supervision strategies 9 (explore trainee feelings concerning specific techniques or interventions) and 10 (encourage trainee self-exploration of confidence and worries in the counseling session) are among those used. The entire exercise takes about 75 minutes.

Next, after a break, trainees present cases and show videotaped segments of their counseling (75 minutes). The supervisor invites the trainees to comment on their own abilities to build counseling relationships at this point in the term. The supervisor asks each trainee which skills feel most comfortable and which seem to require more practice to feel natural. In addition, trainees are asked to assess the effects of using particular skills with the clients they have seen. (This discussion foreshadows next quarter's focus on the client and case conceptualization.)

Finally, the supervisor asks the trainees to summarize their experiences for the day and closes the session.

*To illustrate:*

*[In this situation, a tape segment has just been presented by Trainee 2.]*

*Supervisor:* As we watched that tape, I asked you to focus on your use of the skills you have learned this quarter. What did you see here?

*Trainee 2:* Well, let's see. . . . I maintained eye contact, I leaned forward, I nodded a lot.

*Supervisor:* And what else?

*Trainee 2:* Although I think I ask a lot of questions, I didn't do much of that here. . . . That actually seems like progress. I guess I'm getting better at listening.

*Supervisor:* Yes, I would agree.

*Trainee 2:* I used some paraphrasing and summarization and reflection of feelings.

*Supervisor:* I think you are quite good at picking out the feeling behind all the words of that rather talkative young woman.

*Trainee 1:* Yeah. Me, too. I was kind of wondering where it was going, and then you just pulled it all together when you said, "You sound disappointed."

*Trainee 2:* Yeah.

*Supervisor:* And you hit it exactly! How could you tell?

*Trainee 2:* Because her upper lip started to tremble and her face sort of crumpled.

*Supervisor:* Yes. Not that we want to push for tears, but a change in facial expression is a clear signal that the person has had a reaction to what you have done in the session. . . . Where else could you see that you were going in a useful direction?

*Trainee 2:* When I summarized, she agreed with my summary and then built on it.

*Supervisor:* Yeah, that is a good example of the client's telling you that you are on the right track and that she felt understood. Did you have anything you wanted to add, Trainee 1?

*Trainee 1:* Well, I thought you could have done a confrontation when she said she was really angry at her roommate and smiled while she was saying it.

*Trainee 2:* Yeah, you're right, now that you mention it. . . . I guess I still am pretty uneasy with confrontation.

*Supervisor:* Then that's probably something you need to work with more. . . . Is there anything in particular that makes it difficult for you?

*Trainee 2:* Well, I just don't know how to say it without sounding rude, and so my voice gets all shaky and it doesn't come out right.

*Supervisor:* Okay. Let's work a minute with that. . . . Trainee 1, you play the client, and I'll try some confrontations with you. Then you can see how you feel about them and try the one that fits best for you, Trainee 2.

In this vignette the supervisor elicited the trainee's own response, allowed the other trainee to participate in the discussion, and encouraged the trainees to observe the effects of the interventions on the client. Then the trainees were invited together to define an area that needed additional instruction, which the supervisor provided by modeling. The supervisor acknowledged the trainee's growth to date and provided an opportunity to improve in the use of an underused basic skill that is often difficult for new counselors.

## WEEK A-14. INTERVENING IN INSTITUTIONS ON THE CLIENT'S BEHALF

### Class

*Objectives:*
1. *Present procedures for intervening in institutions on the client's behalf.*
2. *Provide supervision of ongoing clinic cases.*

After a review of the class material from week A-5 on effective collaboration with institutions, the instructor asks the students to imagine client concerns that might lead to intervening in schools, after-school programs, or other agencies on the client's behalf. For each type of concern, students should consider what institutions would be involved, which personnel in those institutions should be contacted, and how the client's family might be involved. A guest speaker from a school might be a rich addition to this class.

Students present cases at the end of the class period. With each case, class members consider whether it could be useful for the counselor to contact an agency, school, or family.

### Supervision

*Objectives:*
1. *Respond to issues as requested by trainees.*
2. *Respond to any trainee feelings associated with their client's experiences.*

With the use of supervision strategy 17 (allow the trainee to structure the supervision session), the supervisor formally encourages the trainees to collaborate on the planning of the supervision session. The trainees are invited to review the past term, to look at areas for growth as in supervision strategy 11 (help the trainee define personal competencies and areas for growth), and to talk together to plan the best use of the session. The supervisor implements strategy 16 (solicit and attempt to satisfy trainee needs during the session) if the trainees find it difficult to structure the entire session. For example, the supervisor might ask whether the trainees have client issues that relate to the class topic. The session then proceeds as proposed.

*To illustrate:*

*[In this situation, the trainee does have a client concern relevant to the weekly class topic.]*

*Trainee 1:* I do have a client situation that might benefit from collaboration with the schools.

*Supervisor:* That's great. Should we start with that today?

*Trainee 1:* It's okay with me. This client is really my most pressing concern.

*Trainee 2:* I have a couple of issues that I'd like to bring up, but I'd be comfortable using the second half of the session.

*Supervisor:* Okay. It sounds as if you would like to split the session between you.

*Trainee 1 and Trainee 2:* Yeah.

*Supervisor:* Great. Trainee 1, which client were you thinking of?

*Trainee 1:* It's a 10-year old kid who was just diagnosed with ADHD [attention deficit hyperactivity disorder] and started on medication by her pediatrician. She is responding well to the Ritalin and she is working well with me in therapy, but I'm worried about her.

*Trainee 2:* What are you worried about? It sounds as if you're doing really well.

*Trainee 1:* Thanks. It's just that I've been reading a lot about ADHD since I was assigned this client, and I know how important, no, how critical, the school environment is for kids like this. I'm worried that her teacher may not know much about how to handle ADHD kids, you know, and perhaps will punish my client for not being more in control all the time or something like that. I don't know. . . .

*Supervisor:* I think your concern is valid. I am a little confused by your apparent hesitation.

*Trainee 1:* Well. I don't know. . . . I have a hard time picturing myself talking to a teacher about this.

*Trainee 2:* You mean because we're still students?

*Trainee 1:* Yeah. I would feel completely intimidated by an experienced teacher in his or her own classroom. I mean, what do I really have to offer?

*Supervisor:* It sounds as if you feel you need to go into the schools in a consultant role and that role feels a little beyond you.

*Trainee 1:* Hmmm. Yeah. I guess my reading has alarmed me and made me think some teachers don't know anything about ADHD. So that makes me think I have to have all the answers if I go talk to her teacher. And that makes me feel young and stupid and pretentious.

*Trainee 2:* I can understand that. I'm older than you are and I have kids in school, and I still sometimes feel intimidated by school teachers.

*[All laugh.]*

*Supervisor:* So a consultant role isn't comfortable for you in this instance. How else might you approach the school?

*Trainee 1:* [Pauses] Well, I honestly want to know what the teacher does know about ADHD and how he or she can help my client do better in school.

*Trainee 2:* So you could frame your visit with the teacher as an information sharing meeting? Would that make you feel more comfortable?

*Trainee 1:* Yes!

*Supervisor:* You still may find yourself in a position to offer the teacher some helpful information. Remember . . . you have been doing some serious study of this disorder.

*Trainee 1:* That's true.

*Trainee 2:* Couldn't you just take the material that you presented in your school counseling class — the handouts and stuff about tips for parents and teachers? Then you could share it if the teacher isn't experienced with ADHD.

*Trainee 1:* Yeah. And I could take a book or two with me like the one by Hallowell and Ratey [1994]. The parents really found that book helpful.

*Supervisor:* Sounds good to me. Do you have a sense of how to go about contacting the teacher?

*Trainee 1:* Yes. The class material was very complete about that. I was just having a hard time picturing myself actually meeting with a teacher. But now I'm kind of excited about the idea!

*Supervisor:* Great!

# WEEK A-15. REVIEWING THE TERM AND EVALUATING THE TRAINEE

## Class

*Objectives:*
1. *Encourage discussion and reflection on students' experiences in the course this term.*
2. *Respond to issues as requested by trainees.*
3. *Respond to any trainee feelings associated with their first encounters with clients.*

Class time is spent in reviewing the term and preparing for individual evaluations. Students are asked to talk about what they have learned and ask any questions that remain. The instructor invites students to evaluate the course as it has been conducted this term.

## Supervision

*Objective:*
1. *Join with the course instructor to provide end-of-term evaluation for trainees.*

Each individual trainee meets with the instructor and the supervisor together. The instructor invites the trainee to tell about his or her experiences during the course, and they share the discussion with the supervisor. The supervisor then asks the trainee to present a self-evaluation. Both supervisor and instructor respond to the trainee's evaluation, asking questions about it and providing some feedback. This is followed by giving the trainee a written evaluation, which includes comments from both the supervisor and the instructor. The trainee has the opportunity to read it and respond. The instructor, supervisor, and trainee sign the evaluation. This indicates only that the trainee has read it, and the supervisor explains that the trainee may file a rebuttal to the evaluation if it does not match the trainee's experience. The trainee keeps a signed copy of the evaluation. Finally, the supervisor asks for the trainee's goals for the next term's work, which may or may not be based on the feedback just given. The instructor checks to make sure that what the instructor and the supervisor have offered has been understood, and they come to a close.

✦

With the evaluation, the first term ends. Although the counseling relationship will continue to be a focus throughout the year, attention in the following term will shift to formal case conceptualization, and use of change theories to plan work with clients and to assess work with clients.

# CHAPTER 6

# SECOND-TERM SESSIONS DESIGNED TO DEVELOP STUDENTS' CASE CONCEPTUALIZATION SKILLS

During the second term of practicum, a number of new concepts are introduced, and students learn to conceptualize cases and plan their work with clients. A great deal of supervision time is spent in the teaching mode in the first term, but more time is spent in the consultant mode in the second term. In general, the supervisor works with the trainee to conceptualize a case and develop a plan for counseling. As Binder (1993) underscored, supervision is where counselors have the opportunity to translate their academic, declarative knowledge into the practical knowledge necessary for expertise.

Because trainees are seeing both volunteer and community clients at this point, what happens in supervision is affected by what is happening in those cases. New and disequilibrating experiences arise for trainees, which provide opportunities for supervisors to use the advanced strategies to encourage trainees' growth as clinical observers and practitioners. For supervisors-in-training, reviewing chapter 4's discussion of advanced supervision and case conceptualization at this time is helpful.

Before the model of case conceptualization is presented, instructors and supervisors focus on students' theories of human change. Trainees, supervisors, and the instructor work together to incorporate their theories of human change into the theoretical orientation used in this course. Attention is given to the idea of an espoused change theory and a practical theory, against which case planning and counseling sessions can be viewed.

Students are asked to consider what information they need about clients and how they use it to plan their work, and this is integrated into the case conceptualization model described in chapter 4. Students learn to incorporate a clinical interview, the client's past history and cultural background, and any formal assessments, to develop a broad picture of the client. In some programs and settings, this may include formal diagnosis. We provide a lesson that allows students to conduct a formal intake, with examples characteristic of our training clinic. Manual users will need to determine whether this lesson fits their training program and site. In our program, students learn to make a formal diagnosis according to the *DSM-IV* (American Psychiatric Association, 1994), and we include that process here. In counseling programs where formal diagnoses are not appropriate, however, this portion may be eliminated. With all of this information in place, students can draw on their theories of human change to plan counseling appropriate for the client, given the nature of the counselor, the client, ethical considerations, and time constraints.

Each class in the case conceptualization unit, except for the first, third, and last of the term, includes a 90-minute lesson on the current topic and an hour of student case presentations. During the week each trainee meets with a supervisor. Supervision in a group of two or more will alternate with individual supervision sessions, to allow adequate time and attention to trainees' individual cases and concerns. All supervision sessions incorporate the presentation of trainees' cases. Ongoing cases are conceptualized according to the model, and reconceptualized when appropriate. Every effort is made to help trainees bring their practical theories into line with their espoused theories, usually the orientation used in the course. Vignettes illustrate the reflective inquiry used to encourage this process.

Trainees' case presentations comprise the largest portion of supervision time. Supervisors provide a range of appropriate feedback to trainees, incorporating both beginning and advanced supervision strategies. Another part of the session is focused on the use of teaching strategies to explore new concepts presented in class. The supervisor makes certain that trainees understand the concepts and then invites the trainees to apply what they can of the model to the clients they are currently seeing.

In general, during case presentations trainees introduce a case, explain any new information about the client, discuss their intentions in the session, and present preselected portions of videotape illustrating the best moments in therapy and any with which the trainee feels the need for assistance. It is helpful for the supervisor to pick one or two random segments to view as well. To the degree that time and facilities allow, supervisors are encouraged to watch at least one full counseling session while it is going on and deliver feedback immediately afterward. Supervisors use supervision strategy 22 (explore the trainee's intentions in a session), as they review the counseling sessions with the trainee.

In the first term, supervision sessions were closely tied to the class presentations, and it is easy to present likely scenarios for supervision sessions in the manual. In this term much of the work is focused on trainees' counseling with clients. Vignettes presented in the manual for each week's supervision show situations associated with that particular week's class presentations. These situations may come up at any time however. They feature clinical and ethical dilemmas faced in practice.

Supervision dialogues employ the case conceptualization model in the analysis of current cases or apply specific supervision strategies to that week's topic in the supervision of a case. Supervisors conduct discussions about cases on the basis of the model for reflective inquiry, described in chapter 1 and in the introduction to part II, to aid students' understanding of the relationship between their espoused theories and their practical theories. Valid information about the client, theories of change, and individual change strategies are modified as a result of work with clients in session.

The term's work finishes with an introduction to counseling strategies for social skills deficits, career planning, depression, anxiety, and family problems. During these lessons, several theoretical approaches are discussed and practiced in addition to the principal orientation for the year's course. Approaches to each disorder will involve two of the following five major counseling theories: behavioral, cognitive, psychodynamic, humanistic, and family systems. In this manner, students can begin to conceptualize cases from a variety of theoretical viewpoints and learn a number of interventions appropriate to treatment of disorders frequently presented in clinical situations.

## WEEK B-1. DEVELOPING CHANGE THEORY

### Class

*Objectives:*
1. *Explore students' theories of personal change in the context of their personal values.*
2. *Introduce the idea of espoused theories and practical theories.*
3. *Integrate the students' personal theories with the theoretical approach used in this course.*

The instructor starts the class by requesting students' first assignments for the term. Students have been asked before class to reflect on their life philosophies and how they believe people change. The instructor asks what each student has written and writes their assumptions about change on the board under the words *espoused theories*. The instructor suggests that students think of something they did to help someone else change; the people they helped may be former clients, friends, colleagues, or family members. Then the instructor asks students what they did and writes down their helpful actions under the words *practical theories*. Students are asked what they make of all this and are encouraged to notice how their espoused theories match their practical theories and how they do not. Toward the end of the discussion, students are questioned about the change theory used in the practicum course. They are invited to explain what the theory espouses and what use of the practical theory might look like. Then they are encouraged to find ways to integrate their personal theories of change with the theory studied in this course. In this way they integrate their declarative knowledge about counseling with the practical knowledge they use in actual work with clients.

## Supervision With Trainees Together

*Objectives:*
1. *Assist trainees to clarify their goals for the term.*
2. *Facilitate the trainee's formulations of change theories with application to cases from last term.*

The supervisor begins by checking in with both trainees and asking them to talk about their goals for the term with each other (45 minutes), using strategy 11 (help the trainee define personal competencies and areas for growth). In this discussion, trainees each talk about goals they set at the end of the previous term. The supervisor asks them if their goals have been modified in any way upon reflection over the break. Trainees respond and explain what they would like from one another and from the supervisor in helping them to meet their goals. This allows trainees to think about what goes into setting goals and meeting goals, a task that is now addressed with clients in mind.

During the next portion of the session (45 minutes), the supervisor explores the trainees' own theories of change, using strategy 9 (explore trainee feelings about specific techniques or interventions). The supervisor asks trainees about their theories' development, and in particular, about personal values and experiences that have influenced their theories. They discuss the ideas of espoused and practical theories and examine together the ways in which their change theories match or do not match the theoretical orientation used in the practicum course. In many ways, this is a personalized and detailed expansion of the classroom portion of the week's lesson.

*To illustrate:*

*Supervisor:* I know that each of you wrote down some things in class about your own philosophy of life and change. Would you tell me about them now?

*Trainee 1:* Well, first we talked about my idea of the purpose of life. *[Laughs]* Just a little topic. . . . You know, though, when I think about the purpose of life, I guess I think we should try to make the world a better place, you know, and help those who are less fortunate to have a better life.

*Supervisor:* Does this have something to do with why you chose to go into this area of study?

*Trainee 1:* Yes, sort of. I was a high school teacher, you know; I taught American history and I was pretty idealistic. I thought I was going to change the world and help a lot of students as well. But then I got pretty frustrated and spent a lot more time talking to my students about their lives than about the Civil War. . . . And then I went to New York and wound up teaching for a while in East Harlem . . . and the whole idea of teaching about American history seemed absurd. . . . The only way I ever seemed to be able to make a difference was with one person at a time. . . . So then I thought I should learn more about helping one person at a time, and that's how I wound up here.

*Trainee 2:* Wow! I didn't realize you had done that!

*Supervisor:* Hmm. It sounds as if you thought a lot about this.

*Trainee 1:* Yes.

*Supervisor:* And how do you think people are helped? That is, how do changes happen in their lives?

*Trainee 1:* Well, this is pretty hard. . . . I think people have to have motivation and opportunity to look at their lives. . . . I mean, if you live in East Harlem and you haven't seen your father for a long time and you see your mother working really hard just cleaning rich people's houses—I don't know how you get an idea of a better life. I mean, it doesn't look as if a person can do anything to have a better life. But some people do.

*Trainee 2:* Yes, but do you think counseling has anything to do with it?

*Trainee 1:* That's where I get pretty confused. . . . I mean, how do you get someone like that into counseling? But let's say that you do. It probably involves respecting and understanding the person and not judging them—accepting them. And then maybe they can think about what they want to do with their lives. And how to go about it. . . . I don't know. I guess I think if you have a new experience with people, you can change how you approach things.

*Supervisor:* Well, let's think about your life for a while. You seem to have gone through some pretty big changes in your life . . . you've changed your career and you've been divorced and remarried. . . . Do you think you have changed as a person as well?

*Trainee 1:* Well, not in terms of basic values. But yes, I think I've changed a lot. I now believe I am more competent than I used to think.

*Supervisor:* And what made the difference?

*Trainee 1:* I had some therapy, and I was able to look at what my family's ideas about life and about me were and how that influenced my view of myself. . . . And then I had a job at a university where we were trying to work with rural school districts, and the people at Bucknell seemed to think I was pretty capable. That's really the first time anyone ever acted as if I were special in some way. . . . And I got thinking that maybe I could do more than I thought, you know, succeed in graduate school and eventually have a bigger impact. I don't know; it gets pretty vague after that.

*Trainee 2:* So that fits pretty well with what you said before. That is, that someone accepted you and respected you in a way that was different from the way your family saw you.

*Trainee 1:* Yeah, and it was pretty important for me to look at just how my family had influenced me too.

*Supervisor:* So knowing your own history and being respected in the present are both important for changing.

*Trainee:* Yes . . . at least, they were for me.

*Supervisor:* And as you think about the theories presented in your theories class, which theory do you think best approximates your ideas about change?

*Trainee:* Well, it's some combination of psychodynamic therapy and person-centered therapy. . . . I definitely wouldn't go for Ellis *[laughs]*. . . .

*Supervisor:* You know, the person-centered people think they're pretty different from the psychodynamic people. That's how Rogers got started. But you're talking about drawing from both, which is, interestingly enough, consistent with the interactional process we have been talking about all year.

*Trainee 1:* Yeah, well, I think understanding the past is pretty important and so is acceptance in the present.

*Trainee 2:* I agree. And talking about what's happening in the present, too.

*Supervisor:* What would you be likely to do in practice to carry out this theory you espouse?

*Trainee 1:* Well, I'd really have to listen carefully and respond empathically.

*Trainee 2:* Which is what we've been working on all year.

*Supervisor:* So when we're watching you work with a client, we need to bear in mind your theory of change. Knowing your intention will help us all to see if what you're doing in practice fits your change theory.

*Trainee 1:* Yeah *[laughs]*. But don't be too hard on me!

*Supervisor:* No. Besides, as we go along, you may find you need to modify your theory of change as you get new information from the client or find that it's not working. You may decide on a whole different theory after a while, but in the meantime, you have a sense of what you want to be doing with clients.

In this vignette, the supervisor encouraged the trainee to think about personal experiences of change and engaged the other trainee in the discussion. After their theoretical discussion, the supervisor supported the trainee's exploration. The supervisor can then go on to repeat the exercise with the second trainee in the next 45 minutes.

At the end of the exploration of the second trainee's theory, the supervisor elicits questions and comments from both trainees on any topic related to theories of change. The session is ended with a brief summary of each trainee's theory as it stands now.

# WEEK B-2. INTRODUCING THE CASE CONCEPTUALIZATION MODEL

## Class

*Objectives:*
1. *Introduce the case conceptualization model.*
2. *Learn how to gather valid information about the client and the problem(s) presented in counseling.*
3. *Examine client on videotape in terms of the model.*

During class the instructor will introduce the model of case conceptualization described in chapter 4, and give its outline (Table 3 in chapter 4) to the students. In particular, students learn to integrate information from the clinical interview, formal assessments, impressions of others in the client's life, and the interviewer's personal reactions to the client to arrive at a picture of the client and the client's present concern. The instructor elaborates the decision points involved in establishing a counseling contract, including goal setting and treatment planning, and illustrates the application of goal-setting strategies to several cases. The instructor points out that a client's goals must be ethically consistent with his or her values and the agency's values; for example, a clinic may refuse to treat a man whose only goal is to remove guilt so that he can more comfortably seduce employees under his direct supervision.

Use of a videotape encourages the use of clinical observation and personal impressions to understand clients shown. Students are encouraged to consider whether formal assessments or others' reports, if available, could provide additional information. This discussion serves as an introduction to learning to gather valid information about clients from a variety of sources.

## Individual Supervision

*Objectives:*
1. *Help trainees apply the case conceptualization model to their own past and current cases.*
2. *Introduce the role of the structured intake in building relationships.*

The supervisor begins by checking in with the trainee (10 minutes). During the following 45 minutes, the supervisor focuses discussion on the case conceptualization model, using strategy 19 (help the trainee conceptualize a case). The trainee is asked for any questions about the case conceptualization material presented in class. After that, the supervisor will request that the trainee apply the model to clients seen during the previous term. After allowing the trainee time to consider the available sources of information, the nature of the client's problem, and the nature of the contract with the volunteer clients, the supervisor will ask the trainee to choose one client to consider more thoroughly.

*To illustrate:*

*[In this situation, the case conceptualization model is applied to a case with a volunteer client the trainee had seen three times. In this segment, the trainee examines the nature of the problem.]*

*Supervisor:* So, now that you've had a chance to think about your clients from last quarter, whom have you selected?

*Trainee:* I've picked Toni, the woman who was trying to decide whether to move in with her boyfriend.

*Supervisor:* And as I recall, you had no strong moral belief about whether she should or shouldn't that might have interfered with counseling her around this issue.

*Trainee:* That's right.

*Supervisor:* Okay. Now, for this exercise, we'll imagine that you are going to keep meeting with her, that the first three sessions were introductory and now you are formulating the case more thoroughly.

*Trainee:* Okay.

*Supervisor:* Why don't you start by giving me your sources of information?

*Trainee:* Well, all I have are the things she told me or the things she showed in the sessions, which I guess could be called a series of clinical interviews.

*Supervisor:* You have what she told you and showed you, but you also have your own reactions to her.

*Trainee:* Oh, yeah, that's right. I guess I still don't think of my reactions as data.

*Supervisor:* Okay. . . . That takes time to learn. You'll want to give more attention to your own reactions. . . . Tell me about her concern.

*Trainee:* Well, she has had this same boyfriend since last spring. He would like her to move in with him next year, and she can't decide what to do.

*Supervisor:* Okay. And why has she come to you to talk about it now?

*Trainee:* She had a chance to get course credit for a counseling experience *[laughs].*

*Supervisor:* Sure. And she decided that this was what she wanted to talk about right now.

*Trainee:* Oh yeah. Well, now that I think about it, he had suggested moving in several months ago, but now she has to decide about it in the next 6 weeks to make arrangements for next year.

*Supervisor:* So that's given it some urgency. What did she tell you about this problem? What does she see as issues in the decision?

*Trainee:* At first she said that she was worried about losing her independence, that if she moved in with him she might stop seeing her friends and pursuing her own interests.

*Supervisor:* Okay. Anything else?

*Trainee:* The second time she came in, she said she'd thought about it, and she decided to talk to her boyfriend, and he encouraged her to keep up her own life even if they lived together. So she felt a little better about that. But before she came back in to talk with me, she woke up in the middle of the night with her heart pounding so hard that she went to the health service the next day. They checked her out and told her that her heart was okay but that she might be pretty anxious about something. That made her think that there was more to this issue than just independence.

*Supervisor:* Yeah, I can imagine. And what did she think that might be?

*Trainee:* She didn't know, but she sure wanted to find out!

*Supervisor:* Okay. Let's look at her history. What do you know about her that might relate to this?

*Trainee:* Well, I know that she is the oldest in a family of four kids, and that her parents got divorced when she was in junior high, and that her father moved away and she has hardly seen him since.

*Supervisor:* Mmm-hmm. And how do you think this could be related to her present dilemma?

*Trainee:* Well, now that I think about it, I remember that she said her mother was really bitter about the divorce. She complained a lot to Toni. The mother said that she hadn't been that anxious to get married, that she had a good job and was having a pretty good time. She said that the father had promised her everything when they got married and then he had gone off with another woman and left her with four kids.

*Supervisor:* So you think some feelings about that might be part of Toni's indecision now?

*Trainee:* Now that I think of it, yes. But I never asked her about that possibility when I was seeing her.

*Supervisor:* What cultural and social factors might play a part here?

*Trainee:* Well, she grew up White and middle class in central Oregon, so I don't suppose she was oppressed because of her race. There is one cultural factor, though. Her family belonged to a strict religious group that believed in male superiority, and that might affect her here. But I don't think it's that big a deal for her because she said her mother left the church when her father took off, and Toni was just starting her teen years.

*Supervisor:* You might want to check that out, nonetheless. Often, early childhood messages about gender relations have a lasting effect. At the same time, you don't want to push your belief about female autonomy on her.

*Trainee:* Right, I wouldn't, though I actually don't think she is still involved with that religion. Now that I think about it, I guess it's true that her early religious life could be more important than I've been thinking. I would want to explore that further if I were seeing her again.

*Supervisor:* Okay. What about her personal characteristics and behaviors? Does she have a pattern of behavior that would affect this problem? How do you experience her as a decision maker in general?

*Trainee:* Well, you know, at first I thought she was sort of passive. She just talked as if she thought I should tell her what to do. But then she thought about it and went and talked to her boyfriend about the independence thing, so I realized she wasn't really passive. . . . And she doesn't seem to have had trouble choosing a major or anything. So I don't know of any consistent personality traits that would contribute to this.

*Supervisor:* It sounds as if you changed your hypothesis after she talked to her boyfriend. Let's think about her personal resources.

*Trainee:* Well, she is introspective and she's pretty willing to look at herself, so that makes her a person who could benefit from counseling. And once she thinks of something, like with the independence thing, then she goes and does something about it, like she did with talking to her boyfriend.

*Supervisor:* So she has some pretty positive patterns of behavior. And does she have any personal deficits in this area?

*Trainee:* Gee, I don't know.

*Supervisor:* Well, let's think for a few minutes. Did you ever notice anything that seemed to create problems for her or contribute to the concerns she had?

*Trainee:* Hmmm . . . I do remember that she didn't ever seem to talk about having any really close friends. I mean, she knew a lot of people, but when I asked her if there were anyone besides her boyfriend she could really confide in or rely on, she couldn't think of anyone.

*Supervisor:* That could be an important piece of information, too. Social support is an important contributor to mental health.

*Trainee:* Oh! Maybe that's one reason she is so worried about being completely dependent on her boyfriend. She doesn't really have anyone else, and if she moved in with him, she wouldn't have anyone else to turn to if he took off.

*Supervisor:* That makes sense. So what hypotheses do you have about that?

*Trainee:* Well, it seems as if she needs more friends, or at least, one more close friend. I mean, if she had other people in her support system, she might not feel that she had to move in with this guy. On the other hand, she might not be afraid to move in with him either.

*Supervisor:* So you have two hypotheses about her, one about her feelings about relying on men that relates to her family of origin, and one about her current social situation.

*Trainee:* Yeah, that's right.

*Supervisor:* Okay. That puts you in a position to think about your contract and goals in a more systematic way.

In this illustration, the supervisor led the trainee through a series of questions, related to the case conceptualization model, which aided the formation of hypotheses about the client and her problem. With this information now more thoughtfully organized, the trainee is in a better position to think about counseling goals and contract decisions with this client. This model also illustrates several ways in which a reflective stance can be developed by trainees, by emphasizing the need to think about and respond to a variety of sources of information.

During the final 30 minutes of the supervision session, the supervisor talks about the establishment of relationships with clients in the initial intake meeting. Supervision strategies 4 (teach, demonstrate, or model intervention techniques) and 5 (explain the rationale behind specific strategies and interventions) may be useful. The supervisor acknowledges that the amount of structure in the intake process can often feel restrictive to trainees. He or she introduces ways in which the trainee can maintain a relational stance with the client, despite needing to handle large amounts of new information. The supervisor also talks about the differences between intake interviews, in which the goal is to gather information, and counseling sessions. Finally, the supervisor helps to prepare the trainee for the upcoming intake training by answering questions and briefly describing the role-play that is to be completed during the upcoming week.

## WEEK B-3. USING INTAKE PROCEDURES THAT FACILITATE GATHERING VALID INFORMATION

### Class

*Objective:*
1. *Provide training on intake procedures.*

During the first half of class, the instructor teaches the trainees how to do an intake interview. Included are general procedures such as making the client comfortable, identifying the presenting problem, negotiating and collecting payment, obtaining informed consent, and closing the intake interview. In addition, agency-specific procedures such as obtaining consent for videotaping and explaining to the client the procedures for case assignment are described. Trainees are instructed in the use of particular assessment instruments and interview strategies. The instructor encourages the trainees to watch a live intake interview prior to the supervision session.

In the second half of class, the instructor and the trainees go to the training clinic. Students learn the location of various intake and assessment materials, and they walk through the intake procedures.

### Supervision With Trainees Together

*Objectives:*
1. *View counseling session tapes.*
2. *Participate in an intake role-play.*

The supervisor checks in with the trainees and explains what will happen during supervision. During the first 60 minutes the supervisor provides brief supervision on each trainee's clinical work with volunteer clients. The following supervision strategies are appropriate for this portion of supervision: 1 (evaluate observed counseling session interactions), 6 (interpret significant events in the counseling session), 7 (explore trainee feelings during the counseling session), and 8 (explore trainee feelings during the supervision session). Due to the brevity of this segment, additional supervision can be scheduled outside of this session to address additional concerns, if necessary.

During the last two hours of the session, one trainee conducts a mock intake interview using the other trainee as the client. The supervisor encourages trainees to make the simulation as realistic as possible, including actually completing the necessary paperwork. The trainee who plays the client is instructed to have a specific presenting problem in mind. This will help the trainees learn to identify and define a problem area. Supervision strategy 10 (facilitate trainee self-exploration of confidence and worries in the counseling session) is emphasized.

Following the role-play, the supervisor invites the trainees to discuss the intake process. In addition, the supervisor provides specific feedback regarding the trainees' comfort with the various assessment tools and the degree of thoroughness with which the intake was conducted. Supervision strategies 1 (evaluate observed counseling session interactions), 4 (teach, demonstrate, or model intervention techniques), and 5 (explain the rationale behind specific strategies and interventions) are important here. Questions can include, "What might you still want to know about this client before making a case assignment?" and "Where are the gaps, if any, in the information?" The supervisor attends to the trainee's ability to gather information and establish a relationship that encourages the client to return for counseling.

Trainees frequently collect information and neglect the relationship or, conversely, engage in more counseling than is appropriate during the intake interview.

*To illustrate:*

*[In this situation, which offers an example of supervision for these errors, the trainees have completed a mock intake interview.]*

*Trainee 1:* It looked really easy when I watched an intake the other day in the clinic, but this was hard.

*Trainee 2:* Yeah. There are really a lot of different things to worry about when you're doing an intake.

*Trainee 1:* I felt as if I were going against all the counseling skills I'd learned. I always had my head down with papers. . . . I didn't even make eye contact.

*Trainee 2:* I know what you mean. But it actually didn't feel bad, and you did get to my problem. And that felt good . . . that you got it. It seemed as if you understood what I was saying and asking for, even though I could tell you were busy with the paperwork and stuff.

*Trainee 1:* Well, thanks. But I still think I could have been smoother with the paperwork, or something. . . . I really felt disconnected, just trying to get information from you. . . . I also wondered if maybe that would be pretty offensive to a client from another culture. Trainee 2, I would really like honest feedback about that. Did I get the information I was looking for in a way that was respectful of your cultural background?

*Trainee 2:* Well, mostly yes. I mean, I could really tell that you wanted to understand me. But there was one question, about my extended family, where I think you might have been relying on some assumptions about Native Americans rather than finding out about my personal experience. It wasn't really offensive, but it did stop me from responding as freely as I might have otherwise. I guess it closed me down a little bit.

*Trainee 1:* Yeah, I think I know which part you mean. I was just sort of condensing stuff in my head, and for a minute I lost track of interacting with you, I think. I appreciate your being honest with me. I want to work on that some more.

*Supervisor:* You've really hit on an important issue with doing intakes. How do you balance establishing a relationship with the client as an individual with getting the information, filling out the paperwork, and using the knowledge you have about counseling people?

*Trainee 1:* I don't know. It feels like you can hardly do all those things and still be a good counselor.

*Trainee 2:* But I didn't really think you were supposed to be a counselor when you're doing an intake.

*Trainee 1:* But the clients come in hurting. You have to do something to help them. How can you not be a counselor?

*Trainee 2:* Well, I don't mean not to be a counselor at all. I just mean that counseling isn't really the primary goal in intakes. We need to use them to gather valid information.

*Supervisor:* Okay, this is an important discussion. Remember, even when you're just getting information, you use a lot of the basic attending skills, especially those that help establish rapport. For people who haven't been listened to before, which is true for many clients, this alone is very therapeutic. But your primary goals are to develop a relationship that gives the client a reason to come back to the clinic and to get the information you need about the client so that you can define the problem and provide basic information for staffing. So, you probably won't use skills like interpretation. Often, the hardest thing can be keeping yourself from trying to jump in and solve the client's problem.

*[Both trainees nod enthusiastically.]*

*Trainee 1:* Yeah, now that we talk about it, I realize that I was kind of wanting to fix things for Trainee 2 when I was doing the intake. I found myself thinking about solutions more than about what I was supposed to be finding out next.

*Supervisor:* A lot of this will come with practice, especially juggling the paperwork with all your other tasks during the intake.

*Trainee 1:* Okay. But how do we know if we're really gathering the right information? We talked a lot in class about "valid information" and learning to pull together a lot of information to get a more complete sense of the client. Sometimes, I felt so overwhelmed with the amount of information I was getting in such a short time that I wondered if it was valid or valuable at all!

*Trainee 2:* Yeah, I have that question too. How do we know when we're going off on tangents or following up on the important things?

*Supervisor:* Well, it's important to recognize that sometimes you will ask questions or follow up a piece of information that doesn't turn out to be important. But, that's really okay. The goal with an intake is to get enough information to form some general impressions and a preliminary diagnosis. If you follow up on something that ends up irrelevant to the client's concerns, then you can always use that information to rule out an issue.

*Trainee 2:* Okay. So there really isn't a "wrong" type of information, as long as I put it all together to help me understand the client.

*Supervisor:* Right.

*Trainee 1:* Oh, that's helpful. Maybe now if I don't worry as much about getting just certain kinds of information, I'll be more able to hear and understand what the client is telling me.

*Supervisor:* Great! That really is the goal here. You have identified a couple of important issues today, and I hope you continue to be aware of the different roles you play with clients in different situations.

Before the session ends, the supervisor addresses any procedural or mechanical errors made in the intake role-play and answers any questions about the assessment tools or other aspects of the intake. During the week, when trainees conduct their first intakes with clients, the supervisor can be available to provide live supervision at prearranged points.

## WEEK B-4. GATHERING VALID INFORMATION IN INSTITUTIONS

### Class

*Objectives:*
1. *Apply the methods for gathering valid information to institutional settings.*
2. *Provide group supervision using videotapes of sessions with clients from the community.*

The class instructor outlines the information a counselor may need from an institutional setting to provide better service to a given client. This might include, but is not limited to, past psychological reports; communication and consultation with previous counselors; communication with a child's teacher about classroom difficulties; direct observation of a client in a relevant home, work, or school setting; consultation with family members; and reports generated by the school or institution relevant to the client's experience there.

During the second portion of the class period, the instructor guides group supervision of community clients. Because this is the first time trainees have shown work with clients who actually represent the public, some apprehension can be expected. In many of the low-cost facilities in which students first practice, the client population can be more difficult than anticipated (Neufeldt, 1994a). The instructor explores trainees' concerns and creates as safe an environment as possible.

### Individual Supervision

*Objectives:*
1. *Provide individual supervision of clients.*
2. *Practice gathering valid information from a representative of an institution.*

After a brief check-in (10 minutes), the supervisor views tapes of the trainee's client session(s) from the previous week (45 minutes). This may be the first time trainees have shown work with community clients who have solicited counseling services. It is not unusual for the trainee to voice new doubts about competence, similar to the doubts experienced early in the first term of practicum. Supervision strategies 7 (explore trainee feeling during the counseling session), 8 (explore trainee feelings during the supervision session), 10 (encourage trainee self-exploration of confidence and worries in the counseling session), and 19 (help the trainee conceptualize a case) are appropriate here.

During the last portion of the session, the supervisor reviews the methods presented in class for gathering information in institutional settings. Then, with the supervisor in the role of a representative from the institution, the trainee conducts a role-play in which he or she works to gather the information needed.

*To illustrate:*

*Supervisor:* I'd like to use the rest of today's session talking more about how to gather valid information from institutional settings. Have you thought at all about questions you might have about that, based on what was discussed in class?

*Trainee:* Yes, actually, I'd like to focus on how to gather information in schools. I'm hoping to see some children as clients this term. I imagine that the chance of needing to work with a school might be pretty good.

*Supervisor:* Great, let's focus on that. First off, why would you approach a school for information about a client?

*Trainee:* Well, I believe that additional information would help me help the child. I guess the specifics would vary with the individual client, but I might need to find out about academic performance, or any trouble the child has in the classroom, or whether he or she has trouble making friends—it seems as if a teacher would know a lot of that information.

*Supervisor:* All right. so you're thinking about talking with a teacher or teachers who work with the child. Is there anyone else you might want to consult?

*Trainee:* Well, I might want to see the school counselor or school pyschologist, especially if the child has had any psychological or cognitive asssessments done.

*Supervisor:* Good. Now, how do you think your approach might change if the school had actually referred the child to you?

*Trainee:* Oh. Well, I haven't thought about that very much. In some situations I suppose I might need to report some things back to them, if I had the permission I needed from the child's family. My feedback to the school would be limited to information necessary for them to help the child.

*Supervisor:* Okay. One thing that is important to keep in mind is that you want to form a collaborative working relationship with anyone you consult with in the school. Both of you need to agree to share information that is helpful and useful, with the permission you were talking about, of course. Also, you want to approach this as colleagues working together, with neither of you assuming an expert role.

*Trainee:* Yes, I can see that. To be the most help to the client, we would really need to work together and respect each other's input.

*Supervisor:* Good. Well, why don't we go ahead and do a role-play with this. I'll serve as the teacher, and you can initiate contact with me regarding the child. Before we start, what do you imagine might be factors for this teacher?

*Trainee:* Well, for one thing, she has lots of kids to think about, so this individual child may not be as central for her as for me, since I would be working with him or her on an individual basis. . . . Also, I imagine the teacher would have a different focus, with an emphasis on learning and the disruption of learning, whereas I'd be attending to the child's emotional state. But I also believe we would both have the best interests of the child in mind, including the child's successful performance in the school environment, so that should allow us to work together fairly well.

*Supervisor:* That's good. It's important to keep in mind that the client isn't the only person of importance in a given setting. I'm glad to see you're sensitive to some of the demands a teacher might be facing. Let's go ahead and do the role-play now.

*[They conduct a brief role-play.]*

*Supervisor:* So, what did you think of that experience?

*Trainee:* Boy, there is a lot of information I might get from a school about a client! In only a few minutes, I was feeling as if there was so much stuff to talk about.

*Supervisor:* What does that mean for you when you think about how you might prepare for an actual meeting with school personnel?

*Trainee:* Well, first of all, I'd definitely need to know in advance what kind of information I needed from them.

*Supervisor:* Yes, and it would probably help if you knew as much as you could about the school itself, because a lot of time could be spent just talking about the structure of class time and stuff like that.

*Trainee:* Good point.

*Supervisor:* Okay, now how might you go about preparing for your school visit?

*Trainee:* Well, I could start by getting some information from my client, so that I'd know where to begin. Then I could develop a list of questions to ask the teacher or school counselor, so that it would be more efficient.

And if I could, I'd find another graduate student who has worked at that school so I could have that information in my head.

*Supervisor:* Good. Those are likely to be helpful strategies.

*Trainee:* Yeah. It's probably going to be a little more complex than I was thinking originally.

*Supervisor:* That's true. And keep in mind, you might also have other options, like visiting the school while your client is there, or getting written reports to help round out the information. There are a lot of things to consider, but I think you've made a good start on recognizing some of the issues involved.

In this segment, the supervisor has relied on supervision strategies 14 (encourage trainee brainstorming of strategies and interventions), 5 (explain the rationale behind specific strategies and interventions), and 16 (solicit and attempt to satisfy trainee needs during the session). Additional information on interviewing school personnel can be found in Sattler (1988). After answering any final questions, the supervisor closes the session.

## WEEK B-5. SETTING THE PROBLEM

### Class

*Objectives:*
*1. Foster the students' development of the ability to formulate a client problem.*

The instructor reminds students to attend to the case conceptualization models previously presented. Information from actual cases is then presented to the class, and if possible, session segments are shown on tape. One case should involve an individual client and the other a school or other agency client. One way to provide videotape demonstrations is to ask the students designated to present cases in class that day, to present their cases at that point.

Students are divided into small groups and asked to set problems to be addressed in therapy, based on the guidelines provided in the second section of the case conceptualization model. Groups report back to the class at the end of the exercise and suggest the nature of the initial contract.

### Supervision With Trainees Together

*Objectives:*
*1. Provide appropriate feedback to students about their clients.*
*2. Encourage students' skill at problem setting with their own cases.*

After trainees have checked in and indicated concerns they have with their clients, they are asked to provide all available information and show tapes. Feedback is given by both the supervisor and the other trainee as appropriate, and then the counselor trainee is encouraged to set a problem according to the model. The other trainee provides assistance, as does the supervisor. The process is then repeated with the second trainee. Applicable beginning supervision strategies as well as advanced supervision strategy 19 (help the trainee conceptualize a case), and perhaps advanced supervision strategies 20 (explore the trainee's feelings to facilitate understanding of the client) and 21 (encourage the trainee's identification and use of cues in the client's and the therapist's behavior) are used. Other advanced strategies are used when appropriate.

*To illustrate:*

*[This situation follows a discussion of a trainee's videotape and issues the trainee has presented.]*

*Supervisor:* So do you feel satisfied with our feedback for right now?

*Trainee 1:* Yes. . . . We can go on.

*Supervisor:* Let's look at this case from the perspective discussed in class. Let's go through a formal process of setting the problem. Remind us of your client's presenting problem and reason for seeking assistance now.

*Trainee 1:* As you know, this is a new client for me, and my first from the community. He came in because his last girlfriend left him after about 6 months and he was devastated. He describes a pattern of getting involved with women, being very emotionally attached, and then feeling crushed when they leave. He says he has had a particularly hard time with this one because he runs into her often at work. He also says he shuts down more after each loss because it hurts so much and he doesn't want to get hurt again.

*Trainee 2:* What led to the break-up?

*Trainee 1:* He's not really sure. He said she just told him she wasn't getting what she needed in the relationship and ended it. He was really surprised.

*Supervisor:* Is that a pattern?

*Trainee 1:* I don't know. What I do know is that he grew up in a military family, and they were always getting transferred to some new place, and he never seemed to know when that was coming. He says that one time he came down to breakfast and his parents said, "You're not going to school today. We're moving."

*Trainee 2:* Wow! That would be awful!

*Supervisor:* That does sound pretty traumatic. Part of his cultural background is simply the military culture, then, with set rules of behavior but uncertainty about how long relationships would last.

*Trainee 1:* Yeah. The other thing that has been helpful for him in that situation but also has complicated things since is his race. Like me, he is African American, and he has strong family ties, especially to his mother. In the military there were a number of other African American families, and he was part of a community. He had a lot of Black friends on the base, and even when he went to school off the base in predominantly White schools, he always had the base to return to and a social structure in which he felt part of the group. At the same time, he learned, especially when he was in the South, to be wary of Whites.

*Supervisor:* So he had some history of social oppression and discrimination, as all African Americans do, probably in the military as well as outside. But he did have a normative, middle-class military group wherever he was

*Trainee 1:* Yeah, and that helped him form a rather solid identity as a person and as a man.

*Trainee 2:* It doesn't sound that different from your background, even though you grew up outside the military.

*Trainee 1:* Yeah, in some ways. But I came from a more communicative family. I mean, my family would never have waited to tell me we were moving on the day that we moved. Still, he does have a strong sense of family. Now he's here, though, and his family is 500 miles away. And this isn't a community with a lot of African Americans in it, and his last two relationships have been with European American women.

*Supervisor:* So how has it been for him to be in this community without many others with racial backgrounds like his?

*Trainee 1:* It's been tough. On the one hand, he works hard just the way his dad did, and they like him at his job. But he is cautious about relationships with Whites.

*Trainee 2:* Sure. And in this society, that makes sense. I'm sometimes surprised just how racist people can be in this supposedly liberal, educated, university town.

*Supervisor:* I agree. How do you sort out what is appropriate caution in relationships and what level of reserve actually interferes with his getting what he wants?

*Trainee 1:* Well, I think it makes sense for him to be wary initially. It takes a while to know when hidden racism is going to show up, even when you think it's not there. But he had been with this woman for months, and nothing he has said about her has indicated that racism was an issue between them.

*Trainee 2:* You know, I'm struck by what you said as we began talking. You said he withdraws each time he gets hurt. How do you feel when you're around him? I mean, do you feel as if you are at a distance, even though you share a racial background?

*Trainee 1:* Well, of course we've only met a couple of times. But yes, I have the feeling he doesn't want to get very involved with me. I feel pretty distant, as if I may never connect with him. For one thing, he almost never looks at me.

*Supervisor:* So one hypothesis might be that the client so fears rejection, he doesn't offer much in a relationship, and then no one really connects with him.

*Trainee 1:* Yeah.

*Supervisor:* And what are his strengths in relating?

*Trainee 1:* Well, you know, he came right in the first time and shook my hand and introduced himself before I'd even finished saying my name. So he knows how to start relationships with people. And he's pretty forthcoming as long as the topic isn't very personal. But as soon as I ask him about his feelings, he gets very quiet.

*Supervisor:* So you hypothesize what?

*Trainee 1:* Well, probably that he never learned to talk about feelings as a kid or that when he did, he was cut off because the family had to get on with other things.

*Supervisor:* Sure. And what's the situation where he works now?

*Trainee 1:* Well, he works at a high-tech firm where they are developing silicon chips. I can't imagine that is exactly a touchy-feely environment!

*Trainee 2:* No. In fact, I worked over there last summer and it was like the home of the automatons. I never did tell them I was studying psychology.

*Trainee 1:* Yeah. Even though they have a good insurance program, he thinks it would be risky to ask for insurance benefits for mental health, and in fact, their visits are pretty limited. That's why he came in here to our training clinic—because we have low fees and the possibility of as many visits as he might want.

*Supervisor:* So what do you hypothesize the problem is?

*Trainee 1:* I think he has never learned how to open up and talk about feelings in a way that helps a relationship develop, and he's afraid to, but at the same time he is starved for an affectionate relationship.

*Supervisor:* Makes sense. You've got a lot of hypotheses here that you will want to check out. Inevitably, you will confirm some and find you need to change others and develop new hypotheses.

*Trainee:* I suppose so.

*Supervisor:* Tell me a little about your initial contract with him.

*Trainee 1:* Right now he's just agreed to come in and talk about his problem. He hasn't asked for any specific techniques and he hasn't mentioned any time limits, so I have decided just to build a relationship with him and work from there.

*Supervisor:* Yes, it will take time to for you both to decide whether to work at a symptomatic level or at a deeper level—or some combination of the two.

In this vignette, the supervisor has worked with the trainee to set the problem by exploring both information about the client and information about the counselor's reaction to the client. Hypotheses have been developed, and the supervisor has reminded the trainee that hypotheses and a contract to work at a specific level are likely to be modified as therapy proceeds.

## WEEK B-6. DEVELOPING CHANGE THEORY AND GOALS FOR A CLIENT

### Class

*Objectives:*
1. *Apply theories of human change to a client issue.*
2. *Introduce new interventions designed to promote client action and change.*
3. *Present the selection of a change strategy and specific goals for change as part of case planning.*

In the class period, the instructor briefly revisits the idea of basic theories of change introduced in week B-1. Then the instructor introduces the idea of selecting a particular change strategy as part of case conceptualization. When it is consistent with the preferred theoretical orientation, the instructor presents new interventions, such as modeling, behavior rehearsal, relaxation training, and cognitive restructuring, as potential action skills (Hill & O'Brien, 1999). The instructor elaborates the decision points in goal setting and treatment planning, and illustrates the application of goal-setting strategies to several cases.

Following this introduction, the trainees form small groups. Each group is presented with client information (from an intake or other source) and asked to apply Section III of the case conceptualization model (develop change strategy) to that client, based on the information presented. Trainees are asked to consider how their own theories of change suggest working with this client, the possible use of action skills to promote change, the importance of matching the client and the change strategy, selection of arenas for change, definition of the therapist's and client's responsibilities in the process, and challenges that might be expected in the course of working with this client in this setting. Finally, the group is asked to develop some outcome goals for this client, by thinking about what they hope the client will come to understand and change during counseling. Students are encouraged to pay attention to the possibility that their own values may influence how they approach the client to set goals.

Group supervision of trainees' cases follows, with an emphasis on the contributions and training of all class members. With each case, the instructor asks the trainee to present a change strategy for the client.

## Individual Supervision

*Objectives:*
1. *Use the trainee's change theory to develop goals for a current client.*
2. *Encourage the trainee to incorporate some action strategies into their plan.*
3. *Supervise any case the trainee may present.*

The supervisor begins by checking in with the trainee briefly. During the next portion of the supervision session (65 minutes), the supervisor and trainee will discuss one client in terms of change strategies and goal setting, similar to the group experience in class. New action interventions will be identified when appropriate, and incorporated at the end. Advanced supervision strategies indicated during this portion include strategies 18 (encourage trainee's exploration of change theory), 19 (help the trainee conceptualize a case), and 23 (help the trainee assess compatibility between in-session behavior and theory of change). Other advanced and beginning supervision strategies can be used as appropriate.

*To illustrate:*

*[In this situation, the trainee has seen the client several times and is having a difficult time deciding how to work with him.]*

*Supervisor:* So, you started working with change strategies and goal setting this week in class. How would you like to apply that information today?

*Trainee:* I think it would be useful for me to try to think about Joe from that perspective. I have a hard time figuring our what my plan is when I work with him, and I think that this approach might give me some help with it.

*Supervisor:* Okay. Sounds good. I'm happy you want to challenge yourself with this, and I think it can be very helpful. Why don't you start by telling me a little bit about how you think of Joe and change?

*Trainee:* All right. . . . I guess that's the hard part, in a way. It's hard for me to see Joe changing very much, for some reason.

*Supervisor:* Well, maybe it'll help to step back a minute. Why don't you think first about the aspects of change that you've already identified as important, and then we'll work on applying those to your work with Joe.

*Trainee:* Well, we've talked about that before, but I think the sort of core ideas I keep coming back to are becoming easier for me to understand and work with. I generally believe that people can change if they're given a lot of support, if they have a clear goal or at least enough of a goal to have a definite direction, and if they are able to see themselves as powerful enough to create some change. I think my role is to offer support and to empower clients so that they can see themselves as able to effect change, and I can also help clarify client goals and directions.

*Supervisor:* Okay. There are several important ideas in that core group. Are there other things you want to add to that?

*Trainee:* Well, when I hear myself say that, it sounds pretty vague, maybe too general to be real counseling. But I can't think of anything else right now.

*Supervisor:* That's fine. As we start to apply this theory to Joe, you may come up with more specific things you want to add. You said that it's hard for you to think of Joe's changing. What has Joe said he wants to change?

*Trainee:* He wants to change two things: his job and his relationship.

*Supervisor:* Those are two broad changes! How can you make them more specific?

*Trainee:* Well, he feels as if right now he is in a rut at work, and he's very tired of the bookkeeping work he's been doing. He seems to want to move into more of a management position, but doesn't really know how to go about doing that.

*Supervisor:* All right. It sounds as if Joe wants to change, and probably feels motivated to change, regarding work, but doesn't have a very clear direction. Now, has Joe actually said he wants to move into management?

*Trainee:* Not in those exact words. But the work he describes wanting to do is definitely management. . . . I guess I haven't really asked him that directly. We mostly talk about how he's dissatisfied with the work he's doing now.

*Supervisor:* Well, that's an important thing to recognize. How would you apply the three ideas crucial to your theory of change to this specific concern of Joe's?

*Trainee:* I'm not sure if I know what you mean.

*Supervisor:* Well, for example, let's start with support. How much support does Joe have to change his work situation?

*Trainee:* Oh, I see. Not very much, really. He has a family to support and they are worried about him giving up a sure job with a decent income. Also, most of his friends work at about the same level as he does, and they don't encourage him to move up. So really, his support is limited. I guess that's a good place for me to start. I can offer support for his goals. And, I guess that takes me to the second issue. He has goals, but they're still pretty vague. It would be important for me to help him clarify those and make sure we both understand them so that we can work together to set specific counseling goals. If I'm thinking he wants to move into management, but we never actually clarify that, it's not a very effective use of our time.

*Supervisor:* Great! I'm glad you can see ways that your response can increase the value of counseling. Now you've covered two of the basic components of your theory of change. What about the issue of empowerment?

*Trainee:* That's a little tougher. Joe must feel somewhat empowered, because he is thinking about changing his work situation, but probably not enough to do anything at this point.

*Supervisor:* Based on that, What might be an initial change strategy?

*Trainee:* Working on ways to help Joe feel more empowered—enough to be able to effect some change. And maybe we could even look at whether he feels entitled to have a higher career position. Perhaps I could work with him on cognitive restructuring.

*Supervisor:* Sure. So now you've really identified a strategy for change. It includes helping Joe clarify his career goals, offering support for those goals, and increasing Joe's sense of empowerment through cognitive restructuring. Does that sound consistent with your theory of change?

*Trainee:* Yes, definitely.

*Supervisor:* All right, then. How does that match with Joe and his current situation?

*Trainee:* Well, it does seem appropriate for the goal that he has, of changing his job situation. It will also fit well within the time limits we are working with, or at least I think it will. None of these things violate anything specific to Joe's cultural background—I know he's talked about his family of origin and their career expectations and achievements, and that feels consistent with what we're talking about. There will probably be some conflict with his family about actually moving to a different job, as I was saying, so dealing with that will need to be a part of our counseling process.

*Supervisor:* And you will need to pay attention to determine whether your belief about his making his own career choices conflicts with any value that Joe might have about his family's coming first. The idea of personal fulfillment is a particularly strong value in European American culture but may conflict with others' cultural or personal values.

*Trainee:* Yeah, I suppose so. That's such an ingrained idea in me that I seldom even notice it as a value.

*Supervisor:* Sure. Now what can you say about the interaction of Joe's personal characteristics with this problem?

*Trainee:* Well, as I was saying at the beginning, it's sort of hard for me to see Joe changing much. I don't know if that's because of his personality or because I was feeling as if I didn't know where we were heading. That's something I'll check out now that I have more of a plan to explore with Joe.

*Supervisor:* Good. That also brings up another important point. Our process and brainstorming is very important, and crucial to supervision, but it won't mean very much if Joe isn't involved. It is very important for the two of you to talk about this and decide whether it fits and who is responsible for what aspects of the strategies you'll be using.

*Trainee:* Yes, I understand that. I think that my responsibilities will be very consistent with my theory. I feel as if I'm responsible for helping Joe clarify his goals, but not for setting them. Also, I can offer support and encouragement, but I can't necessarily give Joe all the support he'll want. He'll have to work on feeling more confident and empowered, with my assistance.

*Supervisor:* Okay. That sounds like a good balance, and a good place to start as you and Joe form an agreement. What about challenges? What do you imagine are some of the obstacles you might face with this strategy?

*Trainee:* Well, there are likely to be times when Joe is very discouraged especially as his current work is increasing his unhappiness. Also, with today's employment patterns, Joe may have a hard time moving up in management regardless of his personal confidence and ability. So, there will definitely be some societal issues to deal with, in addition to some of the family stuff that might feel discouraging at times.

*Supervisor:* Good. I'm glad to see that you're keeping the social environment in mind and acknowledging the context in which Joe lives. Those are all possible challenges, and I'm sure there may be others as well. Let's move on to outcomes. What would you like for Joe to accomplish before the end of counseling?

*Trainee:* Well, regarding work, I'd like him to feel that he has options and doesn't have to stay in a job that makes him unhappy. I think it's important for him to have clear goals and believe that he can move toward those goals in a focused way. If he actually were able to make a job change, that would be great, but I don't think it has to happen for the counseling to be successful. It's probably more important that he be able to start doing things that move him toward a better job and act with a more definite goal in mind.

*Supervisor:* It sounds like you may want to incorporate more of the new action skills you discussed this week.

*Trainee:* Yes, probably.

*Supervisor:* All right. You'll have a lot of important information to share with Joe in your next session regarding work. Once you've done that, and the two of you have come to further agreement, you can begin to consider more specific ways of addressing these changes. Why don't we look more closely now at his relationship concerns?

Although this illustration is abbreviated, it demonstrates several important aspects of planning change strategies for working with a given client. This same technique could be applied to any client, using any theory of change. The supervisor has helped the trainee apply a theory of change to this client in a systematic way. This approach has assisted the trainee to understand the client's issues and plan a more effective strategy for setting goals and reaching the desired outcome. When appropriate, new action skills have been identified as part of the change process, and the trainee and the supervisor rehearse their implementation at the end of this discussion.

In the remainder of the supervision session (20 minutes), the supervisor asks the trainee to show a videotape of any other client. Before the segment is shown, the trainee is asked to reflect on the ways a theory of change influences the sessions. Then they both watch the videotape. The supervisor stops it to ask about the trainee's feelings and intentions, relating them to a theory of change when appropriate.

At the completion of viewing the tape, the supervisor asks the trainee to summarize the session, and they close.

# WEEK B-7. USING THE RELATIONSHIP TO EFFECT CHANGE

## Class

*Objectives:*
1. *Revisit the nature of the therapuetic relationship (including transference and countertransference.)*
2. *Develop ideas for working within the relationship to effect change.*

This lesson depends on the instructor's preferred theoretical orientation. In a psychoanalytic or other dynamic orientation, the dynamics of the personal relationship are primary topics of discussion. In a behavioral counseling relationship, and in Hill and O'Brien's (1999) three-stage model new behaviors are practiced. In either case, the instructor must assist students to address issues within the therapeutic relationship that mimic those that clients have in life. It is recommended that students who present cases this week highlight relationship issues in the segments they show to the class.

## Supervision With Trainees Together

*Objectives:*
1. *Respond to case material in terms of its compatibility with trainees' theories of change.*
2. *Assist trainees to address issues within the therapeutic relationship.*

As they provide feedback on cases presented by trainees, supervisors refer to the trainees' theories of change and help them assess their behavior in session accordingly. In addition, supervisors attend to the therapeutic relationship. They ask trainess about the problems clients have in general in relationships and point out where the clients repeat these patterns in the therapeutic relationship. Both trainees and the supervisor work together to develop responses, consistent with the trainees' theories of change, that are different from those that clients usually encounter in life. Advanced supervision strategies 22 (explore the trainee's intentions in a session), 23 (help trainee assess compatibility between in-session behavior and theory of change), 20 (explore the trainee's feelings to facilitate understanding of the client), and 21 (encourage the trainee's identification and use of cues in the client's and the therapist's behavior) may be used.

*To illustrate attention to the therapeutic relationship:*

*[In this situation, the first trainee has shown a videotape segment that exemplifies relationship difficulties on the job.]*

*Trainee 1:* I am really frustrated with him. He continues to put himself in terrible relationships no matter how much we've talked about it. Now he has a new job where the boss criticizes his every move and even though he complains about it, he also talks about how he is attracted to her.

*Supervisor:* Yes. . . . Tell us something about your feelings when you started out with him.

*Trainee 1:* When we started, I was pretty excited to work with him. He seemed to have a lot of insight about himself and be highly motivated to work on his problems. As you may recall, he said his last therapist was quite hostile to him, and I felt that I could show him another response.

*Supervisor:* So you initially hypothesized that you could work together well. And how were you feeling during the part of the last session that you showed?

*Trainee 1:* I suppose I was quite frustrated. Maybe I felt hostile too. I guess that hypothesis has gone down the drain! I don't really understand how he can keep doing the same things over and over. You know, when he talked about taking this job I was uneasy about it. Now it's turning into the same old stuff, and he's in a crisis, likely to lose his job or have an affair with the boss or both! And I could just shake him! But I don't. . . . I try to stay patient.

*Trainee 2:* You know, when I watched you, I could see how hard you were working at remaining calm. You're obviously aware of some of the ethical components of the problem at work. Yet, you didn't criticize him . . . but you didn't smile much either, the way you usually do with people.

*Trainee 1:* Yeah, you're right.

*Trainee 2:* And there was a place where you were just a tiny bit sarcastic, you know, when you said, "Well, of course you feel sexual tension!"

*Supervisor:* I felt that too, Trainee 2. What's your sense of that, Trainee 1?

*Trainee 1:* I wasn't aware of it then. I thought I was bringing in a little humor. But now that you mention it, I think that's how it came across. But what can I do when he goes on in that crisis mode?

*Supervisor:* This is pretty difficult stuff. It's hard to see yourself in the first place, much less figure out how to change. It seems to me that he has gotten you to respond to him just the way everyone else does. He is showing you his standard behavior pattern. He started out with a therapeutically seductive style—the perfect client who really needs what you can offer. And you were charmed. Then he acts in his same old way and doesn't use anything that you have given him—and presto—what happens?

*Trainee 1:* Oh, I see. I get frustrated with him and feel critical and want to "shake him" or to withdraw from the whole thing.

*Supervisor:* Yeah.

*Trainee 2:* I don't blame you—I'd feel that way too.

*Supervisor:* Of course. He's very good at eliciting those feelings! The trick is to respond to him in a way that's different from his past experiences and help him to see the pattern. That's part of your commitment to provide competent treatment.

*Trainee 1:* I agree, but I'm not sure where to start.

*Supervisor:* Think a bit about that. What were all of you discussing in class this week? Do you have any ideas, Trainee 2?

*Trainee 2:* I don't know . . . well, maybe if you just talked to him about what was happening.

*Trainee 1:* Well, I can't just say "I'm so frustrated that I want to shake you!"

*Supervisor: [Laughs]* No. . . .

*Trainee 1:* I suppose that I could say something about our relationship. I mean, maybe I could say something like, "When we started to work together, I was really excited about it. Now I find myself getting pretty discouraged."

*Supervisor:* You're on the right track. Trainee 2, how might you modify that?

*Trainee 2:* Maybe something to highlight the relationship between you . . . but I'm not sure how to say that.

*Trainee 1:* That's where I'm stuck, too.

*Supervisor:* Well, look at what has happened. What if you said something like, "When we started out, we were both pretty hopeful that therapy would work this time. And now we're both a bit discouraged, and we don't seem to have the same hope and I, at least, feel more distant from you. How do you think we got into this fix?" That highlights what's happening between you and encourages him to address it along with you.

*Trainee 1:* Yeah, I could do that. It doesn't feel so critical when you say that.

*Supervisor:* Remember, though, to use words that are natural to you. How does this seem to you, Trainee 2?

*Trainee 2:* It seems right. I think you could get a dialogue going with that. At least it would make the session different and not just a repeat of the same old stuff!

*Supervisor:* Be aware that when you move into this area, you are talking about more than a symptomatic change, and so you will need to check out with your client how it feels to be talking about your relationship.

In this example, the supervisor explored the trainee's feeling about the client and the relationship, encouraged the second trainee to add to the discussion, and waited until the dynamics were clear before moving to potential interventions. The supervisor highlighted the ethical dimensions. The trainee is reminded that working on the way that this client relates to people in general may require an explicit contract with the client to work at a deeper rather than at a symptomatic level.

## WEEK B-8. UNDERSTANDING THE COURSE OF CHANGE FOR CLIENTS

### Class

*Objectives:*
1. *Present an outline for the course of change that incorporates all change strategies to date.*
2. *Help students recognize small changes that indicate progress.*

The instructor talks with the class about the nature of change and ways it is likely to be manifested within the theoretical approach taken in the course. Students are asked to consider a particular case and anticipate the path of change. Examples are solicited from the class and provided by the instructor as the group considers the modest changes that occur at first. Students are reminded of the challenges they anticipated when they conceptualized the case. Students who present cases are asked to emphasize where change has or has not occurred as anticipated.

### Individual Supervision

*Objectives:*
1. *Provide feedback on counseling sessions.*
2. *Highlight instances of client change and identify likely precipitants of that change.*
3. *Respond to trainees' frustration with the slow pace of change.*
4. *Practice any strategies the trainee wishes to improve and discuss how the trainee feels when using them.*

In this individual session, the trainee presents a case and shows a section of videotape. The supervisor encourages the trainee to structure the supervision meeting (supervision strategy 17) and, as usual, to state what is needed in the way of feedback, discussion, and assistance. When possible, the supervisor highlights elements of change.

*To illustrate:*

*[In this situation, the male trainee has just shown a discussion with the female client in which she has complained that they really have no relationship because "you are just my therapist; you aren't in my life."]*

*Supervisor:* That must have been a difficult session for you, but you handled it very well.

*Trainee:* Thanks. I felt pretty good about staying calm and open—and not panicking when she said she could only feel close if we could have a physical relationship.

*Supervisor:* Yeah. That was real progress for you! I know you have noticed her desire in the past and felt quite uncomfortable about it. Then when you asked her about what was going on between you this time, she just came right out with it. I was kind of surprised, and yet you didn't bat an eye. You just asked her how it felt to tell you that.

*Trainee:* Yes. I have to admit I didn't feel as calm as I looked.

*Supervisor:* And you did a nice job of stating the ethical and professional boundaries when you said later, "How is it for you to be talking to me and knowing that we will not have a physical relationship?"

*Trainee:* Yeah. I think I've made a lot of progress this term! But I have to tell you, I am pretty discouraged with her progress. I mean, I stated the boundaries firmly about 3 months ago, and she keeps coming back to it.

*Supervisor:* What did you anticipate would be happening by now?

*Trainee:* I thought she'd be beyond trying to seduce me—or test me—on this and would be moving in the direction of forming relationships with men in her life. But she still sits at home and thinks about how lonely she is. She doesn't make any moves to have the relationships she can have.

*Supervisor:* Sure. But think about it. What's her history of talking about what's happening in relationships between her and her family or her and anyone close?

*Trainee:* She's never done it.

*Supervisor:* And how was she with you when you first asked about what was happening in your relationship with her?

*Trainee:* Oh! I see what you mean. She used to change the subject or attack me or bring up some crisis whenever I raised the topic. This time she carried out a whole discussion with me about how she felt in our relationship. That is a change. I guess she'd have to learn to do that with me before she could start developing new relationships that would be different from those in her past.

*Supervisor:* Sure. It's natural for you to want to see progress. And you do see progress. Remember, it took 35 years for her to get the way she was when she first came in! If you get this much change in her behavior with you in 3 months, you are really moving!

In this vignette, the supervisor responded to the counselor's increased skill and then moved to his concern with his client's apparent lack of progress. The supervisor emphasized specific elements of change while reiterating that personality change takes time.

After going over the trainee's case, the supervisor invites the trainee to practice any interventions the trainee believes need further work. The supervisor asks the trainee how it feels to use the strategies. Together they consider their appropriateness or timing for use with any current clients.

## WEEK B-9. TERMINATING: PREPARATION AND COMPLETION

### Class

*Objectives:*
1. *Present information on how to prepare for termination.*
2. *Demonstrate a procedure for termination.*
3. *Provide group supervision on selected cases.*

The class instructor provides didactic material about termination procedures, alternatives, and issues. Two advanced students or an advanced student and a supervisor demonstrate a termination session. A videotape of an actual termination session may be useful. They highlight issues of client readiness to terminate and problems associated with termination brought about by the restrictions of the training setting (for example, terminating because the term is ending).

Group supervision emphasizes termination preparation, if appropriate, and proceeds as usual.

### Supervision With Trainees Together

Because trainees may be at different stages with respect to termination with their clients, this supervision session is set up to cover two possible situations: preparing for termination and processing termination. If a trainee is preparing to terminate earlier in the term, section one of this session can be used at that time. Likewise, section two of this session can be used at a later time if appropriate.

After a brief check-in with both trainees, the supervisor will implement one or both of the following procedures.

*Preparing to terminate.* This section emphasizes supervision strategies 6 (interpret significant events in the counseling session), 8 (explore trainee feelings during the supervision session), 12 (provide opportunities for trainee to process his or her own affect and defenses), and 21 (encourage the trainee's identification and use of cues in the client's and the therapist's behavior).

In the first part of the session (30 minutes), the supervisor watches the tape of the previous counseling session and focuses on the client's apparent readiness for termination. The following signals described by Kanfer and Schefft (1988) may be helpful guidelines:

1. *The client's attendance in therapy is inconsistent. This may be demonstrated by missed sessions, late arrival, or frequent attempts to reschedule.*
2. *Client brings up no significant issues.*
3. *Client challenges necessity for or does not complete homework.*
4. *Client shows lack of engagement in therapy.*

In addition, some of the following behaviors may signal readiness: clients report a reduction of presenting symptoms; client goals differ from therapist goals; client initiates discussion of termination. The trainee and supervisor discuss the client's readiness and the trainee's readiness to terminate or, if appropriate, whether the trainee would choose to terminate if time limits were not an issue. In many training and service settings, termination must proceed regardless of the presence of readiness signals from the client.

In this second part of the supervision session, the supervisor reviews specific procedures.

*To illustrate:*

*Supervisor:* Let's review the termination procedures that were discussed in class. Which procedures could you use in a termination session?

*Trainee 1:* Well, I think I could ask my client what reaction she had to termination and I could listen to what she says without being defensive. I'd probably have a harder time expressing my feelings without going overboard.

*Supervisor:* What would going overboard mean to you? Tell me what that would look like?

*Trainee 1:* Well, let's see. Maybe I'd try too hard to let my client know that I felt sad about leaving too—especially since it's sort of an artificial ending. Even though we've known all along that there were time limits, it seems unfinished.

*Trainee 2:* You and Rebecca are just now starting to make some progress with her boyfriend problems, and now you have to quit!

*Supervisor:* Yeah. I can understand your distress. It is a frustrating situation. Aside from the unnatural aspect of this specific termination, are you worried about going overboard?

*Trainee 1:* No. I think I just feel frustrated now that things are going so well with Rebecca.

*Supervisor:* That makes a lot of sense.

*Trainee 2:* You know, this isn't coming as a surprise to Rebecca. You've reached the end of the time you agreed to work together.

*Supervisor:* Yes. How do you think the knowledge that you are ending soon might have been affecting Rebecca?

*Trainee 1:* Well, we have talked about termination before, and I think she's sad to be ending.

*Trainee 2:* You know, it seems to me that she has started to talk more positively about her issues now. Maybe the fact that you'll be ending counseling has something to do with that.

*Supervisor:* That is possible—in fact, it's not at all uncommon for client issues to improve as termination approaches, even if termination doesn't depend on improvement. Of course, it's also true that client concerns can become greater, especially if they feel unprepared to terminate. You might need to check out just how prepared Rebecca is feeling, and do that pretty explicitly.

*Trainee 1:* That makes sense. Maybe I'm just assuming she feels bad about it, when she's actually getting prepared to end. . . . I would like for termination to be a positive experience for her.

*Supervisor:* What are some ways you could make termination positive and extend her growth in the areas you and Rebecca have addressed in your time together?

*Trainee 1:* I really liked the idea of sending the client off with a plan for continued growth.

*Trainee 2:* Yeah.

*Supervisor:* Can you give me an example of a plan that might be helpful for Rebecca?

*Trainee 1:* Well, I'd like her to finish reading the book we were using.

*Supervisor:* That's good. It's important that you check with her, however, on how valuable she finds reading the book.

*Trainee 2:* I think she'd benefit from some group work in the future. What do you think?

*Trainee 1:* That might be a good idea. I'll talk with her about the possibility.

The supervisor repeats this exercise with the other trainee. Then the supervisor takes the next 20 minutes to describe a specific termination procedure in which client and counselor provide each other with feedback about the counseling experience. After that, the supervisor addresses the counselor's responsibilities in termination. He or she reminds counselors to present their own evaluations of client progress to clients. Included in this assessment are client strengths and the kind of work the clients have done that demonstrates their ability to make good use of therapy now and possibly in the future.

The supervisor explains that following discussion of client progress, the counselor should ask the client to evaluate the counseling experience. Some trainees are ready to solicit feedback directly from clients about their counseling experience. For the trainee's first termination experience, however, a counselor may use a pencil and paper assessment outcome evaluation form. This can provide the trainee with useful information in a relatively nonthreatening way. For subsequent termination experiences, the counselor would be expected to ask directly for the client's feedback about what was helpful and difficult in therapy.

At this point, the supervisor takes 30 minutes to do a brief role-play of termination with the trainees. The remaining time is used to explore the trainees' feelings about termination in general, about termination with these clients, and about potential issues associated with termination of supervision.

*Processing termination.* Because this section may need to be added to an existing supervision session when termination occurs, it is one 30-minute exercise to be used as needed. The supervisor uses the following supervision strategies and explores the trainee's success with and feelings about the termination experience:

- Supervision strategy 6 (interpret significant events in the counseling session): How do you think the client felt about termination? How do you think the client reacted to the suggestions for future work?
- Supervision strategy 7 (explore trainee feelings during the counseling session): How were you feeling as you said good-bye to the client? How did you work with those feelings in the counseling session?
- Supervision strategy 8 (explore trainee feelings during the supervision session): How do you feel now that you've ended with this client? What are you feeling as we talk about not seeing this client again?
- Supervision strategy 10 (encourage trainee self-exploration of confidence and worries in the counseling session): How did it go? What went well? What will you do differently next time?

In closing the session, the supervisor asks the trainees for their feelings regarding their work in supervision. The supervisor follows their statements with a reminder that supervision will terminate at some point in the near future as well. This models the termination process and allows the trainees to reflect on the issue for themselves.

## WEEK B-10. LEARNING CONCEPTUALIZATION AND COUNSELING FOR SOCIAL SKILLS NEEDS

### Class

*Objectives:*
1. *Apply the case conceptualization model to social skills building.*
2. *Provide group supervision that applies the model to current clinical cases.*

The instructor discusses the application of the case conceptualization model to social skills building. Student's knowledge of social skills training is solicited. If they offer little here, the instructor can describe basic communication skills (e.g., teaching the use of I-statements) and assertiveness skills as well as cognitive behavioral social training and limit setting. Gambrill and Richey (1985) and Hollin and Trower (1988) have offered useful information. The modeling and behavior rehearsal strategies identified by Hill and O'Brien (1999) may also be appropriate

Group supervision is provided for case presentations and videotapes, with special attention to social skills issues presented by clients.

### Individual Supervision

*Objectives:*
1. *Check-in with attention to concerns with ongoing clients.*
2. *Practice the social skills procedures presented in lecture.*

During the first half of the supervision session (45 minutes), client videotapes are viewed and supervision is offered as appropriate. It is particularly important to pay attention to issues of termination, in terms of both trainee and client feelings.

After responding to case presentations, the supervisor uses the second half of the session to do one or two role-plays with the trainee. In the approach most effective for learning, a trainee plays a client he or she is currently counseling. After the trainee presents the client's initial concerns, the supervisor interrupts the role-play and invites the trainee to conceptualize the case with possible interventions and plans for treatment. Supervision strategies 3 (identify appropriate interventions), 14 (encourage trainee brainstorming of strategies), and 9 (explore trainee feelings concerning specific techniques or interventions) are emphasized. The role-play continues and incorporates some of the planned interventions.

*To illustrate:*

*[This discussion might occur after the role-play experience in which the trainee acted as counselor.]*

*Supervisor:* You did a nice job of introducing me, your client, to the idea of using I-statements. I was very aware of how supportive and nonjudgmental you were, even though you were giving me some very specific information about changing my behavior.

*Trainee:* Thanks. That's good to hear. A few times I felt like I was being too directive—in some ways, I was doing counseling in a way that isn't very natural to me.

*Supervisor:* That's easy to understand. When you start to apply your method of conceptualizing a case, or your change theory, to very specific issues, it can feel a little artificial at first. But, I think you did a good job with that—I felt that you were genuine during the role-play.

*Trainee:* Good. . . . You know, I guess I always think of social skills counseling as being pretty basic, maybe even easy. Like, just helping people learn to be more comfortable in social situations is no big deal compared to some of the issues we work with. But, when I think about it, it's a lot more significant that.

*Supervisor:* In what ways is it more significant?

*Trainee:* Well, first off, people often have to use social skills just to get by. I mean, this client could lose his marriage if he isn't able to change his communication style. For some people, their jobs depend on having adequate social skills, and just having relationships with people depends on being able to interact with them. Really, this could affect every facet of a client's life

*Supervisor:* What you're saying is very important. When clients come in for counseling, it's always because they want help in some way. Regardless of the presenting issue, it's important not to trivialize their concerns.

*Trainee:* Yes, I see that. I guess sometimes it just seems like the clients with severe pathology get more attention.

*Supervisor:* That's true.

*Trainee:* I was thinking, too, that some of the techniques I was using, especially because I felt more directive than usual, might really have different impacts on clients from different backgrounds. I will want to be careful and really check things out with clients when I'm using them—especially with issues like assertiveness training, which we talked about in class.

*Supervisor:* That's a good point. Assertiveness, for example, can mean very different things to people based on their gender, their cultural background, and their family norms. It's important to understand the values each client might attach to it and not impose your own in an inappropriate fashion.

*Trainee:* It also makes me think—sometimes it's confusing—since social skills can affect so many areas of people's lives and can also be so influenced by factors in their lives, how do I know at what depth I should be working?

*Supervisor:* I'm not sure if I know what you mean.

*Trainee:* Well, if a client has some social skills deficit that needs to be addressed but is also moving toward a relationship crisis because of those difficulties with social skills, what kinds of choices should I make about the focus of counseling?

*Supervisor:* Oh, I see. Well, why don't we go back to the case conceptualization model. Based on what you've learned about conceptualizing cases and what you've learned about your own approach with clients, what would you consider in making that choice?

*Trainee:* Well, I guess the first step is to talk with the client these two areas, and see which seems more important to him. I'd also need to consider the terms of our working relationship, and be aware of how much time we'll have to work together and those types of limitations. . . . But I feel as if I'm missing something—I'm not sure what.

*Supervisor:* You started out wondering about the depth at which you should be working. What part of the model addresses that question?

*Trainee:* Oh, I guess I need to think about whether we're working with a first- or second-order focus. On the surface, the client I presented for the role-play seems to have concerns that would involve a first-order focus, working to change communication styles. But, if I had more time with him, it might become more apparent that other changes needed to occur for the communication style to change. Or, it might not—it might be that first-order change would help other areas of his life enough to be a sufficient counseling outcome.

*Supervisor:* And in either case, you would need to check out the client's willingness to work at whichever level you choose. Well, you've done a good job with this! You've integrated the model quite well into your approach to counseling, and now you've used it well with a very specific client issue. Do you see how you can begin to use your skills, ethical understanding, and ability to conceptualize client cases that manifest a variety of issues?

*Trainee:* Yeah—it feels good to have an idea of how to approach new problems.

*Supervisor:* Sure. Well, are there other questions you have about this role-play?

In this vignette, the supervisor has helped the trainee apply a learned model to a new situation and validated the ability to do that. In addition, the supervisor has highlighted the role of making choices about the level at which to work and has reminded the trainee of the choice between a first- or second-order focus for counseling. In addition, the trainee has introduced the issue of responses to diverse clients, and the supervisor has reinforced awareness of this issue. It will, of course, be necessary to follow up on this and other issues in more detail than is allowed in the vignette.

## WEEK B-11. LEARNING CONCEPTUALIZATION AND COUNSELING FOR CAREER PLANNING

### Class

*Objectives:*
1. *Apply the case conceptualization model to problem solving, using career decision making as an example.*
2. *Provide group supervision focused on integration of the model with current client issues.*

This class focuses on career counseling or issues of career decision making. Approaches to career counseling are discussed from an exercise-oriented, largely behavioral perspective (Yost & Corbishley, 1987). One third of the lecture focuses on diversity and gender issues, and special attention is paid to the sociopolitical restrictions placed on people of diverse groups when they are involved in career decision making.

Group supervision emphasizes the contribution of career issues to clients' concerns, as appropriate.

### Supervision With Trainees Together

*Objectives:*
1. *Have the trainees conduct a developmental work history on each other.*
2. *Respond to case presentations.*

After a brief check-in, the trainees are introduced to career counseling by conducting developmental work history interviews with each other (adapted from Yost and Corbishley, 1987). Table 6 provides questions for a practice work history. Supervision strategies 4 (teach intervention techniques) and 9 (explore trainee feelings concerning specific techniques or interventions) are emphasized, as well as the appropriate advanced strategies. The work history exercise will take approximately 1 hour. Following the exercise, the supervisor should allow approximately 30 minutes for the trainees to process the experience.

*To illustrate:*

*Supervisor:* So, now that you've each had a chance to do a little bit of career counseling work, what are your initial reactions?

*Trainee 2:* Well, I'm a little bit surprised. I've always thought that career counseling was a little bit boring, but this was pretty interesting. I enjoyed spending some time thinking about work in the context of my

**TABLE 6.** *Work History Interview*

1. Many children dream of "what I want to be when I grow up." What's the first thing you dreamed of being when you grew up? What other jobs did you imagine doing?

2. Did you know any person (or people) who did those jobs? Who?

3. What kind of work did the people around you do? Your parents? Siblings? Grandparents? Other extended family? Other caretakers? Neighbors? Other people who had an impact on you?

4. What early feelings did you have about "going to work?" Was it joyful, obligatory, anticipated, dreaded, indifferent? How was this expressed in your home?

5. What values about work did you learn as a child? Why did you think work was important when you were growing up? Why do you think work is important now?

6. What kinds of tasks were you responsible for doing as a child, up to junior high school? What did you like about these? What did you dislike about these?

7. What kinds of work or tasks were you responsible for doing during junior high and high school? What did you like about these? What did you dislike about these?

8. What kinds of work or tasks have you done since high school? What did you like about these? What did you dislike about these?

9. Pause for a moment and consider all the information you've explored in the previous questions. What patterns can you identify? What themes do you want to explore, based on what you have learned so far?

family and early beliefs—I could actually see some definite connections between those experiences and what I'm doing now.

*Trainee 1:* I had a similar experience of actually seeing some connections. I guess, though, that this isn't really what I usually think of when I think about career counseling, either. I really like career issues and would like to do more work with career counseling, but I guess I always imagined it as giving clients written assessment, like a Strong Interest Inventory [Strong, Harmon, Hansen, Borgen, & Hammer, 1994] or something, and then just talking to them about their machine-scored profiles. That seems pretty mechanical and not really like counseling.

*Supervisor:* And this type of exercise, which feels more like counseling, doesn't feel like a real assessment, Trainee 1?

*Trainee 1:* Not really . . . although it definitely provides some valid information, and I can use it along with several other assessments to help me form a more complete picture of the client, so I guess really it's a different form of assessment.

*Trainee 2:* Oh, that's an interesting point. This exercise could really help me put a client's career issues in context.

*Supervisor:* You've both said that you didn't really think career counseling was like this. Now, of course, this is just one example of what you might do with a client in career counseling. But, I'm curious, how do you tend to think of career counseling?

*Trainee 2:* Well, I've always thought of it as a very focused, specific type of counseling with clear-cut answers and techniques and not a lot of interesting exploration. I'm not sure where I got that impression, but it has just never seemed as important or interesting as interpersonal counseling.

*Supervisor:* Okay. How about you, Trainee 1?

*Trainee 1:* Well, as I said, I tend to think of the assessment part of career counseling. But, I guess I also think of career counseling as a pretty specific approach that only impacts one facet of the client's life—I just happen to think it's a really interesting facet!

*Supervisor:* You've both described career counseling as something that only affects part of the client's life. But I wonder if career dissatisfaction, or career satisfaction, might not affect quite a large portion of a client's experience.

*Trainee 2:* Oh, that makes me think of an exercise we did in class. We figured out how many hours we might spend working over the rest of our lives—I think my total was something like 80,000 hours! Now, when I think about that, I can see that career counseling with clients can have a huge impact on their lives—I mean, they might be working more than anything else they do. So, I guess, when I do career counseling, I'm actually doing counseling that affects the client's whole life.

*Supervisor:* Exactly. And whether or not people are happy during those 80,000 or so hours is likely to have a pretty large impact on the rest of their personal functioning.

*Trainee 1:* Boy, that's for sure. I have a client now who is really anxious and sad, and it's almost all because of her situation at work. She came in because of stress with her partner, but I wonder if maybe we might need to focus more on her career life.

*Supervisor:* Well, that is certainly worth checking out, Trainee 1. In fact, if you have a tape of her today, we might want to explore your work with her in that context.

Following a short break, the remainder of the session (approximately 80 minutes) focuses on the presentation of client cases. Advanced supervision strategies 22 (explore the trainee's intentions in a session) and 21 (encourage the trainee's identification and use of cues in the client's and the therapist's behavior) might be useful emphases. In addition, if not already addressed with the trainees, advanced supervision strategy 26 (use parallel process to model appropriate strategies for dealing with clients) may provide helpful training.

At this point in the term, trainees should have definitive plans for termination with some clients. With other clients, trainees need to develop plans for referring the client to another counselor or continuing to work with the client. It is also important to assess the feelings trainees have about termination of supervision, both with the supervisor and with each other. At the close of the session, the supervisor continues to model good termination procedures by reminding the trainees of how many individual and group supervision sessions remain.

## WEEK B-12. LEARNING CONCEPTUALIZATION AND COUNSELING FOR DEPRESSION

### Class

*Objectives:*
1. *Apply the case conceptualization model to depression.*
2. *Introduce the ways in which depression is manifested in adolescents.*
3. *Present some treatment strategies for adolescent and adult depression.*
4. *Provide group supervision for ongoing clients, emphasizing depressive symptoms where appropriate.*

After briefly describing the clinical category of depression, the class instructor introduces two theoretical interventions for this common problem. It is recommended that the instructor provide the students with the sense that these are simply two technical examples, and that their own orientation may not use either of these techniques. Interventions can include cognitive-behavioral (Beck, 1995) and existential (Norcross, 1987; Yalom, 1980) approaches. The instructor also discusses possible concerns about the use of these interventions with diverse clients. In addition, the instructor describes likely causes for adolescent depression and the symptoms demonstrated by adolescents who are depressed. Particular attention is paid to the ways in which adolescents may subtly, rather than directly, signal depression. The instructor also addresses the ethical responsibilities associated with contacting parents of depressed adolescents.

Group supervision emphasizes the model's applicability to ongoing clinical cases. If possible, the instructor attends to clients who are currently demonstrating symptoms of depression. Students are encouraged to discuss these client symtoms using the framework provided by the case conceptualization model.

## Individual Supervision

*Objectives:*
1. *Provide individual supervision for ongoing clients.*
2. *Explore a relevant advanced supervision strategy.*
3. *Discuss in depth the material on depression presented in lecture.*

The trainee presents clinical concerns and portions of videotape. The supervisor helps the trainee conceptualize a case using supervision strategies 19 (help the trainee conceptualize a case) and 20 (explore the trainee's feelings to facilitate understanding of the client).

After this exploration, the supervisor implements a supervision strategy relevant to the concerns presented by the trainee. When appropriate, the supervisor uses supervision strategy 24 (present a developmental challenge) to encourage the trainee to reflect on unexpected events in counseling sessions. The trainee should be invited to consider how the material presented in recent weeks enables him or her to form richer case conceptualizations.

The final segment of supervision is used to explore the didactic material presented on depression. The supervisor takes a few minutes to discuss the trainee's knowledge of depression. Next they discuss the two approaches described in class. The supervisor encourages the trainee to consider the two treatment approaches in terms of theories of counseling. The remainder of the time is used to explore how either or both fit the trainee's experience with depressed clients. Specifically, the supervisor asks how the interventions match or conflict with the supervisee's theories of client change.

*To illustrate:*

*[In this situation, the supervisee is torn between the two demonstrated interventions.]*

*Supervisors:* You look a little confused, Trainee.

*Trainee:* Well, I liked both of the interventions described in class. I don't know how to choose between the two.

*Supervisor:* It might be interesting to see how each intervention resonates with your view of how clients change.

*Trainee:* Hmmm. The existential one is easy since I've always thought of myself as an existentialist. I think clients can change when they are willing to take responsibility for their lives and are able to accept the existential givens of life. But what really appealed to me was the idea of the power of engagement to lift the sense of depression. I would be excited about helping a client discover that.

*Supervisor:* So you would enjoy modeling engagement and working to get the client moving into life?

*Trainee:* Yes, I really would. But I've had some experience with depressed clients, and I think the cognitive-behavioral intervention might work better . . . or at least faster.

*Supervisor:* And speed would seem important to you with a depressed client?

*Trainee:* Well . . . yes and no. I wouldn't want to go for quick fix if it wouldn't last.

*Supervisor:* So you feel the cognitive-behavioral work might not be as permanent?

*Trainee:* Distorted cognitions might be all that's underlying the depression with some clients. I just wouldn't know which ones.

*Supervisor:* It seems as if you have two dilemmas: how to choose the intervention that best fits your personal view of the world, and how to choose the intervention that best fits your client.

*Trainee:* Yes.

In this vignette, the supervisor encouraged the trainee's reflection on the relationship between material presented in class, experience with clients, and the trainee's worldview.

Following this, the supervisor checks out briefly with the trainee and ends the session.

# WEEK B-13. LEARNING CONCEPTUALIZATION AND COUNSELING FOR ANXIETY

## Class

*Objectives:*
1. *Apply the case conceptualization model to anxiety in adults.*
2. *Introduce the ways in which anxiety is manifested in children.*
3. *Present some treatment strategies for childhood anxiety.*
4. *Provide group supervision with emphasis on the application of the model to clinical case issues.*

The instructor elicits the different forms of anxiety (generalized anxiety, panic disorders, and phobias) from the class and provides a list of references for a more comprehensive study of anxiety. The instructor also highlights ways in which gender, cultural factors, and religious background can affect the manifestation of anxiety. This is followed by a discussion of basic information about the treatment of generalized anxiety from a cognitive-behavioral model (Butler, Fennell, Robson, & Gelder, 1991) and a psychodynamic model (Milrod & Shear, 1991).

In the discussion of anxiety in children, the instructor treats those students with extensive child experience as consulting experts. They are asked how children's anxieties and fears occur in patterns characteristic of their ages, and the instructor provides additional information as necessary. Discussion illuminates some of the reasons children are anxious, the ways in which their anxiety is apparent to others, variations as a function of gender and ethnicity, and some strategies for working with anxious children. Gender, ethnic, religious, and cultural factors are considered in treatment for anxiety in both children and adults.

The last portion of the class is devoted to case presentation. If a child interview is presented, the instructor encourages the class members to provide feedback on rapport-building skills and the use of age-appropriate language with the child in question. The instructor points out that the same basic skills used in working with adults are also used with children, but in a more active fashion.

## Supervision With Trainees Together

*Objectives:*
1. *Integrate the trainees' theoretical knowledge, personal theories of change, and new information about anxiety and depression.*
2. *Use a relevant advanced supervision strategy.*
3. *Focus on trainees' current clinical cases.*

At this point in the term, the trainees will have received a large amount of information about the treatment of anxiety and depression, two complex and significant client issues. To provide a context for this information, it is important to revisit the trainees' earlier training. Therefore, following a brief check-in, the first half of this session is focused on consolidating the trainees' beginning understanding of anxiety and depression. Trainees are encouraged to integrate this new information with material they have recieved in course work on theories, and particularly to integrate it with their personal theories of change, as explored in week B-1. Supervision strategy 9 (explore trainee feelings concerning specific techniques or interventions) is used throughout the session.

During the first 45 minutes, the supervisor explores the trainees' understanding of anxiety and depression. Questions such as the following encourage discussion:

- What questions do you have about the information that's been presented to you in the class lecture?
- How could you identify anxiety or depression in a client?
- How might that identification differ for male and female clients?
- How might it differ for clients of various ethnic or cultural backgrounds?
- What types of behavior might you expect to see accompanying depression or anxiety?
- How might anxiety or depression develop according to behavioral or cognitive-behavioral theories of change? According to psychodynamic theories of change? According to humanistic theories of change?

*To illustrate:*

*Supervisor:* I know you've heard a lot of information about treatment in the last couple of lectures, especially about anxiety and depression. I'm wondering how this is coming together for you, and if you can give me an idea of what it all means in your own words.

*Trainee 1:* Well, it's a little overwhelming. I feel as if I'm supposed to learn everything there is to know about anxiety in just a couple of hours, and that doesn't seem possible.

*Trainee 2:* Boy, I know what you mean! I feel the same way. There's just so much to bring together. But I do feel as if I'm starting to understand a little bit, especially with depression, because I've had a little more time to think about that.

*Supervisor:* Yes, I know it can seem overwhelming. That's why I'm hoping that we can use part of our time today to consolidate some of this for you, and clear up at least some of the questions you may have.

*Trainee 1:* Well, I'm starting to understand how to talk with children. I have no younger brothers or sisters, and until now, I've never worked with children. In the school where I work now, I see that some children's behavior can be explained by anxiety.

*Supervisor:* Yes. It's surprising just how anxious many children are.

*Trainee 1:* I'm starting to realize that depression can take a lot of different forms. I know that a person might be depressed even if he or she laughs a lot, and things like that. I think I'd have an easier time identifying depression in my clients now than I would have a few weeks ago. I still have some questions about choosing the right intervention, though.

*Supervisor:* Okay, well, let's talk about that a little bit. What kinds of questions do you have?

*Trainee 2:* Well, we heard about two different interventions in class, cognitive-behavioral and existential. It sounds to me as if the cognitive-behavioral stuff might be easier to use, and might even be more effective, but I really think that the existential approach gets to the heart of the issue the best. I feel as if I'd like to use some kind of combination of the two.

*Supervisor:* What do you think about that idea, Trainee 1?

*Trainee 1:* It sounds interesting, but I guess I don't see those two approaches as very compatible, so I don't really know how I could use both.

*Supervisor:* I think that there are several options in this situation that one could use. Why don't you tell us a little bit about how you could imagine using the two approaches together, Trainee 2.

The supervisor continues to explore this and other questions with both trainees. It is important that they appreciate the variety of approaches to client issues and the decisions involved in a given situation. Although every question won't be answered in this session, trainees can practice the application of theoretical understanding to specific cases.

During the next 45 minutes, the supervisor reminds trainees of their previous work to develop their own theories of change and helps trainees examine again whether their own theories match any known counseling theories. The supervisor asks trainees about new developments in their personal change theories and requests that the trainees consider how they each might integrate new information they have received about depression and anxiety into their theories, and how they plan to approach counseling for these two problems. Each trainee is asked to describe his or her refined theory of change, and comments, reactions, and questions are invited from the other trainee. Again, what is important here is not that trainees leave with all the answers but that they feel they are able to approach these issues in ways that suit them and their philosophies of human change.

During the last half of the session, the supervisor works with the trainees on their cases. Trainees should be encouraged to think about how the materials presented the previous 2 weeks might enable them to form richer conceptualizations about current clients. In addition, the supervisor may want to emphasize supervision strategies 22 (explore the trainee's intentions in a session) or 21 (encourage the trainee's identification and use of cues in the client's and the therapist's behavior) in the context of current clinical cases.

## WEEK B-14. INTRODUCING FAMILY COUNSELING

### Class

*Objectives:*
1. *Introduce the relationship skills involved in interviewing a family as a unit.*
2. *Present the complexities of interviewing more than one person at a time.*
3. *Provide case supervision for trainees on their ongoing cases.*

The instructor provides a videotape or written transcript of the first counseling session with a family. Skills for managing a family session and eliciting information from all family members are demonstrated. Reflections, questions and feedback are invited from students. The instructor reminds students that one class cannot prepare a person for skillful family counseling, and at the same time encourages the trainees by pointing out how many of the specific proficiencies they have already acquired. The instructor explains that the family interview uses skills for interviewing children, for interviewing adults, and for working with groups. The instructor who delivers this lesson should have specialized training in family work.

During the last hour of class, students present cases for discussion and evaluation. Reference is made to current family issues or those associated with the client's family of origin, as each case is discussed. The instructor explores the potential benefits or contraindications for involving a client's family members in therapy.

### Individual Supervision

*Objectives:*
1. *Consider the complexities of forming a working alliance with a family.*
2. *Provide feedback on trainee's cases, highlighting family cases if available.*

The first segment after the check-in is devoted to discussion of the family interview. The supervisor elicits reactions about the family interventions as suggested by supervision strategy 9 (explore trainee feelings concerning specific techniques or interventions). After responding to questions and concerns, the supervisor asks the trainee to consider how a working alliance might be formed with a family and its members. Particular attention is paid to the development of bonds, goals, and tasks in a family context.

*To illustrate:*

*Supervisor:* As you observed the demonstration and participated in class discussion, what were your thoughts and feelings about the process of interviewing a family?

*Trainee:* It all makes sense, but I just felt that it would be difficult to work with more than one person in the room. How could you pay attention to all those people at once? And what would you do if they all started fighting?

*Supervisor:* It sounds as if you're worried about setting boundaries and managing the session more than anything.

*Trainee:* Yeah.

*Supervisor:* As I recall, you taught school for a while, didn't you?

*Trainee:* Yeah.

*Supervisor:* Well, maybe learning to work with a whole family after learning how to work with one person is a little like learning to teach a whole class after doing some one-on-one tutoring.

*Trainee:* Oh, you know, that's probably right. . . . You have to set a lot more rules and boundaries when you meet with a whole class. . . . and maybe that's what you do with a family. . . .

*Supervisor:* Sure. And it's different with the use of counseling techniques, but in some ways, the goals are rather similar—to unravel what is interfering with the development of the family members and to teach the family new skills to live more effectively.

*Trainee:* Yeah, I can see that too. . . . But I still am concerned about working with them all when they may have different goals. I mean, in a classroom, there is agreement that everyone needs to learn to read.

*Supervisor:* So what you're worrying about, to some extent, is how to get enough agreement on goals to facilitate the formation of a good working alliance.

*Trainee:* Yes.

*Supervisor:* Well, let's think about how a working alliance is formed with a family. . . . First of all, who is considered to be the client?

*Trainee:* The family itself.

*Supervisor:* Yeah. And so your alliance has to be formed with the whole family, because that's the client. So as you think about that, how can goals be set for a whole family? Usually the family can agree on only one thing.

*Trainee:* Yeah, often everyone agrees that they don't like things the way they are now.

*Supervisor:* Yes—although there are exceptions. However, the adolescents and the adults might disagree about the causes of the problem or even what the solution might look like, but they all agree it ought to be better than it is. So that's a goal you can access and make explicit with them.

*Trainee:* But what about the tasks? I mean, one family member might think someone else should do more work around the house and so on, but someone else could want the way they talk together to change.

*Supervisor:* So it sounds as if they might want to find a way to resolve their various disagreements.

*Trainee:* Oh yeah, you're probably right about that.

*Supervisor:* Sure! And the first task is to build a bond with the family.

*Trainee:* Well, I suppose you have to show respect and empathy to build that bond, just as you do with an individual client. But what if the family members start shouting at one another? I mean, you can't just keep nodding and going "Mmm-hmm" in those circumstances. And if you stop someone, you're likely to be seen as on someone else's side.

*Supervisor:* That's one of the issues. . . . But think how relieved a class is when the teacher takes charge and insists on everyone's getting a respectful hearing without abusing anyone else. . . .

*Trainee:* Yeah, I see what you mean. Even though a person doesn't like to be cut off, the whole group feels more comfortable if the teacher takes charge in a responsible way.

*Supervisor:* Sure. . . . And just one lecture won't make you a family therapist, but I can see that you have some sense of how a working alliance might be formed with a family.

In this vignette, the supervisor has assisted the trainee in considering the formation of a working alliance with a family by making an analogy to the trainee's previous experience. Encouraging a trainee to reflect on past experiences helps him or her to conceptualize the new material and at the same time be reminded of their own competence in a similar arena.

Most of the session is used for supervision of cases. The supervisor facilitates reflection on the trainee's work with clients, and then asks the trainee to summarize the session. The trainee is reminded that all trainees meet with the course instructor for evaluations during the upcoming week and that their last session together follows. The trainee is asked to prepare a self-evaluation and set goals for the future based on it. The supervisor lets the trainee know that they will take time to process the end of their work together.

## WEEK B-15. REVIEWING THE COURSE AND TERMINATING SUPERVISION

### Class

*Objectives:*
1. *Summarize the aspects of the counseling relationship and skills involved in its formation.*
2. *Summarize the application of the case conceptualization model.*
3. *Explore the ways trainees have learned to think about their clients and themselves in the counseling process.*
4. *Encourage students to evaluate the course and their learning during the two terms.*

The instructor invites the trainees to discuss the concepts of working alliance, transference, and the counseling relationship and give examples of each from their casework. This is followed by a discussion of selected cases from the perspective of the case conceptualization model. Students are asked to consider which aspects of the model they use most often and how they conceptualize cases differently after two terms of experience with clients. In the process of exploring the counseling relationship and case conceptualization, the instructor inquires frequently about the ways students think about their work with clients.

This discussion is followed by an evaluation of the course from the trainees' point of view. The instructor closes by presenting a videotape of a client at intake for the class to conceptualize according to the model.

### Supervision With Individual and Group Aspects

Trainees meet individually with the instructor and the supervisor for evaluation. Then two trainees meet together with their supervisor to complete their work and terminate as a group.

*Objectives:*
1. *Allow the trainees to assess their own work.*
2. *Encourage the trainees' establishment of goals for the future.*
3. *Allow the trainees to end their work with one another and with the supervisor and to say good-bye in a manner that illustrates a good termination.*

In the initial segment of supervision, each trainee meets separately with the instructor and the supervisor. Evaluation proceeds as it did at the end of the first term (week A-15). At the close of the evaluation meeting, the instructor and trainee formally end their work together in practicum.

After this has occurred with each trainee, trainees from each supervision group meet with their student supervisor. The supervisor checks to see how they are feeling about the end of the term in general and then moves on to explore their feelings about the end of supervision. Each trainee is encouraged to respond to the other's work and contribution to the supervision process. Both assess, to the extent that they are comfortable doing so, the supervisor's contribution to their development. The supervisor responds to their statements. In addition, the supervisor emphasizes particular attributes of the trainees that have made them able to learn in this setting, to work with others in a counseling situation, and to reflect on their work and their own growth. It is important for the supervisor to acknowledge the resolution of any difficulties during supervision and the feelings of sadness and satisfaction associated with ending.

*To illustrate:*

*[This dialogue represents the latter part of the supervision session, after the trainees have made their statements.]*

*Supervisor:* I am delighted to hear your impressions of what we have accomplished together! It sounds as if you are both feeling a bit weary at the end of the year, and yet you're able to see what you have learned in practicum.

*Trainee 1 and Trainee 2:* Yeah.

*Supervisor:* I am really pleased that you seem to have developed a way of thinking through your cases and reflecting on them, because that will be useful to you during your professional life.

*Trainee 1:* Yeah, I agree. In some ways, learning to think about things was the most fun part.

*Supervisor:* I'm glad. You know, though, at the beginning of the quarter we had a pretty difficult time when you were both angry with one another and with me. I'd like to know how you are feeling about that now.

*Trainee 1:* Well, you know, I didn't like it that you were confronting me about not showing my tapes in joint supervision. And I was pretty afraid to show my tapes in front of Trainee 2 because he seemed so critical.

*Trainee 2:* Yeah, I see that now. I didn't know I was coming across as such a critic. . . . I guess I was just trying to show the supervisor what I could see and wasn't paying much attention to how you felt about it.

*Supervisor:* When we talked about it, you both seemed relieved, though.

*Trainee 1:* Well, you know, we talked about how competitive we felt with one another. . . . I mean, we both were used to being stars, and in this program it's hard to be a star.

*Supervisor:* Sure. Everyone who comes in here is a star of sorts.

*Trainee 1:* And then, you're our supervisor; you're the one person who seems really focused on us.

*Trainee 2:* And I, at least, wanted to be your favorite. Well, we talked about that.

*Trainee 1:* And so did I. But after we talked about it, I remembered that we could be support for each other.

*Trainee 2:* And I got the idea that part of our job in group supervision was to help each other feel important and competent. I hadn't thought about that as part of what I was supposed to be doing as a good supervisee. So I was pretty mad at both of you for making me feel that I was an inadequate member of the group!

*Supervisor:* Understandably so! And how are you both feeling about all of this now, as we end?

*Trainee 2:* I feel much better! It seems like a long time ago. I really began to rethink what I'm doing in this program and in this profession. . . . You know, to get here, I had to be ambitious and somewhat competitive for grades and stuff. . . . What I see now is that I can be ambitious and succeed without beating everyone else out . . . at least, sometimes I can see that *[laughs]*. In any event, Trainee 1, I've found that I can respond to you in a positive way and not feel diminished myself.

*Trainee 1:* Yeah, I have felt your support. And I've gotten much braver about showing my screw-ups in counseling, not just because you are less critical but because when I have shown bad sections, I have learned more from it than from the good ones. And you, Supervisor, have helped me to feel that my showing some of my less-than-great work is an achievement in itself. So I appreciate that.

*Supervisor:* It sounds as if you have both made some significant progress with issues that have been with you a long time in your academic careers.

*Trainee 1 and Trainee 2:* Yeah.

*Supervisor:* Great! So one of the ways you've used supervision is to develop personally and as professionals in general, beyond just learning skills. I imagine that you will continue to do that as you go through this program and beyond. . . . And now we need to say good-bye. How are you both feeling about that?

*Trainee 2:* Well, I'm so tired that I'm really looking forward to summer! But I have gotten awfully used to the comfort and familiarity of our meetings this year, and I wonder what it will be like to have an experienced professional as my supervisor next year.

*Trainee 1:* Yeah, I wonder about that too. It has felt good to meet with a more advanced student. I think I got just the right supervisor for me, and I'm going to miss working with you. I know you have a busy year ahead with internship, but it will be strange to be here without seeing you.

*Supervisor:* I feel the same way. We can all look forward to the next steps along the professional path, but I have really liked supervising you this year, and I will miss you, too. On the other hand, it is nice to move to the stage of colleagueship. I will be here this summer and back from time to time next year. Because I will no longer be your supervisor, we can just have coffee or lunch or whatever we choose on a collegial basis. But it is a change and an opportunity for you to take what you have learned into your work with a new supervisor.

The supervisor continues to talk with the trainees about their feelings about the end of supervision as they move toward a close of the session and their time as a group. It is important for the trainees to say good-bye to one another as members of the same supervision group, even though they will continue to be colleagues in subsequent years.

◆

At the end of the first year, trainees are just beginning to appreciate the complexity of counseling. Like Skovholt and Rønnestad's (1992, 1995) stage 3 counselors, most have acquired enough skills to imitate the experts in whatever setting they enter next. More important most trainees have learned to reflect continuously on their professional lives so that further development is ensured.

At the same time, supervisors can also reflect on their own development. With good mentoring, they have progressed not only as therapists but also as educators. Because they have attended to the process of reflective inquiry with their trainees, supervisors should have increased their capacity for reflection and reached a level of greater professional autonomy in their work with both clients and trainees.

# REFERENCES

American Association for Marriage and Family Therapy. (1991). *AAMFT code of ethics*. Washington, DC: Author.

American Counseling Association. (1995). *Code of ethics and standards of practice*. Alexandria, VA: Author.

American Psychiatric Association. (1994) *DSM-IV: Diagnostic and statistical manual of mental disorders*. Washington, DC: Author.

American Psychiatric Association. (1995). *The principles of medical ethics with annotations especially applicable to psychiatry*. Washington, DC: Author.

American Psychological Association. (1992). Ethical principles of psychologists and code of conduct. *American Psychologist, 47*, 1597–1611.

American Psychological Association. (1993). Guidelines for providers of psychological services to ethnic, linguistic, and culturally diverse populations. *American Psychologist, 48*, 45–48.

American School Counselor Association. (1992). Ethical standards for school counselors. *ASCA Counselor, 29*, 13–16.

Argyris, C., & Schön, D. A. (1974). *Theory in practice: Increasing professional effectiveness*. San Francisco: Jossey-Bass.

Association for Counselor Education and Supervision. (1995). Ethical guidelines for counseling supervisors. *Counselor Education and Supervision, 34*, 270–276.

Atkinson, D. R., & Lowe, S. M. (1995). The role of ethnicity, cultural knowledge, and conventional techniques in counseling and psychotherapy. In J. G. Ponterotto, J. M. Casas, L. A. Suzuki, & C. M. Alexander (Eds.), *Handbook of multicultural counseling* (pp. 386–414). Thousand Oaks, CA: Sage.

Atkinson, D. R., Morten, G., & Sue, D. W. (1998). *Counseling American minorities: A cross-cultural perspective* (5th ed.). Dubuque, IA: Brown & Benchmark.

Beck, J. S. (1995). *Cognitive therapy: Basics and beyond*. New York: Guilford.

Berliner, D. C. (1988, February). *The development of expertise in pedagogy*. Charles W. Hunt Memorial Lecture presented at the annual meeting of the American Association of Colleges for Teacher Education, Washington, DC: AACTE.

Bernard, J. M. (1979). Supervisor training: A discrimination model. *Counselor Education and Supervision, 19*, 60–68.

Bernard, J. M., & Goodyear, R. K. (1998). *Fundamentals of clinical supervision* (2nd ed.). Needham Heights, MA: Allyn & Bacon.

Beutler, L. E., & Clarkin, J. F. (1990). *Systematic treatment selection: Toward targeted therapeutic interventions*. New York: Brunner/Mazel.

Beutler, L. E., Machado, P. P. P., & Neufeldt, S. A. (1994). Therapist variables. In A. E. Bergin & S. L. Garfield (Eds.), *Handbook of psychotherapy and behavior change* (3rd ed., pp. 229–269). New York: Wiley.

Binder, J. L. (1993). Is it time to improve psychotherapy training? *Clinical Psychology Review, 13,* 301–318.

Binder, J. L., & Strupp, H. H. (1997). Supervision of psychodynamic psychotherapies. In C. E. Watkins, Jr. (Ed.), *Handbook of psychotherapy supervision* (pp. 44–62). New York: Wiley.

Blocher, D. H. (1983). Toward a cognitive developmental approach to counselor supervision. *The Counseling Psychologist, 11*(1), 27–34.

Borders, L. D. (1989). Developmental cognitions of first practicum supervisees. *Journal of Counseling Psychology, 36,* 163–169.

Borders, L. D. (1992). Learning to think like a supervisor. *Clinical Supervisor, 10*(2), 135–148.

Borders, L. D., Bernard, J. M., Dye, H. A., Fong, M. L., Henderson, P., & Nance, D. W. (1991). Curriculum guide for training counseling supervisors: Rationale, development, and implementation. *Counselor Education and Supervision, 31,* 209–218.

Borders, L. D., & Fong, M. L. (1994). Cognitions of supervisors-in-training: An exploratory study. *Counselor Education and Supervision, 33,* 280–293.

Butler, G., Fennell, M., Robson, P., & Gelder, M. (1991). Comparison of behavior therapy and cognitive behavior therapy in the treatment of generalized anxiety disorder. *Journal of Consulting and Clinical Psychology, 59,* 167–175.

Collins, W. D., & Messer, S. B. (1991). Extending the plan formulation method to an object relations perspective: Reliability, stability, and adaptability. *Psychological Assessment: A Journal of Consulting and Clinical Psychology, 3,* 75–81.

Cook, D. A. (1994). Racial identity in supervision. *Counselor Education and Supervision, 34,* 132–141.

Copeland, W. T., Birmingham, C., de la Cruz, E., & Lewin, B. (1993). The reflective practitioner in teaching: Toward a research agenda. *Teaching and Teacher Education, 9,* 349–359.

Corey, G., Corey, M. S., & Callanan, P. (1998). *Issues and ethics in the helping professions* (5th ed.). Pacific Grove, CA: Brooks/Cole.

Dawes, R. M. (1994). *House of cards: Psychology and psychotherapy built on myth.* New York: Free Press.

Elliott, R. (1984). A discovery-oriented approach to significant events in psychotherapy: Interpersonal process recall and comprehensive process analysis. In L. Rice & L. Greenberg (Eds.), *Patterns of change* (pp. 249–286). New York: Guilford.

Ericsson, K. A., Krampe, R. T., & Tesch-Romer, C. (1993). The role of deliberate practice in the acquisition of expert performance. *Psychology Review, 100,* 363–406.

Ericsson, K. A., & Lehmann, A. C. (1996). Expert and exceptional performance: Evidence of maximal adaptation to task constraints. *Annual Review of Psychology, 47,* 273–305.

Fischer, A. R., Jome, L. M., & Atkinson, D. R. (1998). Reconceptualizing multicultural counseling: Universal healing conditions in a culturally specific context. *The Counseling Psychologist, 26,* 525–588.

Flavell, J. H. (1985). *Cognitive development* (2nd ed.). Englewood Cliffs, NJ: Prentice Hall.

Fogel, M. S. (1990, May/June). Supervisors should not dominate but doubt, reflect, innovate. *Family Therapy News,* 5–6.

Fong, M. L., Borders, L. D., Ethington, C. A., & Pitts, J. H. (1997). Becoming a counselor: A longitudinal study of student cognitive development. *Counselor Education and Supervision, 37*, 100–114.

Fong, M. S., & Lease, S. H. (1997). Cross-cultural supervision: Issues for the White supervisor. In D. B. Pope-Davis & H. L. K. Coleman (Eds.), *Multicultural counseling competencies: Assessment, education and training, and supervision* (pp. 387–405). Thousand Oaks, CA: Sage.

Freire, P. (1993). *Pedagogy of the oppressed.* (Rev. ed.; M. B. Ramos, Trans.). New York: Continuum.

Friedlander, M. L., Siegel, S. M., & Brenock, K. (1989). Parallel processes in counseling and supervision: A case study. *Journal of Counseling Psychology, 36*, 149–157.

Gambrill, E., & Richey, C. (1985). *Taking charge of your social life.* Belmont, CA: Wadsworth.

Gelso, C. J., & Carter, J. A. (1985). The relationship in counseling and psychotherapy: Components, consequences, and theoretical antecedents. *The Counseling Psychologist, 13*, 155–243.

Gelso, C. J., & Carter, J. A. (1994). Components of the psychotherapy relationship: Their interaction and unfolding during treatment. *Journal of Counseling Psychology, 41*, 296–306.

Gilligan, C. (1982). *In a different voice: Psychological theory and women's development.* Cambridge, MA: Harvard University Press.

Ginsburg, H., & Opper, S. (1969). *Piaget's theory of intellectual development: An introduction.* Englewood Cliffs, NJ: Prentice Hall.

Glickauf-Hughes, C., & Campbell, L. F. (1991). Experiential supervision: Applied techniques for a case presentation approach. *Psychotherapy, 28*, 625–635.

Goodyear, R. K. (1982). *Psychotherapy supervision by major theorists* [Videotape series]. Manhattan, KS: Instructional Media Center. (Note: For further information, contact the author at the University of Southern California.)

Goodyear, R. K., & Sinnett, E. D. (1984). Current and emerging ethical issues for counseling psychologists. *The Counseling Psychologist, 12*, 87–98.

Grace, M., Kivlighan, D. M., Jr., & Kunce, J. (1995). The effect of nonverbal skills training on counselor trainee nonverbal sensitivity and responsiveness and on session impact and working alliance ratings. *Journal of Counseling & Development, 73*, 547–552.

Greenberg, L., & Goldman, R. L. (1988). Training in experiential therapy. *Journal of Consulting and Clinical Psychology, 56*, 696–702.

Hallowell, E. M., & Ratey, J. J. (1994). *Driven to distraction.* New York: Pantheon.

Henry, W. P., Schacht, T. E., Strupp, H. H., Butler, S. F., & Binder, J. L. (1993). Effects of training in time-limited dynamic psychotherapy: Mediators of therapists responses to training. *Journal of Consulting and Clinical Psychology, 61*, 441–447.

Henry, W. P., Strupp, H. H., Butler, S. F., Schacht, T. E., & Binder, J. L. (1993). Effects of training in time-limited dynamic psychotherapy: Changes in therapist behavior. *Journal of Consulting and Clinical Psychology, 61*, 434–440.

Heppner, P. P., & Roehlke, H. J. (1984). Differences among supervisees at different levels of training: Implications for a developmental model of supervision. *Journal of Counseling Psychology, 31*, 76–90.

Hill, C. E., Charles, D., & Reed, K. G. (1981). A longitudinal analysis of changes in counseling skills during doctoral training in counseling psychology. *Journal of Counseling Psychology, 28*, 428–436.

Hill, C. E., Helms, J. E., Tichenor, V., Spiegel, S. B., O'Grady, K. E., & Perry, E. S. (1988). Effects of therapist response modes in brief psychotherapy. *Journal of Counseling Psychology, 35,* 222–233.

Hill, C. E., & O'Brien, K. M. (1999). *Helping skills: Facilitating exploration, insight, and action.* Washington, DC: American Psychological Association.

Hill, C. E., & O'Grady, K. E. (1985). List of therapist intentions illustrated in a case study and with therapists of varying theoretical orientations. *Journal of Counseling Psychology, 32,* 3–22.

Hogan, R. A. (1964). Issues and approaches in supervision. *Psychotherapy: Theory, Research, and Practice, 1,* 139–141.

Hollin, C. R., & Trower, P. (1988). *Handbook of social skills training: Applications across the life span.* New York: Pergamon.

Holloway, E. L. (1987). Developmental levels of supervision: Is it development? *Professional Psychology: Research and Practice, 18,* 209–216.

Holloway, E. L. (1992a, April). *Beneath the words of supervision: Research awards address.* Paper presented at the annual meeting of the American Educational Research Association, San Francisco.

Holloway, E. L. (1992b). Supervision: A way of teaching and learning. In S. D. Brown & R. W. Lent (Eds.), *Handbook of counseling psychology* (2nd ed., pp. 177–214). New York: Wiley.

Holloway, E. L. (1995). *Clinical supervision: A systems approach.* Ventura, CA: Sage.

Holloway, E. L., & Hosford, R. E. (1983). Towards developing a prescriptive technology of counselor supervision. *The Counseling Psychologist, 11(1),* 73–77.

Holloway, E. L., & Neufeldt, S. A. (1995). Supervision: Its contributions to treatment efficacy. *Journal of Consulting and Clinical Psychology, 63,* 207–213.

Holloway, E. L., & Wampold, B. E. (1983). Patterns of verbal behavior and judgments of satisfaction in the supervision interview. *Journal of Counseling Psychology, 30,* 227–234.

Holloway, E. L., & Wampold, B. E. (1986). Relation between conceptual level and counseling-related tasks: A meta-analysis. *Journal of Counseling Psychology, 33,* 310–319.

Ivey, A. E., Ivey, M. B., & Simek-Morgan, L. (1993). *Counseling and psychotherapy: A multicultural perspective* (3rd ed.) Boston: Allyn & Bacon.

Jennings, L., & Skovholt, T. M. (1999). The cognitive, emotional and relational characteristics of master therapists. *Journal of Counseling Psychology, 43,* 3–11.

Kagan, N. (1983). Classroom to client: Issues in supervision. *The Counseling Psychologist, 11(1),* 69–72.

Kanfer, F. H., & Schefft, B. K. (1988). *Guiding the process of therapeutic change.* Champaign, IL: Research.

Kiesler, D. J. (1982). Interpersonal theory for personality and psychotherapy. In J. C. Anchin & D. J. Kiesler (Eds.), *Handbook of interpersonal psychotherapy* (pp. 3–24.) New York: Pergamon.

Kitchener, K. S. (1984). Intuition, critical evaluation and ethical principles: The foundation for ethical decisions in counseling psychology. *The Counseling Psychologist, 12,* 43–55.

Kitchener, K. S. (1988). Dual role relationships: What makes them so problematic? *Journal of Counseling and Development, 67,* 217–221.

Kleintjes, S., & Swartz, L. (1996). Black clinical psychology trainees at a "White" South African University: Issues for clinical supervision. *Clinical Supervisor, 22,* 489–495.

Knapp, S., & VandeCreek, L. (1997). Ethical and legal aspects of clinical supervision. In C. E. Watkins, Jr. (Ed.), *Handbook of psychotherapy supervision* (pp. 589–599). New York: Wiley.

Kohlberg, L. (1984). *Essays on moral development: Vol. 2. The psychology of moral development.* New York: Harper & Row.

Kurtz, R. (1990). *Body-centered psychotherapy: The Hakomi method.* Mendocino, CA: Life Rhythm.

Ladany, N., Hill, C. E., Corbett, M. M., & Nutt, E. A. (1996). Nature, extent, and importance of what psychotherapy trainees do not disclose to their supervisors. *The Counseling Psychologist, 43*, 10–24.

Ladany, N., Lehrman-Waterman, D., Molinaro, M., & Wolgast, B. (in press). Psychotherapy supervisor ethical practices: Adherence to guidelines, the supervisor working alliance, and supervisee satisfaction. *The Counseling Psychologist.*

Ladany, N., O'Brien, K. M., Hill, C. E., Melincoff, D. S., Knox, S., & Petersen, D. A. (1997). Sexual attraction toward clients, use of supervision, and prior training: A qualitative study of predoctoral psychology interns. *Journal of Counseling Psychology, 44*, 413–424.

LaFromboise, T. D., & Foster, S. L. (1992). Cross-cultural training: Scientist-practitioner model and methods. *The Counseling Psychologist, 20*, 472–489.

Lambert, M. J., & Arnold, R. C. (1987). Research and the supervision process. *Professional Psychology: Research and Practice, 18*, 217–224.

Larrabee, M. J., & Miller, G. M. (1993). An examination of sexual intimacy in supervision. *Clinical Supervisor, 11*(2), 103–126.

Leong, F. T. L., & Wagner, N. S. (1994). Cross-cultural counseling supervision: What do we know? What do we need to know? *Counselor Education and Supervision, 34*, 117–131.

Linehan, M. M. (1993). *Cognitive-behavioral therapy of borderline personality disorder.* New York: Guilford.

Lippitt, G., & Lippitt, R. (1986). *The consulting process in action* (2nd ed.) La Jolla, CA: University Associates.

Loganbill, C., Hardy, E., & Delworth, U. (1982). Supervision: A conceptual model. *The Counseling Psychologist, 10*(1), 3–42.

Mahoney, M. J. (1991). *Human change processes: The scientific foundations of psychotherapy.* New York: Basic.

McNeill, B. W., & Worthen, V. (1989). The parallel process in psychotherapy supervision. *Professional Psychology: Research and Practice, 20*, 293–333.

Meara, N. M., Schmidt, L. D., & Day, J. D. (1996). Principles and virtues: A foundation for ethical decisions, policies, and character. *The Counseling Psychologist, 24*, 4–77.

Miller, G. M., & Larrabee, M. J. (1995). Sexual intimacy in counselor education and supervision: A national survey. *Counselor Education and Supervision, 34*, 332–343.

Milrod, B., & Shear, M. K. (1991). Dynamic treatment of panic disorder: A review. *Journal of Nervous and Mental Disease, 179*, 741–743.

Monahan, J. (1993). Limiting therapist exposure to *Tarasoff* liability: Guidelines for risk containment. *American Psychologist, 48*, 242–250.

National Association of Social Workers. (1996). *Code of ethics.* Washington, DC: Author.

Nelson, M. L., & Holloway, E. L. (1990). The relation of gender to power and involvement in supervision. *Journal of Counseling Psychology, 37*, 473–481.

Neufeldt, S. A. (1994a). Preparing counselors to work with today's clinic clients. In

J. Myers (Ed.), *Developing and directing counselor education laboratories* (pp. 107–113). Alexandria, VA: American Counseling Association.

Neufeldt, S. A. (1994b). Use of a manual to train supervisors. *Counselor Education and Supervision, 33,* 327–336.

Neufeldt, S. A. (1997). A social constructivist approach to counseling supervision. In T. L. Sexton & B. L. Griffin (Eds.), *Constructivist thinking in counseling practice, research, and training* (pp. 191–210). New York: Teachers College.

Neufeldt, S. A. (1999). Training in reflective processes in supervision. In M. Carroll & E. L. Holloway (Eds.), *Educating clinical supervisors* (pp. 92–105). London: Sage.

Neufeldt, S. A., Doucette-Gates, A., & Carvalho, J. (1998 August). *Replicating the supervision training model: Comparisons, contrasts, and research directions.* Paper presented at the annual meeting of the American Psychological Association, San Francisco.

Neufeldt, S. A., & Forsyth, L. E. (1993, November). *Supervision for reflective practice: Facilitating clinical and scientific inquiry.* Paper presented at the annual meeting of the Western Association for Counselor Education and Supervision, Berkeley, CA.

Neufeldt, S. A., Karno, M. P., & Nelson, M. L. (1996). A qualitative study of experts' conceptualization of supervisee reflectivity. *Journal of Counseling Psychology, 43,* 3–9.

Neufeldt, S. A., & Nelson, M. L. (in press). When is counseling an appropriate and ethical supervision function? *The Clinical Supervisor.*

Norcross, J. C. (1987). A rational and empirical analysis of existential psychotherapy. *Journal of Humanistic Psychology, 27,* 41–68.

Palmer, P. J. (1998a). *The courage to teach: Exploring the inner landscape of a teacher's life.* San Francisco: Jossey-Bass.

Palmer, P. J. (1998b, September). The grace of great things: Reclaiming the sacred in knowing, teaching, and learning. *The Sun,* pp. 24–28.

Pedersen, P. B. (1991). Multiculturalism as a generic approach to counseling. *Journal of Counseling and Development, 70,* 6–12.

Pedersen, P. B. (1994). *A handbook for developing multicultural awareness* (2nd ed.). Alexandria, VA: American Counseling Association.

Persons, J. B., Curtis, J. T., & Silberschatz, G. (1991). Psychodynamic and cognitive-behavioral formulations of a single case. *Psychotherapy, 28,* 608–617.

Pope, K. S., Levenson, H., & Schover, L. R. (1979). Sexual intimacy in psychology training: Results and implications of a national survey. *American Psychologist, 34,* 682–689.

Priest, R. (1994). Minority supervisor and majority supervisee: Another perspective of clinical reality. *Counselor Education and Supervision, 34,* 152–158.

Rambo, A. H., & Shilts, L. (1997). Four supervisory practices that foster respect for difference. In T. C. Todd & C. L. Storm (Eds.), *The complete systemic supervisor* (pp. 83–92). Needham Heights, MA: Allyn & Bacon.

Reising, G. N., & Daniels, M. H. (1983). A study of Hogan's model of counselor development and supervision. *Journal of Counseling Psychology, 30,* 235–244.

Rønnestad, M. H., & Skovholt, T. M. (1993). Supervision of beginning and advanced graduate students of counseling and psychotherapy. *Journal of Counseling and Development, 71,* 396–405.

Rønnestad, M. H., & Skovholt, T. M. (1998). Berufliche Entwicklung und Supervision von Psychotherapeuten [The professional development and supervision of psychotherapists]. *Psychotherapeut, 42,* 299–306.

Rosen, H. (1985). *Piagetian dimensions of clinical relevance.* New York: Columbia University Press.

Rosenberg, J. I. (1998, August). *Reconstructing supervision training: How cognitive psychology informs clinical practice.* Paper presented at the annual meeting of the American Psychological Association, San Francisco.

Rosenblatt, A., & Mayer, J. E. (1975). Objectionable supervisory styles: Students' views. *Social Work, 20,* 184–189.

Satir, V. (1967). *Conjoint family therapy.* Palo Alto, CA: Science and Behavior.

Sattler, J. (1988). *Assessment of children* (3rd ed.). San Diego: Sattler.

Schön, D. A. (1983). *The reflective practitioner: How professionals think in action.* New York: Basic.

Schön, D. A. (1987). *Educating the reflective practitioner.* San Francisco: Jossey-Bass.

Sexton, T. L., & Whiston, S. C. (1994). The status of the counseling relationship: An empirical review, theoretical implications, and research directions. *The Counseling Psychologist, 22,* 6–78.

Shaw, B. F. (1984). Specification of the training and evaluation of cognitive therapists for outcome studies. In J. B. W. Williams & R. L. Spitzer (Eds.), *Psychotherapy research: Where are we and where should we go?* (pp. 173–188). New York: Guilford.

Skovholt, T. M., & Rønnestad, M. H. (1992). Themes in therapist and counselor development. *Journal of Counseling and Development, 70,* 505–515.

Skovholt, T. M., & Rønnestad, M. H. (1995). *The evolving professional self: Stages and themes in therapist and counselor development.* Chichester: Wiley.

Skovholt, T. M., Rønnestad, M. H., & Jennings, L. (1997). Searching for expertise in counseling, psychotherapy, and professional psychology. *Educational Psychology Review, 9,* 361–369.

Smith, P. H. (1994). Reaction: On-campus practicum and supervision. In J. Myers (Ed.), *Developing and directing counselor education laboratories* (pp. 115–117). Alexandria, VA: American Counseling Association.

Stenack, R. J., & Dye, H. A. (1982). Behavioral descriptions of counseling supervision roles. *Counselor Education and Supervision, 21,* 295–304.

Stoltenberg, C. D., & Delworth, U. (1987). *Supervising counselors and therapists.* San Francisco: Jossey-Bass.

Stoltenberg, C. D., McNeill, B. W., & Crethar, H. C. (1994). Changes in supervision as counselors and therapists gain experience: A review. *Professional Psychology: Research and Practice, 25,* 416–449.

Stoltenberg, C. D., McNeill, B., & Delworth, U. (1998). *IDM supervision: An integrated developmental model for supervising counselors and therapists.* San Francisco: Jossey-Bass.

Stone, G. L. (1997). Multiculturalism as a context for supervision: Perspectives, limitations, and implications. In D. B. Pope-Davis & H. L. K. Coleman (Eds.), *Multicultural counseling competencies: Assessment, education and training, and supervision.* (pp. 263—289). Thousand Oaks, CA:Sage.

Strong, S. R. (1968). Counseling: An interpersonal influence process. *Journal of Counseling Psychology, 15,* 215–224.

Strong, S. R., & Claiborn, C. D. (1982). *Change through interaction: Social psychological processes of counseling and psychotherapy.* New York: Wiley.

Strong, E. K., Harmon, L. W., Hansen, J. C., Borgen, F. H., & Hammer, A. L. (1994). Strong Interest Inventory. Palo Alto, CA: Consulting Psychologists.

Sue, D. W., & Sue, D. (1990). *Counseling the culturally different: Theory and practice* (2nd ed.). New York: Wiley.

Szasz, T. S. (1974). *The myth of mental illness: Foundation of a theory of personal conduct.* New York: Harper & Row.

Tanaka-Matsumi, J., & Draguns, J. G. (1997). Culture and psychopathology. In J. W. Berry, M. H. Segall, & C. Kagitcibasi (Eds.), *Handbook of cross-cultural psychology (Vol. 3): Social behavior and applications* (pp. 449–491). Boston: Allyn & Bacon.

Teyber, E. (1997). *Interpersonal process in psychotherapy: A guide for clinical training* (3rd ed.). Pacific Grove, CA: Brooks/Cole.

Vaillant, G. E. (1977). *Seasons of a man's life.* Boston: Little Brown.

Vasquez, M. J. T. (1992). Psychologist as clinical supervisor: Promoting ethical practice. *Professional Psychology: Research and Practice, 23,* 196–202.

Wampold, B. E., Mondin, G. W., Moody, M., Stitch, F., Benson, K., & Ahn, H. (1997). A meta-analysis of outcome studies comparing bonafide psychotherapies: Empirically, "all must have prizes." *Psychological Bulletin, 122,* 226–230.

Watkins, C. E., Jr. (1995). Researching psychotherapy supervisor development: Four key considerations. *Clinical Supervisor, 13*(2), 111–118.

Watkins, C. E., Jr. (1997a). Defining psychotherapy supervision and understanding supervisor functioning. In C. E. Watkins, Jr. (Ed.), *Handbook of psychotherapy supervision* (pp. 1–10). New York: Wiley.

Watkins, C. E., Jr. (Ed.). (1997b). *Handbook of psychotherapy supervision.* New York: Wiley.

Whiston, S. C., & Emerson, S. (1989). Ethical implications for supervisors in counseling of trainees. *Counselor Education and Supervision, 28,* 318–325.

Wiley, M. O., & Ray, P. B. (1986). Counseling supervision by developmental level. *Journal of Counseling Psychology, 33,* 439–445.

Worthington, E. L., Jr. (1987). Changes in supervision as counselors and supervisors gain experience: A review. *Professional Psychology: Research and Practice, 18,* 189–208.

Worthington, E. L., Jr., & Roehlke, H. J. (1979). Effective supervision as perceived by counselors-in-training. *Journal of Counseling Psychology, 26,* 64–73.

Worthington, R. L., & Gugliotti, T. (1997, August). *Toward guidelines for ethical behavior among supervisory trainees.* Paper presented at the annual meeting of the American Psychological Association, Chicago.

Yalom, I. D. (1980). *Existential psychotherapy.* New York: Basic.

Yost, E. B., & Corbishley, M. A. (1987). *Career counseling: A psychological approach.* San Francisco: Jossey-Bass.